**ALL-IN-ONE**
Student Workbook
Version A

MW00991646

**2013**
Edition

Prentice Hall

# Course 1
# MATHEMATICS
## Common Core

Taken from:

*Prentice Hall Mathematics, Course 1, All-in-One Workbook,* Version A

**PEARSON**

Front Cover: Wolfgang Kaehler/CORBIS
Back Cover: Ian Cartwright/Getty Images.

Taken from:
*Prentice Hall Mathematics Course 1: ALL-IN-ONE Student Workbook Version A*, Global Edition
Copyright © 2010 by Pearson Education, Inc.
Published by Prentice Hall
Upper Saddle River, New Jersey 07458

Pearson Learning Solutions, 501 Boylston Street, Suite 900, Boston, MA 02116
A Pearson Education Company
www.pearsoned.com

Printed in the United States of America

8 9 10 V011 17 16 15 14

000200010271665667

SD

ISBN 10: 1-256-73721-6
ISBN 13: 978-1-256-73721-6

# Daily Notetaking Guide

# Daily Notetaking Guide (continued)

# Practice, Guided Problem Solving, Vocabulary

## Chapter 1: Number Properties and Decimals

## Chapter 2: Expressions and Equations

# Chapter 3: Number Theory

# Chapter 4: Fraction Operations

# Chapter 5: Ratios and Percents

# Chapter 6: Integers and Rational Numbers

## Chapter 7: The Coordinate Plane

## Chapter 8: Geometry and Measurement

# Chapter 9: Data and Graphs

## A Note to the Student:

This section of your workbook contains notetaking pages for each lesson in your student edition. They are structured to help you take effective notes in class. They will also serve as a study guide as you prepare for tests and quizzes.

Name _____ Class _____ Date _____

# Lesson 1-1

**Properties of Numbers**

| Lesson Objective | Common Core State Standards |
|---|---|
| To understand and use the properties of operations | Equations and Expressions: 6.EE.2.b, 6.EE.3 |

## Key Concepts

### Properties of Addition

**Commutative Property of Addition**

Changing the [ ] of the addends does not change the sum.

$9 + 5 = \square + \square$

**Associative Property of Addition**

Changing the [ ] of the addends does not change the sum.

$9 + (5 + 4) = \left(\square + \square\right) + 4$

**Identity Property of Addition**

The sum of $\square$ and any number is that number.

$0 + 9 = \square$

### Properties of Multiplication

**Commutative Property of Multiplication**

Changing the [ ] of factors does not change the product.

$4 \times 6 = \square \times \square$

**Associative Property of Multiplication**

Changing the [ ] of factors does not change the product.

$4 \times (6 \times 2) = \left(\square \times \square\right) \times 2$

**Identity Property of Multiplication**

The product of $\square$ and any number is that number.

$4 \times 1 = \square$

Name _____ Class _____ Date _____

## Examples

**❶ Using the Properties of Addition** Use mental math to find $64 + 26$.

Look at the addends and notice that they end in 6 and 4, which combine to make ⬚.

**What you think**

First I will think of 64 as $\left(60 + \boxed{\phantom{xx}}\right)$. Next, I will add $4 + 26$ to get $\boxed{\phantom{xx}}$.

$60 + 30$ is $\boxed{\phantom{xx}}$. So $64 + 26 = \boxed{\phantom{xx}}$.

**Why it works**

$$64 + 26 = \left(\boxed{\phantom{xxx}} + 4\right) + 26 \qquad \leftarrow \text{Rewrite 64 as } \left(\boxed{\phantom{xxx}} + 4\right).$$

$$= 60 + \left(\boxed{\phantom{x}} + \boxed{\phantom{x}}\right) \qquad \leftarrow \text{Use the Associative Property of Addition.}$$

$$= 60 + \left(\boxed{\phantom{xx}}\right) \qquad \leftarrow \text{Add inside the parentheses first.}$$

$$= \boxed{\phantom{xx}} \qquad \leftarrow \text{Simplify.}$$

**❷ Using the Properties of Multiplication** Find $25 \times 7 \times 4$.

**What you think**

First I will multiply 25 and 4.

$25 \times 4 = \boxed{\phantom{xxx}}$, and $\boxed{\phantom{xxx}} \times 7 = \boxed{\phantom{xxx}}$.

**Why it works**

$$25 \times 7 \times 4 = 25 \times 4 \times 7 \qquad \leftarrow \boxed{\phantom{xxxxxxxxxx}} \text{ Property of Multiplication}$$

$$= (25 \times 4) \times 7 \qquad \leftarrow \boxed{\phantom{xxxxxxxxxx}} \text{ Property of Multiplication}$$

$$= \boxed{\phantom{xxx}} \times 7 \qquad \leftarrow \text{Multiply inside the parentheses.}$$

$$= \boxed{\phantom{xxx}} \qquad \leftarrow \text{Simplify.}$$

## Quick Check

**1. Mental Math** Find the sum $36 + 25 + 34$.

**2. Mental Math** Find $20 \times (6 \times 5)$.

# Lesson 1-2

**Order of Operations**

| Lesson Objective | Common Core State Standards |
|---|---|
| To use the order of operations to simplify expressions and solve problems | Equations and Expressions: 6.EE.2.b, 6.EE.2.c |

## Vocabulary and Key Concepts

**Order of Operations**

1. Do all operations within [　　　　] first.

2. [　　　　] and [　　　　] in order from left to right.

3. [　　　　] and [　　　　] in order from left to right.

An expression is _____

_____

## Example

**① Finding the Value of Expressions** Find the value of each expression.

a. $(5 + 7) \div 6 \times 3 = \boxed{\phantom{00}} \div 6 \times 3$  ← **Add 5 and 7 within the parentheses.**

$= \boxed{\phantom{00}} \times 3$  ← **Divide 12 by $\boxed{\phantom{0}}$.**

$= \boxed{\phantom{00}}$  ← **Multiply.**

b. $20 - 5 \times 8 \div 2 = 20 - \boxed{\phantom{00}} \div 2$  ← **Multiply 5 by $\boxed{\phantom{0}}$.**

$= 20 - \boxed{\phantom{00}}$  ← **Divide $\boxed{\phantom{0}}$ by 2.**

$= \boxed{\phantom{00}}$  ← **Subtract.**

## Quick Check

1. Find the value of each expression.

a. $17 - 4 \times 2$

b. $34 + 5 \times 2 - 17$

c. $(6 + 18) \div 3 \times 2$

Name _____ Class _____ Date _____

## Example

❷ **Using Expressions to Solve Problems** The table shows items Sandy bought at the hardware store. What is the total cost of Sandy's purchase (do not include tax)?

| Items Purchased | |
|---|---|
| 1 Bottle Glue | @ $3.00 each |
| 8 Decals | @ $1.00 each |
| 2 Coupons | @ $4.00 each |

**A.** $3     **B.** $7     **C.** $8     **D.** $11

Write an expression to help you find the total cost.

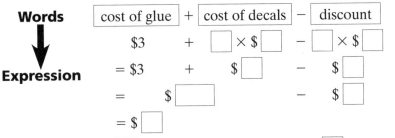

**Words**    cost of glue $+$ cost of decals $-$ discount

$$\$3 \quad + \quad \boxed{\phantom{x}} \times \$\boxed{\phantom{x}} \quad - \quad \boxed{\phantom{x}} \times \$\boxed{\phantom{x}}$$

**Expression**    $= \$3 \quad + \quad \$\boxed{\phantom{x}} \quad - \quad \$\boxed{\phantom{x}}$    ← **Multiply.**

$= \quad \$\boxed{\phantom{x}} \quad - \quad \$\boxed{\phantom{x}}$    ← **Add.**

$= \$\boxed{\phantom{x}}$    ← **Subtract.**

The total cost is $ \boxed{\phantom{x}} . The correct answer is choice \boxed{\phantom{x}} .

## Quick Check

**2.** You are paid $7 per hour to rake leaves. Your brother is paid $5 per hour. You worked 4 hours and your brother worked 3 hours. How much did the two of you earn together?

<br><br><br><br><br>

# Lesson 1-3

**Understanding Decimals**

**Lesson Objective**

To read, write, and round decimals

---

## Examples

❶ **Writing a Decimal in Words** Write 1.0936 in words.

Begin by writing 1.0936 in a place value chart

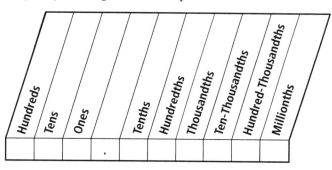

1.0936 ⌐ **Four decimal places indicate ten-thousandths.**

[ ] and [ ] ten-thousandths

❷ **Standard Form and Expanded Form** There are four thousand five hundred thirty-six ten-thousandths kilograms in one pound. Write this number in standard form and in expanded form.

[ ]. ← Write the whole number part. Place the decimal point.

0. [■][■][■][■] ← Ten-thousandths is [ ] places to the right of the decimal point.

0. [ ] ← Place 4536.

**Standard form:** [ ]

**Expanded form:** [ ] + [ ] + [ ] + [ ]

© Pearson Education, Inc., publishing as Pearson Prentice Hall.

Name _____ Class _____ Date _____

**❸ Rounding Decimals** Round 20.32 to the nearest tenth.

20.32 ← **Look at the digit to the** ☐ **of the** ☐ **place.**

↑

2 ☐ **5, so round** ☐ .

So 20.32 rounded to the nearest tenth is 20.3.

## Quick Check

**1.** Write each decimal in words.

  **a.** 67.3

☐

  **b.** 6.734

☐

  **c.** 0.67

☐

**2.** The winning car in a race won by fifteen hundredths of a second. Write the decimal in standard and expanded forms.

☐

**3.** Round each decimal to the underlined place.

  **a.** 2.3<u>4</u>28

☐

  **b.** 0.173<u>4</u>7

☐

  **c.** 9.<u>0</u>53

☐

# Lesson 1-4

**Adding and Subtracting Decimals**

| Lesson Objective | Common Core State Standards |
|---|---|
| To add and subtract decimals and to solve problems involving decimals | The Number System: 6.NS.3 |

## Example

❶ **Finding Decimal Sums** Find 6.8 + 4.65 + 2.125.

**Step 1** Estimate 6.8 + 4.65 + 2.125 ≈ ☐ + ☐ + ☐ , or ☐

**Step 2** Add.

```
    6 . 8  0  0      ← Line up the decimal points.
    4 . 6  5  0      ← Write zeros so that all decimals have
 +  2 . 1  2  5        the same number of digits to the right
 ┌──┬──┐.┌──┬──┬──┐    of the decimal point.
 └──┴──┘ └──┴──┴──┘
```

### Check for Reasonableness

The sum ☐ is reasonable since it is close to ☐ .

## Quick Check

1. Find 0.84 + 2.0 + 3.32. Estimate first.

## Examples

**❷ Using Front-End Estimation** A lemonade costs $1.79, sodas cost $1.29, and water costs $1.49. Use front-end estimation to estimate the total cost of buying one of each drink.

**Step 1** Add the front-end digits. These are the the dollar amounts.

$$\begin{array}{r} \$1.79 \\ 1.29 \\ +\ 1.49 \\ \hline \$\ \boxed{\phantom{0}} \end{array}$$

**Step 2** Estimate the total cents. Then adjust dollar amounts.

$$\begin{array}{r} \$1.79 \\ 1.29 \end{array}\Big\} \leftarrow \text{about } \$\ \boxed{\phantom{0}}$$
$$+\ 1.49 \leftarrow \text{about } \$\ \boxed{\phantom{0}}$$
$$\$3 \leftarrow \text{about } \$\ \boxed{\phantom{0}}$$

The total cost is about $ $\boxed{\phantom{0}}$ + $ $\boxed{\phantom{000}}$ , or $ $\boxed{\phantom{000}}$ .

**❸ Finding a Difference** First estimate and then find $16 - 8.79$.

**Estimate** $16 - 8.79 \approx \boxed{\phantom{0}} - \boxed{\phantom{0}}$, or $\boxed{\phantom{0}}$

**Write 16 with a decimal point and two zeros.**

$$\begin{array}{r} 16.00 \\ -\ 8.79 \end{array}$$

**Rename 16 as 15 and** $\boxed{\phantom{0}}$ **tenths.**

$$\begin{array}{r} \overset{15\ 10}{\cancel{16}.00} \\ -\ 8.79 \end{array}$$

**Rename 10 tenths as 9 tenths and 10** $\boxed{\phantom{00000}}$.

$$\begin{array}{r} \overset{9}{\underset{}{}} \\ \overset{15\ \cancel{10}\ 10}{\cancel{16}.\cancel{00}} \\ -\ 8.79 \\ \hline \boxed{\phantom{000}} \end{array} \leftarrow \text{Subtract.}$$

**Check for Reasonableness** The difference $\boxed{\phantom{00}}$ is reasonable since it is close to $\boxed{\phantom{00}}$ .

## Quick Check

**2.** Use front-end estimation to estimate the total cost of one small popcorn and two large popcorns.

**3.** Use the graph at the right. How much greater is the women's record discus throw than the men's throw?

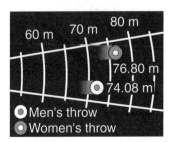

# Lesson 1-5
**Multiplying Decimals**

| Lesson Objective | Common Core State Standards |
|---|---|
| To multiply decimals and to solve problems by multiplying decimals | The Number System: 6.NS.3<br>Equations and Expressions: 6.EE.2.b |

## Examples

**❶ Multiplying by a Decimal** Find the product $2.73 \times 4$.

$$2.73 \leftarrow \boxed{\phantom{0}} \text{ decimal places}$$
$$\times \quad 4 \leftarrow + \boxed{\phantom{0}} \text{ decimal places}$$
$$\boxed{\phantom{0}}\boxed{\phantom{0}}.\boxed{\phantom{0}}\boxed{\phantom{0}} \leftarrow \boxed{\phantom{0}} \text{ decimal places}$$

**❷ Multiplying Decimals** Find the product $0.6 \times 0.42$.

$$0.42 \leftarrow \boxed{\phantom{0}} \text{ decimal places}$$
$$\times \quad 0.6 \leftarrow + \boxed{\phantom{0}} \text{ decimal places}$$
$$\boxed{\phantom{0}}.\boxed{\phantom{0}}\boxed{\phantom{0}}\boxed{\phantom{0}} \leftarrow \boxed{\phantom{0}} \text{ decimal places}$$

## Quick Check

**1. a.** Find $6 \times 0.13$

**b.** Find $4.37 \times 5$.

**c.** Find $7 \times 0.8$

**d.** Find $0.22 \times 3$.

**2.** Find each product.

**a.** $0.3(0.2)$

**b.** $1.9 \cdot 5.32$

**c.** $0.9 \times 0.14$

Name _____ Class _____ Date _____

## Example

❸ Cameron can read 196 words in a minute. Robert reads 1.6 times as fast. How many words can Robert read in a minute?

**Estimate**  196 × [    ]  ≈ 200 × 1.5, or [    ].

```
        1  9  6   ←  [  ]  decimal places
     ×  1. 6      ←  [  ]  decimal place
     1  1  7  6
   + 1  9  6
   ───────────
   [ ][ ][ ].[ ]  ←  [  ]  decimal place
```

Robert can read about [        ] words in a minute.

**Check for Reasonableness** [        ] is reasonable since it is close to [        ].

## Quick Check

3. One pound of tomatoes costs $1.29. To the nearest cent, how much do 2.75 pounds of tomatoes cost?

[                                                    ]

# Lesson 1-6

**Dividing Decimals**

| Lesson Objective | Common Core State Standards |
|---|---|
| To divide decimals and to solve problems by dividing decimals | The Number System: 6.NS.2, 6.NS.3<br>Equations and Expressions: 6.EE.2.b |

## Examples

**❶ Dividing Whole Numbers** There are 836 middle school students and 76 high school students going on a field trip. If each bus holds 48 passengers, how many buses are needed?

Total passengers: 836 + 76 = ☐

You need to divide ☐ into equal groups of 48.

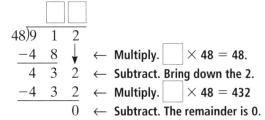

48)9  1  2
  −4  8 ↓   ← **Multiply.** ☐ × **48 = 48.**
    4  3  2  ← **Subtract. Bring down the 2.**
  −4  3  2  ← **Multiply.** ☐ × **48 = 432**
          0  ← **Subtract. The remainder is 0.**

So ☐ buses are needed.

**❷ Dividing a Decimal by a Whole Number** A class of 27 students held a picnic. They purchased food and drinks for the picnic for a total cost of $93.15. What was the price for each student's meal?

Since you are looking for prices of equal meals, you need to divide.

**Estimate** 93.15 ÷ 27 ≈ ☐ ÷ ☐ , or ☐ .

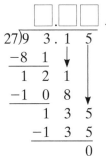

27)9  3 . 1  5   ← **Divide as with whole numbers. Place**
  −8  1 ↓           **the decimal point in the quotient above**
    1  2  1 ↓        **the decimal point in the dividend.**
  −1  0  8 ↓
       1  3  5
     −1  3  5
             0

Each student's meal cost $ ☐ .

**Check for Reasonableness** ☐ is reasonable since it is close to ☐ .

Name _____ Class _____ Date _____

**❸ Dividing a Decimal by a Decimal** Find the quotient $9.674 \div 0.7$.

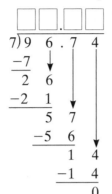

$0.7\overline{)9.674}$ ⟶

Since the divisor has ☐ decimal place, multiply the dividend and the divisor by ☐ so that the divisor is a whole number.

$$
\begin{array}{r}
\phantom{7)}\,\square\,\square\,.\,\square\,\square \\
7\overline{)9\ \ 6\,.\,7\ \ 4} \\
-7\phantom{\ \ \ \ \ \ \ \ } \\
\hline
2\ \ 6\phantom{\ \ \ \ \ } \\
-2\ \ 1\phantom{\ \ \ \ \ } \\
\hline
5\ \ 7\phantom{\ \ } \\
-5\ \ 6\phantom{\ \ } \\
\hline
1\ \ 4 \\
-1\ \ 4 \\
\hline
0
\end{array}
$$

← Divide as with whole numbers. Place the decimal point in the quotient above the decimal point in the dividend.

## Quick Check

**1. a.** $3,348 \div 9$

**b.** $27\overline{)378}$

**2. a.** Find $8\overline{)385.6}$

**b.** Find $9.12 \div 6$.

**3.** You have $2.75. You want to buy trading cards that cost $0.25 each. How many can you buy?

# Lesson 2-1
**Variables and Expressions**

| Lesson Objective | Common Core Standards |
|---|---|
| To evaluate algebraic expressions | Expressions and Equations: 6.EE.2.c, 6.EE.6 |

## Vocabulary

A numerical expression is _____

_____

A variable is _____

_____

An algebraic expression is a _____

_____

To evaluate an algebraic expression is to _____

_____

## Example

**1** **Modeling with Algebra Tiles** Model the expression $2x + 3$ with algebra tiles.

2 [_____] tiles represent **2x**, and

3 [_____] tiles represent **3**.

## Quick Check

**1.** Draw algebra tiles to model the expression $x + 2$.

## Examples

❷ **Evaluating an Algebraic Expression** Evaluate $8x + 2$ for $x = 3$.

$8x + 2 = 8\left(\boxed{\phantom{x}}\right) + 2$  ← **Replace x with** $\boxed{\phantom{x}}$.

$\quad\quad = \boxed{\phantom{xx}} + 2$  ← **Multiply 8 and 3.**

$\quad\quad = \boxed{\phantom{xx}}$  ← **Add 24 and 2.**

❸ **Canoe Rental** The cost to rent a canoe at the lake is a $6 basic fee plus $4 for each hour $h$ the canoe is rented. The expression for the total cost of a canoe rental is $6 + 4h$. Complete the table for the given number of hours.

| Hours | Total Cost |
|-------|------------|
| $h$   | $6 + 4h$   |
| 1     |            |
| 2     |            |
| 3     |            |

**Substitute each number of hours for h.**

 ← **6 + 4 ×** ☐

 ← **6 + 4 ×** ☐

 ← **6 + 4 ×** ☐

## Quick Check

**2.** Evaluate each expression for $x = 7$.

**a.** $3x + 15$

**b.** $5x \div 7$

**c.** $56 - 4x$

**3.** In Example 3, how much will it cost to rent a canoe for 6 hours?

# Lesson 2-2

**Writing Algebraic Expressions**

| Lesson Objective | Common Core Standards |
|---|---|
| To write algebraic expressions and use them to solve problems | Expressions and Equations: 6.EE.2.a, 6.EE.2.b, 6.EE.6 |

## Examples

**❶ From Words to Expressions** Write an expression for "the quotient when $y$ is divided by 12."

**❷ Retail** A newspaper advertisement reads, "Buy 3 T-shirts of the same kind, take $5 off the total price." Let $t$ represent the cost of one T-shirt. Write an algebraic expression that describes the situation.

| Total Cost | 5 |
|---|---|
| $t$ | $t$ | $t$ |

Write the full cost of 3 T-shirts as [  ] .

An expression of the discounted price is [  ] – [  ] .

## Quick Check

**1.** Write an expression for "2 more than $x$."

**2.** Brandon is 28 years younger than his father. Write an expression using Brandon's age to describe his father's age.

Name _____ Class _____ Date _____

## Example

❸ **From a Pattern to an Expression** Write an expression to describe the relationship of the data in the table.

| $n$ | ■ |
|-----|-----|
| 1 | 3 |
| 4 | 12 |
| 5 | 15 |

$1 \times \boxed{\phantom{0}} = 3$   ← **Multiplying each number in**
$4 \times \boxed{\phantom{0}} = 12$   **the first column by** $\boxed{\phantom{0}}$ **gives**
$5 \times \boxed{\phantom{0}} = 15$   **you the number in the**
  **second column.**

The expression $\boxed{\phantom{0000}}$, or $\boxed{\phantom{0000}}$, describes the pattern.

## Quick Check

**3.** Write an algebraic expression to describe the relationship in each table.

a.

| $n$ | ■ |
|-----|-----|
| 2 | 1 |
| 6 | 3 |
| 9 | 4.5 |

$\boxed{\phantom{00000000}}$

b.

| $n$ | ■ |
|-----|-----|
| 2 | 6 |
| 5 | 9 |
| 7 | 11 |

$\boxed{\phantom{00000000}}$

Name _____ Class _____ Date _____

# Lesson 2-3

| Lesson Objective | Common Core Standards |
|---|---|
| To use mental math to estimate and solve problems | Expressions and Equations: 6.EE.5, 6.EE.6, 6.EE.7 |

## Vocabulary and Key Concepts

**Number Properties**

**Identity Properties**

The sum of 0 and any number is [     ] .

**Arithmetic** $0 + 9 =$ [  ]      **Algebra** $0 + a =$ [  ]

The product of 1 and any number is [     ] .

**Arithmetic** $1 \cdot 9 =$ [  ]      **Algebra** $1 \cdot a =$ [  ]

**Commutative Properties**

Changing the [     ] of the addends or factors does not change the sum or the product.

**Arithmetic** $9 + 6 =$ [  ] $+$ [  ]      $9 \cdot 6 =$ [  ] $\cdot$ [  ]

**Algebra** $a + b =$ [  ] $+$ [  ]      $a \cdot b =$ [  ] $\cdot$ [  ]

**Associative Properties**

Changing the [     ] of numbers does not change the sum or the product.

**Arithmetic** $9 + (6 + 4) =$ [     ] $+$ [  ]      $9 \cdot (6 \cdot 4) =$ [     ] $\cdot$ [  ]

**Algebra** $a + (b + c) =$ [     ] $+$ [  ]      $a(bc) =$ [     ] $\cdot$ [  ]

An equation is _____

An open sentence is _____

A solution of an equation is _____

## Example

**❶ True Equations and False Equations** Is the equation $24 - 16 = 8$ true or false?

$24 - 16 \overset{?}{=} 8$  ← **Write the equation.**

[  ]  ← **Subtract 16 from 24.**

[  ] $\overset{?}{=} 8$  ← **Compare.**      The equation is [     ] .

•••••••••••••••••••••••••••••••••••••••••••••••••• *Course 1 Lesson 2-3*                    Daily Notetaking Guide

Name _____ Class _____ Date _____

## Examples

❷ **Using Mental Math** Use mental math to solve each equation.

**a.** $y - 7 = 15$

**b.** $d \div 9 = 6$

**What you think**

[    ] $- 7 = 15$, so the solution is [    ].

**What you think**

[    ] $\div 9 = 6$, so the solution is [    ].

❸ **Guess, Check, and Revise** Use the strategy *Guess, Check, and Revise* to solve $n + 14 = 42$.

**Estimate** Round numbers to get a good starting point.

$n + 14 = 42$

↓   ↓   ↓

$n + 10 = 40$

**What you think**

Using mental math, you know [    ] $+ 10 = 40$, so $n$ is close to [    ].

I can try substituting $n =$ [    ] in the equation: [    ] $+ 14 =$ [    ].

The number [    ] is too high. I will try $n = 25$:   $25 + 14 =$ [    ].

The number 25 is [    ]. I will try $n = 28$:   $28 + 14 =$ [    ].

Since $28 + 14 = 42$ is [    ], the solution of $n + 14 = 42$ is [    ].

## Quick Check

**1.** Tell whether each equation is true or false.

**a.** $7 \times 9 = 63$

**b.** $4 + 5 = 45$

**c.** $70 - 39 = 41$

**2. Mental Math** Solve each equation.

**a.** $17 - x = 8$

**b.** $w \div 4 = 20$

**c.** $4.7 + c = 5.9$

**3.** Use the strategy *Guess, Check, and Revise* to solve $k + 39 = 82$.

# Lesson 2-4                              **Solving Addition Equations**

| Lesson Objective | Common Core Standards |
|---|---|
| To use subtraction to solve equations | Expressions and Equations: 6.EE.5, 6.EE.6, 6.EE.7 |

## Vocabulary and Key Concepts

**Subtraction Property of Equality**

If you ☐ the same value from each side of an equation, the
two sides remain equal.

| **Arithmetic** | **Algebra** |
|---|---|
| $2 \cdot 3 = 6$, so $2 \cdot 3 - 4 = 6 - $ ☐ . | If $a = b$, then $a - c = b - $ ☐ . |

Inverse operations are _____

## Example

❶ **Solving Equations by Subtracting** Solve $h + 9 = 14$.
   Get $h$ alone on one side of the equation.

$$h \; + \; 9 \; = \; 14$$
$$\underline{\quad - \;\square \quad - \;\square \quad}$$
$$h \; = \; \square$$

← Subtract ☐ from each side to undo the
   ☐ and get $h$ by itself.

← Simplify.

**Check**   $h + 9 = 14$

← Check your solution in the original
   equation.

☐ $+ 9 \stackrel{?}{=} 14$   ← Substitute ☐ for $h$.

☐ $= 14$ ✓

## Quick Check

**1.** Solve $w + 4.3 = 9.1$. Check the solution.

Name _____ Class _____ Date _____

## Example

❷ **Growth** Rita's height in first grade was 44 inches. In the fourth grade, Rita's height was 51 inches. How many inches did Rita grow between the first and fourth grades?

| Height in fourth grade | |
|---|---|
| Height in first grade | Inches grown |

Let $h$ = the number of inches grown.

| 51 | |
|---|---|
| | |

The equation $\boxed{\phantom{00}} + \boxed{\phantom{00}} = \boxed{\phantom{00}}$ models this situation.

$$44 + h = 51$$

$$44 + h - \boxed{\phantom{0}} = 51 - \boxed{\phantom{0}} \qquad \leftarrow \textbf{Subtract } \boxed{\phantom{0}} \textbf{ from both sides}$$
$$\textbf{to undo the } \boxed{\phantom{000}}.$$

$$h = \boxed{\phantom{0}} \qquad \leftarrow \textbf{Simplify.}$$

Rita grew $\boxed{\phantom{0}}$ inches.

## Quick Check

2. A cat has gained 1.8 pounds in a year. It now weighs 11.6 pounds. Write and solve an equation to find how much it weighed one year ago. Check the solution.

# Lesson 2-5

**Solving Subtraction Equations**

| Lesson Objective | Common Core Standards |
|---|---|
| To use addition to solve equations | Expressions and Equations: 6.EE.5, 6.EE.6, 6.EE.7 |

## Key Concepts

**Addition Property of Equality**

If you [ ] the same value to each side of an equation, the two sides remain equal.

| **Arithmetic** | **Algebra** |
|---|---|
| $2 \cdot 3 = 6$, so $2 \cdot 3 + 4 = 6 + \boxed{\phantom{x}}$. | If $a = b$, then $a + c = b + \boxed{\phantom{x}}$. |

## Example

① **Solving an Equation by Adding** Solve $p - 22.3 = 5.08$.

$$p - 22.3 + \boxed{\phantom{xxxx}} = 5.08 + \boxed{\phantom{xxxx}}$$   ← Add $\boxed{\phantom{xxx}}$ to undo the $\boxed{\phantom{xxxxxxx}}$.

$$p = \boxed{\phantom{xxxx}}$$   ← Simplify.

## Quick Check

**1.** Solve each equation.

**a.** $n - 53 = 28$

**b.** $x - 43 = 12$

## Example

❷ **Entertainment** The sale price of a CD is \$11.49. This is \$3.50 less than the regular price (*r*) of the CD. What is the regular price of the CD?

**Words** | sale price | is | \$3.50 | less than | regular price

Let ☐ = the regular price.

**Equation** ☐ = ☐ − ☐

$$r - 3.50 = 11.49 \quad \leftarrow \text{ Write the equation.}$$

$$+ \boxed{\phantom{xx}} \qquad + \boxed{\phantom{xx}} \quad \leftarrow \text{ Add } \boxed{\phantom{xx}} \text{ to each side to undo the } \boxed{\phantom{xx}}.$$

$$r = \boxed{\phantom{xx}} \quad \leftarrow \text{ Simplify.}$$

The regular price of the CD is ☐ .

## Quick Check

2. The temperature dropped 9°F between 7 P.M. and midnight. It was 54°F at midnight. Write an equation to find the temperature at 7 P.M.

# Lesson 2-6

**Solving Multiplication and Division Equations**

| Lesson Objective | Common Core Standards |
|---|---|
| To use multiplication and division to solve equations | Expressions and Equations: 6.EE.5, 6.EE.6, 6.EE.7 |

## Key Concepts

**Division Property of Equality**

If you [____] each side of an equation by the same nonzero number, the two sides remain equal.

**Arithmetic**

$4 \times 2 = 8$, so $4 \times 2 \div 2 = 8 \div$ [__].

**Algebra**

If $a = b$ and $c \neq 0$, then $a \div c = b \div$ [__].

**Multiplication Property of Equality**

If you [____] each side of an equation by the same number, the two sides remain equal.

**Arithmetic**

$6 \div 2 = 3$, so $(6 \div 2) \times 2 = 3 \times$ [__].

**Algebra**

If $a = b$, then $a \cdot c = b \cdot$ [__].

## Example

**1 Solving an Equation by Dividing** Solve $6x = 144$.

$$6x \div \boxed{\phantom{x}} = 144 \div \boxed{\phantom{x}}$$    ← Divide each side by [__] to undo the [_____] and get *x* alone on one side.

$$x = \boxed{\phantom{x}}$$    ← Simplify.

**Check**    $6x = 144$    ← Check your solution in the original equation.

$$6 \times \boxed{\phantom{x}} \overset{?}{=} 144$$    ← Replace *x* with [__].

$$\boxed{\phantom{x}} = 144 \checkmark$$

## Quick Check

**1.** Solve $0.8p = 32$. Then check the solution.

[box for work]

## Examples

❷ **Entertainment** The cost of a pay-per-view concert on television is $39.95. Five friends decide to watch the concert together and split the cost equally. What amount will each friend pay?

Use a diagram to help write an equation.

| Total Cost | | | | |
|---|---|---|---|---|
| $c$ | $c$ | $c$ | $c$ | $c$ |

Let $c$ = each person's share of the cost of the concert.

The equation [    ] = [    ] models this situation.

$5c = 39.95$       ← **Write the equation.**

$5c \div$ [  ] $= 39.95 \div$ [  ]    ← **Divide each side by** [  ] **to undo the**
[            ].

$c =$ [        ]    ← **Simplify.**

Each friend's share is [        ].

❸ **Solving an Equation by Multiplying** Solve $x \div 6.3 = 9$.

$x \div 6.3 \times$ [    ] $= 9 \times$ [    ]    ← **Multiply by** [    ] **to undo the** [        ] **and get x alone.**

$x =$ [        ]    ← **Simplify.**

## Quick Check

**2.** A club sells greeting cards for a fundraiser. The profit for each card sold is $.35. The club's total profit is $302.75. Use an equation to find the total number of cards the club sells.

[                                                                    ]

**3.** Solve $w \div 1.5 = 10$. Then check the solution.

[                                                                    ]

# Lesson 3-1

**Divisibility and Mental Math**

**Lesson Objective**

To check for divisibility using mental math and to use divisibility to solve problems

## Vocabulary and Key Concepts

**Divisibility of Whole Numbers**

**A whole number is divisible by**

- ☐ , if the number ends in 0, 2, 4, 6, or 8.

- ☐ , if the sum of the number's digits is divisible by 3.

- ☐ , if the number ends in 0 or 5.

- ☐ , if the sum of the number's digits is divisible by 9.

- ☐ , if the number ends in 0.

One whole number is ☐ by a second whole number if the

remainder is ☐ when the first number is divided by the second number.

An even number is _____

An odd number is _____

## Example

❶ **Using Mental Math for Divisibility**

**a.** Is 46 divisible by 3?

  **Think** Since $3 \times 15 =$ ☐ ,

  and $3 \times 16 =$ ☐ · ,

  46 ☐ divisible by 3.

**b.** Is 63 divisible by 7?

  **Think** Since $7 \times 9 =$ ☐ ,

  63 ☐ divisible by 7.

## Quick Check

**1. a.** Is 64 divisible by 6? ☐

**b.** Is 93 divisible by 3? ☐

## Examples

❷ **Divisibility by 2, 3, 5, and 10** Test 580 for divisibility by 2, 3, 5, and 10.

2: 580 is an [＿＿＿] number. So 580 [＿＿＿] divisible by 2.

3: Find the sum of the digits in 580.

$5 + 8 + 0 =$ [＿＿＿]

The sum of the digits is [＿＿], which [＿＿＿] divisible by 3.

So 580 [＿＿＿] divisible by 3.

5: 580 ends in [＿]. So 580 [＿＿＿] divisible by 5.

10: 580 ends in [＿]. So 580 [＿＿＿] divisible by 10.

❸ **Divisibility by 9** A baker sells muffins in boxes that contain exactly 9 muffins each. Can the baker place 576 muffins in boxes of 9 with none left over?

If 576 is divisible by 9, then there will be no muffins left over.

$5 + 7 + 6 =$ [＿＿＿]  ← **Find the sum of the digits in 576.**

$18 ÷ 9 =$ [＿＿]  ← **The sum** [＿＿＿] **divisible by 9.**

So, 576 [＿＿＿] divisible by 9. There [＿＿＿] muffins left over.

## Quick Check

2. Test each number for divisibility by 2, 3, 5, and 10.

   **a.** 150   **b.** 1,021   **c.** 2,112

   [＿＿＿＿]   [＿＿＿＿]   [＿＿＿＿]

3. **Music** A high school marching band has 126 members. Each row in the band formation on the field has 9 musicians. Will everyone in the band fit in a nine-person row with none left over?

   [＿＿＿＿＿＿＿＿＿＿＿＿＿＿＿＿＿＿＿＿]

# Lesson 3-2                                                        Exponents

| Lesson Objective | Common Core Standards |
|---|---|
| To use exponents and to simplify expressions with exponents | Expressions and Equations: 6.EE.1, 6.EE.2, 6.EE.2.c |

## Vocabulary and Key Concepts

**Order of Operations**

1. Do all operations within ⬚ first.

2. Do all work with exponents.

3. ⬚ and ⬚ in order from left to right.

4. ⬚ and ⬚ in order from left to right.

An ⬚ tells you how many times

a number, or ⬚, is used as a factor.

$8 \times 8 \times 8 = 8^3$ ← ⬚

↑

⬚

A power is _____

## Example

❶ **Using Exponents** Write $5 \times 5 \times 5 \times 5$ using an exponent. Name the base and the exponent.

$5 \times 5 \times 5 \times 5 = 5^{⬚}$     ← $5^4$ means that ⬚ is used as a factor ⬚ times.

The base is ⬚ and the exponent is ⬚.

## Quick Check

1. Write each expression using an exponent. Name the base and the exponent.

   **a.** $3.94 \times 3.94$       **b.** $7 \times 7 \times 7 \times 7$       **c.** $x \cdot x \cdot x$

## Examples

❷ **Simplifying a Power** What is the value of $6^3$?

$6^3 = 6 \times 6 \times 6 =$ ⬚    ← **The base** ⬚ **is used as a factor** ⬚ **times.**

❸ **Simplifying an Expression** Simplify $24 - (8 - 1.2 \times 5)^2$.

$24 - \left(8 - \boxed{\phantom{x}}\right)^2$    ← **Simplify within parentheses. Simplify 1.2 × 5.**

$24 - \left(\boxed{\phantom{x}}\right)^2$    ← **In parentheses, simplify 8 − 6.**

$24 - \boxed{\phantom{x}}$    ← **Simplify $2^2$.**

$\boxed{\phantom{xx}}$    ← **Subtract 4 from 24.**

## Quick Check

2. **Astronomy** Phobos, the largest of Mars' moons, has a diameter of $3^3$ kilometers. What is the value of $3^3$?

[ ]

3. **a.** Simplify $2^3 - 6 \div 3$.

[ ]

**b.** Simplify $5 + (2 + 1)^2$.

[ ]

# Lesson 3-3

**Prime Numbers and Prime Factorization**

**Lesson Objective**

To factor numbers and to find the prime factorization of numbers

## Vocabulary

A factor is _____

_____

A composite number is _____

_____

A prime number is _____

_____

A prime factorization is _____

_____

## Example

**❶ Finding Factors** List the factors of each number.

**a.** 24

$1 \times 24$  ← Write each pair of factors. Start with 1.

$2 \times \boxed{\phantom{0}}, 3 \times \boxed{\phantom{0}}, 4 \times \boxed{\phantom{0}}$  ← $\boxed{\phantom{0}}, \boxed{\phantom{0}},$ and $\boxed{\phantom{0}}$ are factors. Skip 5, since 24 is not divisible by 5.

$6 \times \boxed{\phantom{0}}$  ← Stop when you repeat factors.

The factors of 24 are $\boxed{\phantom{0}}, \boxed{\phantom{0}}, \boxed{\phantom{0}}, \boxed{\phantom{0}}, \boxed{\phantom{0}}, \boxed{\phantom{0}}, \boxed{\phantom{0}},$ and $\boxed{\phantom{0}}$.

**b.** 35

$1 \times 35$  ← Write each pair of factors. Start with 1.

$\boxed{\phantom{0}} \times 7$  ← Skip 2, 3, and 4, since 35 is not divisible by 2, 3, or 4. $\boxed{\phantom{0}}$ is a factor. Skip 6, since 35 is not divisible by 6.

$7 \times \boxed{\phantom{0}}$  ← Stop when you repeat factors.

The factors of 35 are $\boxed{\phantom{0}}, \boxed{\phantom{0}}, \boxed{\phantom{0}},$ and $\boxed{\phantom{0}}$.

## Quick Check

**1.** A gift box must hold the same number of pears in each row. You have 24 pears. What arrangements can you use?

_____

## Examples

❷ **Prime or Composite?** Is the number prime or composite? Explain.

   **a.** 61 [＿＿＿＿] ; 61 has [＿＿] factors, [＿＿] and [＿＿].

   **b.** 65 [＿＿＿＿] ; 65 is divisible by [＿＿], so 65 has more than [＿＿] factors.

❸ **Prime Factorization** Write the prime factorization of 90 using exponents.

**Method 1** Use a division ladder

   2)90     ← **Divide 90 by the prime number 2. Work down.**

   3)[＿＿]   ← **The result is** [＿＿]. **Divide by the prime number 3.**

   3)[＿＿]   ← **The result is** [＿＿]. **Divide by 3 again.**

    [＿＿]   ← **The prime factorization is** [＿] × [＿] × [＿] × [＿].

**Method 2** Use a factor tree

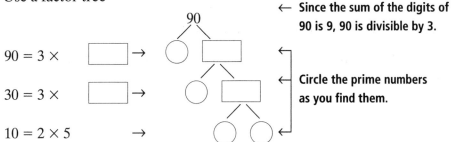

← **Since the sum of the digits of 90 is 9, 90 is divisible by 3.**

90 = 3 × [＿＿] →

30 = 3 × [＿＿] →

← **Circle the prime numbers as you find them.**

10 = 2 × 5 →

The prime factorization of 90 is [＿] × [＿] × [＿] × [＿], or [＿] × [＿]$^2$ × [＿].

## Quick Check

**2.** Is the number prime or composite? Explain.

   **a.** 39

   [＿＿＿＿＿＿＿＿＿＿＿＿＿＿＿＿＿＿＿＿＿]

   **b.** 47

   [＿＿＿＿＿＿＿＿＿＿＿＿＿＿＿＿＿＿＿＿＿]

   **c.** 63

   [＿＿＿＿＿＿＿＿＿＿＿＿＿＿＿＿＿＿＿＿＿]

**3.** Find the prime factorization of 27.

   [＿＿＿＿＿＿＿＿＿＿＿＿]

# Lesson 3-4

Greatest Common Factor

| Lesson Objective | Common Core Standard |
|---|---|
| To find the GCF of two or more numbers | The Number System: 6.NS.4 |

## Vocabulary

A common factor is _____

_____

The greatest common factor (GCF) of two or more numbers is _____

_____

## Example

**1** **Using Lists of Factors** Find the greatest common factor of 48 and 64.

List the factors of 48 and the factors of 64. Then circle the common factors.

Factors of 48: 1, 2, 3, 4, 6, 8, 12, 16, 24, 48

Factors of 64: 1, 2, 4, 8, 16, 32, 64      ← **The common factors are**

The greatest common factor (GCF) is ☐.      ☐, ☐, ☐, ☐, and ☐.

## Quick Check

**1.** List the factors to find the GCF of each pair of numbers.

**a.** 6, 21   factors of 6: ☐, ☐, ☐, ☐

factors of 21: ☐, ☐, ☐, ☐      GCF of 6 and 21: ☐

**b.** 18, 49   factors of 18: ☐, ☐, ☐, ☐, ☐, ☐

factors of 49: ☐, ☐, ☐      GCF of 18 and 49: ☐

**c.** 14, 28   factors of 14: ☐, ☐, ☐, ☐

factors of 28: ☐, ☐, ☐, ☐, ☐, ☐      GCF of 14 and 28: ☐

Name _____ Class _____ Date _____

## Examples

❷ **Using a Division Ladder** Find the GCF of 84 and 90. Use a division ladder.

2) 84   90   ← **Divide by** ☐ **, a common factor of 84 and 90.**
3)☐ ☐   ← **Divide by** ☐ **, a common factor of 42 and 45.**
☐ ☐   ← **14 and 15 have** ☐ **common factors.**
—————— **Multiply the common factors:** ☐ × ☐ = ☐ .

The GCF of 84 and 90 is ☐ .

❸ **Using Factor Trees** Use factor trees to find the GCF of 28 and 42.

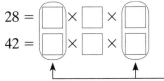

28          42
/\          /\
2  ☐        2  ☐     ← **Make a factor tree**
   /\          /\        **for each number.**
  2  ☐       ☐   7

28 = ☐ × ☐ × ☐
42 = ☐ × ☐ × ☐     ← **Write the prime factorization**
                        **for each number.**

———————— **Identify common factors.**
☐ × ☐ = ☐     ← **Multiply the common factors.**

The GCF of 28 and 42 is ☐ .

## Quick Check

**2.** You want to cut two ribbons into pieces of equal length with nothing left over. The ribbons are 18 and 42 inches long. What is the longest possible length of ribbon you can cut?

☐

**3.** Use factor trees to find the GCF.

**a.** 48, 80, 128

**b.** 36, 60, 84

# Lesson 3-5
**Least Common Multiple**

| Lesson Objective | Common Core Standard |
|---|---|
| To find the LCM of two or more numbers | The Number System: 6.NS.4 |

## Vocabulary

A multiple of a number is _____

_____

A common multiple is _____

_____

The least common multiple (LCM) of two or more numbers is _____

_____

## Examples

❶ **Finding the LCM Using Lists of Multiples** Find the least common multiple of 6 and 9.

multiples of 6: ☐ , ☐ , ☐ , ☐ , ☐ , ☐     ← **List multiples of each number.**

multiples of 9: ☐ , ☐ , ☐ , ☐     ☐ **and** ☐ **are common multiples.**

The least common multiple is ☐ .

❷ **Using Prime Factorizations** Use prime factorizations to find the LCM of 6, 9, and 15.

Write the prime factorizations for 6, 9, and 15. Then circle each different factor where it appears the greatest number of times.

$6 = $ ☐ $\times$ ☐     ← **2 appears** ☐ **.**

$9 = $ ☐ $\times$ ☐     ← **3 appears the most often here** (☐) **.**

$15 = $ ☐ $\times$ ☐     ← **5 appears** ☐ **· Don't circle 3 again.**

☐ $\times$ ☐ $\times$ ☐ $\times$ ☐ $=$ ☐     ← **Multiply the circled factors.**

The LCM of 6, 9, and 15 is ☐ .

Name _____ Class _____ Date _____

## Quick Check

1. List multiples to find the LCM.

   **a.** 10, 12

   multiples of 10: ⬚ , ⬚ , ⬚ , ⬚ , ⬚ , ⬚

   multiples of 12: ⬚ , ⬚ , ⬚ , ⬚ , ⬚ , ⬚

   The LCM of 10 and 12 is ⬚ .

   **b.** 7, 10

2. Use prime factorizations to find the LCM of 6, 8, and 12.

Name _____ Class _____ Date _____

# Lesson 3-6
**The Distributive Property**

| Lesson Objective | Common Core Standards |
|---|---|
| To use the Distributive Property to simplify expressions in problem solving situations | Expressions and Equations: 6.EE.2b, 6.EE.3, 6.EE.4 |

## Vocabulary and Key Concepts

**Distributive Property of Multiplication**

**Over Addition**

$a(b + c) = \boxed{\phantom{xxx}} + \boxed{\phantom{xxx}}$

**Over Subtraction**

$a(b - c) = \boxed{\phantom{xxx}} - \boxed{\phantom{xxx}}$

**Equivalent expressions** have the same _____

## Example

❶ **Using the Distributive Property with Algebraic Expressions** Write an equivalent expression for $3(9x + 3)$.

$3(9x + 3) = \left(\boxed{\phantom{xx}} \times \boxed{\phantom{xx}}\right) + \left(\boxed{\phantom{xx}} \times \boxed{\phantom{xx}}\right)$ ← Use the Distributive Property.

$\qquad = \boxed{\phantom{xx}} + \boxed{\phantom{xx}}$ ← Multiply.

**Check**

$3(9x + 3) \overset{?}{=} \boxed{\phantom{xxxxx}}$ ← Check if the two expressions are equivalent.

$3\left(9 \cdot \boxed{\phantom{xx}} + 3\right) \overset{?}{=} \boxed{\phantom{xxxxx}}$ ← Substitute a value, such as 2, for $x$.

$\boxed{\phantom{xxx}} = \boxed{\phantom{xxx}}$ ← Simplify.

## Quick Check

1. Simplify each expression.

a. $4(3n + 6)$

b. $8(7 - 3m + 4p)$

c. $12(2a + 3b - 5)$

Name _____ Class _____ Date _____

### Example

❷ **Factoring Expressions** Factor $40 + 16$.

$40 = $ [_____]     ← Write the prime factors of 40 and 16.
                              Then determine the GCF.

$16 = $ [_____]

$40 + 16 = $ [_____]   ← Write each term as a product of the GCF and
                                  its remaining factors.

$= $ [_____]        ← Use the Distributive Property.

### Quick Check

2. Factor each expression.

   **a.** $18 + 24$        **b.** $56 + 49$        **c.** $84 + 60$

### Example

❸ **Factor Algebraic Expressions** Factor $20x + 8 + 12y$.

$20x = 2 \cdot 2 \cdot 5 \cdot x$

$8 = $ [_____]        ← Write the prime factors of 20x, 8, and 12y.

$12y = $ [_____]      ← The GCF is $2 \cdot$ _____ = _____.

$20x + 8 + 12y = $ [_____]   ← Write each term as a product of the GCF and its
                                          remaining factors.

$= $ [_____]        ← Use the Distributive Property.

### Quick Check

3. Factor each expression.

   **a.** $3n + 21$        **b.** $72 + 16h$        **c.** $48y + 80z + 64$

# Lesson 3-7

**Simplifying Algebraic Expressions**

| Lesson Objective | Common Core Standards |
|---|---|
| To simplify algebraic expressions | Expressions and Equations: 6.EE.2b, 6.EE.3, 6.EE.4 |

## Vocabulary and Key Concepts

**Properties for Simplifying Algebraic Expressions**

| Property | Addition | Multiplication |
|---|---|---|
| [ ] | $a + b = b + a$ | $ab = ba$ |
| Associative | [ ] | $(ab)c = a(bc)$ |

| | Addition | Subtraction |
|---|---|---|
| Distributive | $a(b + c) = ab + ac$ | [ ] |

A **term** is _____

_____

A **coefficient** is _____

## Example

❶ **Generating Equivalent Expressions** Simplify $8k + (5k + 7 + 11k)$ by combining like terms.

$8k + (5k + 7 + 11k) = 8k + \left( \boxed{\phantom{xxxxxxxx}} \right)$  ← Commutative Property.

$= \left( \boxed{\phantom{xxxxxxxx}} \right) + 7$  ← Associative Property.

$= k(8 + 5 + 11) + 7$  ← $\boxed{\phantom{xxxxxxxx}}$

$= k(24) + 7$  ← Simplify.

$= 24k + 7$  ← $\boxed{\phantom{xxxxxxxx}}$

Daily Notetaking Guide

Name _____ Class _____ Date _____

## Quick Check

1. Find an equivalent expression for each expression by simplifying.

   **a.** $2b + 3b + 4b$

   **b.** $2c + 8 + 4c - c$

## Example

❷ **Application: Perimeter** The playground at a park has the dimensions shown in the figure. What is the perimeter of the playground?

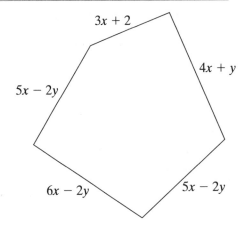

$3x + 2 + 4x + y + 5x - 2y + 6x - 2y + 5x - 2y$    ← **Write an expression for the perimeter.**

$\left(\underline{\hspace{3cm}}\right) + \left(\underline{\hspace{3cm}}\right) + 2$    ← **Use the Commutative Property to group like terms.**

$x\left(\underline{\hspace{3cm}}\right) + y\left(\underline{\hspace{3cm}}\right)$    ← **Distributive Property.**

$x(23) + y(-5)$    ← **Simplify.**

$23x - 5y$    ← $\underline{\hspace{4cm}}$

## Quick Check

2. A drawing of Mrs. Stefano's yard is shown in the figure at the right. What is the perimeter of her yard?

# Lesson 4-1

Multiplying Fractions and Mixed Numbers

**Lesson Objective**

To solve problems by multiplying fractions and multiplying mixed numbers

## Key Concepts

**Multiplying Fractions**

**Arithmetic**

$$\frac{3}{4} \times \frac{1}{2} = \frac{3 \times 1}{4 \times 2} = \frac{3}{8}$$

**Algebra**

$\frac{a}{b} \cdot \frac{c}{d} = \frac{ac}{bd}$, where $b$ and $d$ are not zero.

## Example

**❶ Multiplying Two Fractions** Find $\frac{5}{6}$ of $\frac{3}{8}$.

$$\frac{5}{6} \cdot \frac{3}{8} = \frac{5 \cdot \boxed{\phantom{0}}}{\boxed{\phantom{0}} \cdot 8} \quad \leftarrow \text{ Multiply the numerators.}$$
$$\leftarrow \text{ Multiply the denominators.}$$

$$= \frac{\boxed{\phantom{0}}}{\boxed{\phantom{0}}} \quad \leftarrow \text{ Find the two products.}$$

$$= \frac{\boxed{\phantom{0}}}{\boxed{\phantom{0}}} \quad \leftarrow \text{ Simplify.}$$

## Quick Check

**1. a.** Find $\frac{3}{5} \cdot \frac{1}{4}$.

**b.** Find $\frac{2}{9} \times \frac{5}{7}$.

Name _____ Class _____ Date _____

**Example**

❷ **Multiplying a Whole Number** Find $\frac{2}{5}$ of 30.

$\frac{2}{5} \cdot 30 = \frac{2}{5} \cdot \dfrac{\boxed{\phantom{x}}}{\boxed{\phantom{x}}}$  ← Write 30 as $\dfrac{\boxed{\phantom{x}}}{\boxed{\phantom{x}}}$.

$= \dfrac{\boxed{\phantom{x}}}{\boxed{\phantom{x}}} \cdot \overset{\boxed{\phantom{x}}}{\underset{1}{\cancel{30}}}$  ← Divide 30 and 5 by their GCF, $\boxed{\phantom{x}}$.

$= \dfrac{\boxed{\phantom{x}}}{\boxed{\phantom{x}}}$  ← Multiply the numerators and denominators.

$= \boxed{\phantom{x}}$  ← Simplify.

**Quick Check**

**2.** A baby alligator is $\frac{5}{6}$ foot long. An adult alligator is 12 times as long as the baby alligator. How long is the adult alligator?

**Example**

❸ **Multiplying Mixed Numbers** Find the product $3\frac{3}{8} \times 1\frac{5}{9}$.

**Estimate** $3\frac{3}{8} \times 1\frac{5}{9} \approx \boxed{\phantom{x}} \times \boxed{\phantom{x}}$, or $\boxed{\phantom{x}}$.

$3\frac{3}{8} \times 1\frac{5}{9} = \dfrac{\boxed{\phantom{x}}}{8} \times \dfrac{\boxed{\phantom{x}}}{9}$  ← Write the mixed numbers as improper fractions.

$= \dfrac{\boxed{\phantom{x}}}{\boxed{\phantom{x}}} \times \dfrac{\boxed{\phantom{x}}}{\boxed{\phantom{x}}}$  ← Divide 27 and 9 by their GCF, $\boxed{\phantom{x}}$. Divide 8 and 14 by their GCF, $\boxed{\phantom{x}}$.

$= \dfrac{\boxed{\phantom{x}}}{\boxed{\phantom{x}}}$, or $\boxed{\phantom{x}}\dfrac{\boxed{\phantom{x}}}{\boxed{\phantom{x}}}$  ← Multiply the numerators and denominators. Then write as a mixed number.

**Check for Reasonableness** $\boxed{\phantom{x}}\dfrac{\boxed{\phantom{x}}}{\boxed{\phantom{x}}}$ is near the estimate of $\boxed{\phantom{x}}$.

**Quick Check**

**3. a.** Find $10\frac{1}{4} \times 2\frac{3}{4}$.

**b.** Find $7\frac{1}{3} \times 3\frac{3}{4}$.

Daily Notetaking Guide  Course 1 Lesson 4-1  **41**

# Lesson 4-2                                         Modeling Fraction Division

| Lesson Objective | Common Core State Standard |
|---|---|
| To use models to interpret and perform fraction division and to solve word problems involving fraction division | The Number System: 6.NS.1 |

## Example

**❶ Dividing a Whole Number by a Unit Fraction** Make a model to represent the expression $2 \div \frac{1}{6}$. Then find the quotient.

**Step 1** Draw [ ] congruent circles to represent the dividend 2.

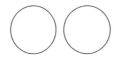

**Step 2** Divide each circle into [ ] to represent the divisor $\frac{1}{6}$.

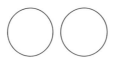

**Step 3** Find the total number of pieces you have. You have 2 circles. Each circle is divided into sixths. So you have [ ] pieces altogether.

**Step 4** This shows that $2 \div \frac{1}{6} = $ [ ]

## Quick Check

**1.** Make a model to represent the expression $8 \div \frac{1}{4}$. Then find the quotient.

## Example

❷ **Dividing a Mixed Number by a Unit Fraction** Suppose you have $3\frac{2}{3}$ loaves of banana bread to share. Use a model to find how many sixths you can cut from the loaves. Then write the division problem shown in the model.

**Step 1** In the top row, use [ ] unit bars to represent the $3\frac{2}{3}$ loaves.

**Step 2** Place [ ] bars in the second row to represent the sixths you can cut from the loaves.

| 1 | 1 | 1 | |
|---|---|---|---|
| $\frac{1}{6}$ $\frac{1}{6}$ $\frac{1}{6}$ $\frac{1}{6}$ $\frac{1}{6}$ $\frac{1}{6}$ | $\frac{1}{6}$ $\frac{1}{6}$ $\frac{1}{6}$ $\frac{1}{6}$ $\frac{1}{6}$ $\frac{1}{6}$ | $\frac{1}{6}$ $\frac{1}{6}$ $\frac{1}{6}$ $\frac{1}{6}$ $\frac{1}{6}$ $\frac{1}{6}$ | $\frac{1}{6}$ $\frac{1}{6}$ |

**Step 3** Find the number of $\frac{1}{6}$ bars that make up the $3\frac{2}{3}$ unit bars.
The model shows that there are [ ] $\frac{1}{6}$-bars that make up the $3\frac{2}{3}$ unit bars.

**Step 4** Write the division problem. This shows that $3\frac{2}{3} \div \frac{1}{6} =$ [ ].

## Quick Check

2. Suppose you have $1\frac{3}{4}$ sheets of wrapping paper to cut for wrapping gifts. Use a model to find how many eighths you can cut from the sheets. Then write the division problem shown in the model.

# Lesson 4-3

**Dividing Fractions**

| Lesson Objective | Common Core State Standard |
|---|---|
| To divide fractions and to solve problems by dividing fractions | The Number System: 6.NS.1 |

## Vocabulary and Key Concepts

**Dividing Fractions**

**Arithmetic**

$$\frac{3}{5} \div \frac{1}{3} = \frac{3}{5} \times \frac{3}{1}$$

**Algebra**

$$\frac{a}{b} \div \frac{c}{d} = \frac{a}{b} \times \frac{d}{c}, \text{where } b, c, \text{ and } d \text{ are not } 0.$$

Two numbers are reciprocals if _____

## Example

❶ **Writing a Reciprocal** Write the reciprocal of each number.

**a.** $\frac{4}{9}$

Since $\frac{4}{9} \times \dfrac{\boxed{\phantom{0}}}{\boxed{\phantom{0}}} = \dfrac{\boxed{\phantom{0}}}{\boxed{\phantom{0}}}$ or 1, the reciprocal is $\dfrac{\boxed{\phantom{0}}}{\boxed{\phantom{0}}}$.

**b.** 5

Write 5 as $\frac{5}{1}$.

Since $\frac{5}{1} \times \dfrac{\boxed{\phantom{0}}}{\boxed{\phantom{0}}} = \dfrac{\boxed{\phantom{0}}}{\boxed{\phantom{0}}}$ or 1, the reciprocal is $\dfrac{\boxed{\phantom{0}}}{\boxed{\phantom{0}}}$.

## Quick Check

**1. a.** Find the reciprocal of $\frac{3}{4}$.

**b.** Find the reciprocal of 7.

Name _____ Class _____ Date _____

## Examples

❷ **Dividing with Fractions** Find $\frac{3}{8} \div \frac{7}{12}$.

$\frac{3}{8} \div \frac{7}{12} = \frac{3}{8} \times \frac{12}{7}$  ← Multiply by $\dfrac{\boxed{\phantom{x}}}{\boxed{\phantom{x}}}$, the reciprocal of $\frac{7}{12}$.

$= \dfrac{3}{\underset{\boxed{}}{8}} \times \dfrac{\overset{\boxed{}}{12}}{7}$  ← Divide 8 and 12 by their GCF, $\boxed{\phantom{x}}$.

$= \dfrac{\boxed{\phantom{x}}}{\boxed{\phantom{x}}}$  ← Multiply.

❸ **Recipes** Chris uses $\frac{3}{4}$ cup of brown sugar in each batch of his banana muffins. He has a total of 5 cups of brown sugar. How many batches of banana muffins can Chris bake?

You want to find out how many $\frac{3}{4}$-cup portions are in 5 cups, so divide 5 by $\frac{3}{4}$.

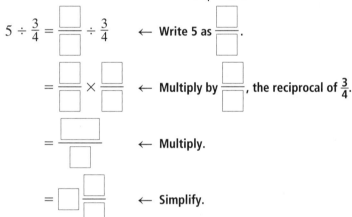

$5 \div \frac{3}{4} = \dfrac{\boxed{\phantom{x}}}{\boxed{\phantom{x}}} \div \frac{3}{4}$  ← Write 5 as $\dfrac{\boxed{\phantom{x}}}{\boxed{\phantom{x}}}$.

$= \dfrac{\boxed{\phantom{x}}}{\boxed{\phantom{x}}} \times \dfrac{\boxed{\phantom{x}}}{\boxed{\phantom{x}}}$  ← Multiply by $\dfrac{\boxed{\phantom{x}}}{\boxed{\phantom{x}}}$, the reciprocal of $\frac{3}{4}$.

$= \dfrac{\boxed{\phantom{x}}}{\boxed{\phantom{x}}}$  ← Multiply.

$= \boxed{\phantom{x}} \dfrac{\boxed{\phantom{x}}}{\boxed{\phantom{x}}}$  ← Simplify.

Chris has enough brown sugar to bake $\boxed{\phantom{x}} \dfrac{\boxed{\phantom{x}}}{\boxed{\phantom{x}}}$ batches of banana muffins.

## Quick Check

**2. a.** Find $\frac{9}{16} \div \frac{3}{4}$.

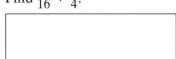

**b.** Find $\frac{4}{5} \div \frac{1}{3}$.

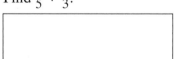

**3.** Your art teacher cuts $\frac{5}{6}$ yard of fabric into five equal pieces. How long is each piece of fabric?

# Lesson 4-4

**Dividing Mixed Numbers**

| Lesson Objective | Common Core State Standard |
|---|---|
| To estimate and compute the quotient of mixed numbers | The Number System: 6.NS.1 |

## Examples

❶ **Estimating Quotients** Paulo wants to put a row of decorative tiles along a wall. The wall is $72\frac{3}{8}$ inches wide. Each tile is $3\frac{3}{4}$ inches wide. Estimate the number of tiles he will need. Draw a diagram to model the situation.

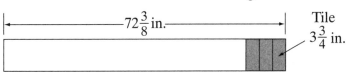

Tile
$3\frac{3}{4}$ in.

$72\frac{3}{8} \div 3\frac{3}{4}$    ← **Round each mixed number to the nearest whole number.**

$\boxed{\phantom{x}} \div \boxed{\phantom{x}} = \boxed{\phantom{x}}$    ← **Divide.**

Paulo needs about $\boxed{\phantom{x}}$ tiles.

❷ **Multiple Choice** Shaleen has enough oatmeal to make 5 batches of cookies. She wants to distribute $3\frac{1}{3}$ cups of raisins equally among the 5 batches. What amount of raisins should she put into each batch?

**A.** $\frac{1}{4}$ cup       **B.** $\frac{1}{3}$ cup       **C.** $\frac{2}{3}$ cup       **D.** $\frac{3}{4}$ cup

$\boxed{\phantom{xxx}} \div \boxed{\phantom{xxx}}$    ← **Divide the number of cups by the number of batches.**

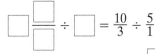

$\boxed{\phantom{x}}\frac{\boxed{\phantom{x}}}{\boxed{\phantom{x}}} \div \boxed{\phantom{x}} = \frac{10}{3} \div \frac{5}{1}$    ← **Substitute. Then write the numbers as improper fractions.**

$= \frac{10}{3} \times \frac{\boxed{\phantom{x}}}{\boxed{\phantom{x}}}$    ← **Multiply by** $\frac{\boxed{\phantom{x}}}{\boxed{\phantom{x}}}$ **, the reciprocal of 5.**

$= \frac{\boxed{\phantom{x}}\cancel{10}}{3} \times \frac{1}{\cancel{5}\boxed{\phantom{x}}}$    ← **Divide 10 and 5 by their GCF,** $\boxed{\phantom{x}}$ **.**

$= \frac{\boxed{\phantom{x}}}{\boxed{\phantom{x}}}$    ← **Multiply.**

Each batch of cookies gets $\frac{\boxed{\phantom{x}}}{\boxed{\phantom{x}}}$ cups of raisins. The correct answer is choice $\boxed{\phantom{x}}$.

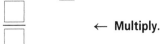

**Check for Reasonableness** You can estimate $3\frac{1}{3} \div 5$. The result is $3 \div 5$ or

$\frac{\boxed{\phantom{x}}}{\boxed{\phantom{x}}}$, so $\frac{\boxed{\phantom{x}}}{\boxed{\phantom{x}}}$ cup is a reasonable answer.

Name _____ Class _____ Date _____

**❸ Dividing Mixed Numbers** Find $6\frac{1}{4} \div 1\frac{7}{8}$.

$$6\frac{1}{4} \div 1\frac{7}{8} = \frac{25}{4} \div \frac{15}{8}$$  ← **Write the numbers as improper fractions.**

$$= \frac{25}{4} \times \frac{\boxed{\phantom{0}}}{\boxed{\phantom{0}}}$$  ← **Multiply by $\dfrac{\boxed{\phantom{0}}}{\boxed{\phantom{0}}}$, the reciprocal of $\frac{15}{8}$.**

$$= \frac{\overset{5}{\cancel{25}}}{1\,\cancel{4}} \times \frac{\overset{2}{\cancel{8}}}{\cancel{15}\,3}$$  ← **Divide 25 and 15 by their GCF, $\boxed{\phantom{0}}$.**
**Divide 4 and 8 by their GCF, $\boxed{\phantom{0}}$.**

$$= \frac{\boxed{\phantom{0}}}{\boxed{\phantom{0}}}, \text{ or } \boxed{\phantom{0}}\frac{\boxed{\phantom{0}}}{\boxed{\phantom{0}}}$$  ← **Multiply and simplify.**

## Quick Check

**1. a.** Estimate $7\frac{2}{5} \div 1\frac{3}{7}$.

**b.** Estimate $14\frac{9}{16} \div 3\frac{8}{19}$.

**2.** The baker has $3\frac{3}{4}$ cups of walnuts to make three batches of muffins. How many cups of walnuts should go into each batch?

**3. a.** Find $7 \div 1\frac{1}{6}$.

**b.** Find $6\frac{5}{6} \div 3\frac{1}{3}$.

# Lesson 4-5                                    Equations With Fractions

| Lesson Objective | Common Core State Standards |
|---|---|
| To solve equations with fractions | Expressions and Equations: 6.EE.6, 6.EE.7 |

## Examples

❶ **Using Mental Math in Equations** Solve $x + 3\frac{4}{9} = 12\frac{7}{9}$ using mental math.

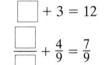

$$\boxed{\phantom{x}} + 3 = 12$$

$$\frac{\boxed{\phantom{x}}}{\boxed{\phantom{x}}} + \frac{4}{9} = \frac{7}{9}$$

← **Use mental math to find the missing whole number and the missing fraction.**

$$x = \boxed{\phantom{x}}\frac{\boxed{\phantom{x}}}{\boxed{\phantom{x}}}$$

← **Combine the two parts.**

$$= \boxed{\phantom{x}}\frac{\boxed{\phantom{x}}}{\boxed{\phantom{x}}}$$

← **Simplify.**

❷ **Solving Equations with Fractions** Solve $x - \frac{1}{8} = \frac{3}{4}$.

$$x - \frac{1}{8} + \frac{\boxed{\phantom{x}}}{\boxed{\phantom{x}}} = \frac{3}{4} + \frac{\boxed{\phantom{x}}}{\boxed{\phantom{x}}}$$

← **Add $\frac{\boxed{\phantom{x}}}{\boxed{\phantom{x}}}$ to each side.**

$$x = \frac{\boxed{\phantom{x}}}{8} + \frac{1}{8}$$

← **The LCD is $\boxed{\phantom{x}}$. Write $\frac{3}{4}$ as $\frac{\boxed{\phantom{x}}}{8}$**

$$x = \frac{\boxed{\phantom{x}}}{\boxed{\phantom{x}}}$$

← **Add.**

## Quick Check

1. Solve each equation using mental math.

   a. $x - 1\frac{3}{8} = 1\frac{3}{8}$          b. $14\frac{1}{4} + x = 25\frac{1}{2}$          c. $5\frac{5}{6} - x = 2\frac{1}{6}$

2. a. Solve $n + \frac{1}{3} = \frac{11}{12}$.          b. Solve $\frac{2}{5} + a = \frac{13}{20}$.

## Examples

**❸ Solving Equations by Multiplying** Solve $\frac{c}{3} = 14$.

**A.** 42        **B.** 45        **C.** 47        **D.** 50

$$\frac{c}{3} = 14$$

$$\boxed{\phantom{x}} \cdot \frac{c}{3} = \boxed{\phantom{x}} \cdot 14 \quad \leftarrow \text{ Multiply each side by } \boxed{\phantom{x}} \text{ to undo the division and get } c \text{ by itself.}$$

$$\frac{\boxed{\phantom{x}}}{\cancel{3}} \cdot \frac{c}{\cancel{3}}_{\boxed{\phantom{x}}} = \boxed{\phantom{x}} \quad \leftarrow \text{ Write 3 as } \frac{3}{1}. \text{ Simplify.}$$

$$\frac{\boxed{\phantom{x}}}{1} = \boxed{\phantom{x}} \quad \leftarrow \text{ Multiply the numerators and the denominators.}$$

$$c = \boxed{\phantom{x}} \quad \leftarrow \text{ Simplify.}$$

The solution is $\boxed{\phantom{x}}$. So the correct answer is choice $\boxed{\phantom{x}}$.

**❹ Writing and Solving Equations** Mai Li worked $7\frac{1}{2}$ hours and earned $150. What amount did she earn per hour?

**Words** | hours worked | × | earnings per hour | = | amount earned |

Let $\boxed{m}$ = earnings per hour.

**Equation**    $\boxed{\phantom{xx}}$    ×    $\boxed{\phantom{xx}}$    =    $\boxed{\phantom{xx}}$

$$7\frac{1}{2}m = 150 \quad \neg \text{ Write the equation.}$$

$$\frac{\boxed{\phantom{x}}}{\boxed{\phantom{x}}}m = \frac{150}{1} \quad \leftarrow \text{ Write } 7\frac{1}{2} \text{ as an improper fraction. Write 150 as } \frac{150}{1}.$$

$$\frac{\boxed{\phantom{x}}}{\boxed{\phantom{x}}} \cdot \left(\frac{15}{2}m\right) = \frac{\boxed{\phantom{x}}}{\boxed{\phantom{x}}} \cdot \frac{150}{1} \quad \leftarrow \text{ Multiply each side by } \frac{\boxed{\phantom{x}}}{\boxed{\phantom{x}}}, \text{ the reciprocal of } \frac{15}{2}.$$

$$m = \frac{2}{\cancel{15}}_{\boxed{\phantom{x}}} \cdot \frac{\cancel{150}^{\boxed{\phantom{x}}}}{1} \quad \leftarrow \text{ Multiply.}$$

$$m = \boxed{\phantom{x}} \quad \neg \text{ Simplify.}$$

Mai Li earned \$$\boxed{\phantom{x}}$ per hour.

## Quick Check

**3.** Solve $\frac{x}{2} = 15$.

$\boxed{\phantom{xxxxxxxxxxxxxx}}$

**4.** Solve $\frac{7}{8}x = 42$.

$\boxed{\phantom{xxxxxxxxxxxxxx}}$

# Lesson 5-1

**Ratios**

| Lesson Objective | Common Core State Standards |
|---|---|
| To write ratios to compare real-world quantities | Ratios and Proportional Relationships: 6.RP.1, 6.RP.3 |

## Vocabulary

A ratio is _____

_____

A tape diagram is _____

_____

A double number line diagram is _____

_____

## Example

**❶ Three Ways to Write a Ratio** During a school trip, there are 3 teachers and 25 students on each bus. Write each ratio in three ways.

**a.** teachers to students

There are ⬜ teachers and ⬜ students on each bus.

**teachers to students** → 3 to ⬜ or 3 : ⬜ or $\dfrac{3}{\boxed{\phantom{x}}}$

**b.** students to teachers

There are ⬜ students and ⬜ teachers on each bus.

**students to teachers** → 25 to ⬜ or 25 : ⬜ or $\dfrac{25}{\boxed{\phantom{x}}}$

## Quick Check

**1.** Use the recipe at the right to write each ratio in three ways.

**a.** pretzels to cereal

```



```

**b.** pretzels to party mix

```



```

PARTY MIX
Makes 6 cups
4 cups  cereal
2 cups  pretzels
3 tbsp Worcestershire
       sauce

Name _____ Class _____ Date _____

## Examples

❷ **Ratios on a Tape Diagram** The tape diagram shows the ratio of male
to female puppies in a litter. Describe the ratio of male to female puppies.

Male Puppies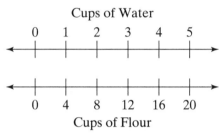

Female Puppies

The ratio of male puppies to female puppies is ☐ : ☐ .

For every ☐ male puppies in the litter, there are ☐ female puppies.

❸ **Using a Double Number Line Diagram** Jesse mixed water and flour to
make clay. Use the double number line to describe the ratio of water to
flour that Jesse used.

Cups of Water

```
0   1   2   3   4   5
←―――+―――+―――+―――+―――+―――→
```

```
←――+―――+―――+―――+―――+――→
   0   4   8   12  16  20
```
Cups of Flour

The ratio of cups of water to cups of ☐ is ☐ : ☐ .

For every ☐ cup(s) of ☐ , he used ☐ cup(s) of ☐ .

## Quick Check

2. The tape diagram below shows the ratio of dollars earned to dollars
saved. How can you describe this ratio?

Dollars Earned

Dollars Saved

The ratio of dollars earned to _____

For every _____

3. The double number line shows Emma's speed
during a track event. Describe this ratio.

The ratio of _____

For every _____

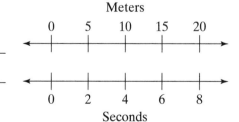

# Lesson 5-2

**Unit Rates**

| Lesson Objective | Common Core State Standards |
|---|---|
| To find and use unit rates and unit costs | Ratios and Proportional Relationships: 6.RP.2, 6.RP.3, 6.RP.3.b |

## Vocabulary

A rate is _____

_____

A unit rate is _____

_____

A unit cost is _____

_____

## Example

**❶ Finding a Unit Rate** Find the unit rate for typing 145 words in 5 minutes.

Divide 145 by 5:

145 words ÷ 5 minutes = [  ] words per minute

The unit rate is [  ] words per minute.

## Quick Check

**1.** Find the unit rate for $2.37 for 3 pounds of grapes.

Name _____ Class _____ Date _____

## Examples

**❷ Comparing Unit Cost** The same brand of pretzels comes in two sizes: a 10-ounce bag for $.99, and an 18-ounce bag for $1.49. Which size is a better buy? Round each unit price to the nearest cent.

Divide to find the unit price of each size.

price → $.99
size → 10 oz  ≈ $⬚ per ounce

price → $1.49
size → 18 oz  ≈ $⬚ per ounce

The better buy costs less per ounce. Since ⬚ is less than ⬚ ,

the ⬚ -ounce bag is the better buy.

**❸ Using a Unit Rate** Apples cost $1.49 for 1 pound. How much do 5 pounds of apples cost?

**A.** $6.25          **B.** $7.45          **C.** $8.15          **D.** $8.85

Multiply the price for 1 pound of apples by the number of pounds.

$⬚ × ⬚ pounds = $⬚

Five pounds of apples cost ⬚ . The correct answer is choice ⬚ .

## Quick Check

2. You can buy 6 ounces of yogurt for $.68 or 32 ounces of yogurt for $2.89. Find each unit cost. Which is the better buy?

3. Solve the problem using unit rates.

   **a.** You can earn $5 in 1 hour. How much do you earn in 5 hours?

   **b.** You type 25 words in 1 minute. How many words can you type in 10 minutes?

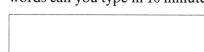

# Lesson 5-3

**Equivalent Ratios and Rates**

| Lesson Objective | Common Core State Standards |
|---|---|
| To use equivalent ratios and rates to solve real-world and mathematical problems | Ratio and Proportional Relationships: 6.RP.3, 6.RP.3.a |

## Vocabulary

Equivalent ratios are _____

## Example

❶ **Using a Multiplication Table** Yellow and blue paint are mixed in a ratio of 2 to 5. Use a multiplication table to write five ratios equivalent to the ratio 2 to 5.

| × | 1 | 2 | 3 | 4 | 5 | 6 |
|---|---|---|---|---|---|---|
| **1** | 1 | 2 | 3 | 4 | 5 | 6 |
| **2** | 2 | 4 | 6 | 8 | 10 | 12 |
| **3** | 3 | 6 | 9 | 12 | 15 | 18 |
| **4** | 4 | 8 | 12 | 16 | 20 | 24 |
| **5** | 5 | 10 | 15 | 20 | 25 | 30 |
| **6** | 6 | 12 | 18 | 24 | 30 | 36 |

Make a table of equivalent ratios.

Use the rows for ☐ and ☐ in the multiplication table.

Complete the table.

| **Yellow** | 2 | 4 | | | 12 |
|---|---|---|---|---|---|
| **Blue** | 5 | | 20 | | |

Look at the ratios for yellow to ☐ to write equivalent ratios for 2 to 5.

These are equivalent ratios.

4 to ☐        6 to ☐        8 to ☐        10 to ☐        12 to ☐

## Quick Check

**1.** White and green paint are mixed in a ratio of 2 to 3. Use a multiplication table to write two equivalent ratios for the ratio 2 to 3.

_____

### Example

**❷ Solving Rate Problems** Maria can make 2 bows in 5 minutes. At that rate, how many bows can she make in 25 minutes?

Bows Made

2    4    ☐    8    ☐    12

Complete a double number line to show equivalent ratios.

On the top number line show the number of ☐.

5    ☐    15    20    25    ☐

On the bottom number line shows the number of ☐.

The number lines show that the ratio of bows made to ☐ is 2 to ☐.

For every ☐ bows made it takes ☐ minutes.

The double number line shows that Maria can make ☐ bows in ☐ minutes.

### Quick Check

2. Sonia can read 3 pages in 8 minutes. At that rate, how many pages will she read in 24 minutes?

### Example

**❸ Using a Tape Diagram** The ratio of round beads to square beads in a bracelet is 4 : 5. The total number of beads is 27. How many round beads are there?

Complete a tape diagram.

The diagram shows 4 parts for round beads and ☐ parts for _____ beads

The diagram shows ☐ parts in all.

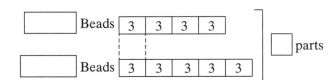

☐ Beads | 3 | 3 | 3 | 3 |

☐ Beads | 3 | 3 | 3 | 3 | 3 |

☐ parts

Think:

☐ parts → 27 beads

1 part → 27 beads ÷ 9 = ☐ beads

4 parts → 4 × 3 beads = ☐ beads

There are ☐ round beads.

### Quick Check

3. The ratio of nickels to dimes in a coin bank is $\frac{5}{3}$. The total number of nickels and dimes is 40. How many nickels are there?

Name _____ Class _____ Date _____

# Lesson 5-4                Using Ratios to Convert Measurement Units

| Lesson Objective | Common Core State Standard |
|---|---|
| To use ratios to convert from one unit of measure to another | Ratio and Proportional Relationships: 6.RP.3.d |

## Example

**1** **Using Ratios to Convert Measures** Kade needs 64 ounces of potatoes for a potato salad recipe. How many pounds of potatoes does he need?

First, write a ratio to of equivalent measurements. Write the new unit, pound, in the numerator.

$\dfrac{1 \boxed{\phantom{xx}}}{\boxed{\phantom{xx}} \text{ ounces}}$

Then, multiply the given measurement by the ratio.

64 ounces = 64 ounces × $\dfrac{\boxed{\phantom{xx}}}{\boxed{\phantom{xx}}}$

= 64 ~~ounces~~ × $\dfrac{\boxed{\phantom{xx}}}{\boxed{\phantom{xx}}}$

= $\dfrac{64 \text{ pounds}}{16}$

= $\boxed{\phantom{xxx}}$

Kade needs $\boxed{\phantom{xxx}}$ of potatoes.

## Quick Check

1. A piece of ribbon is 72 inches long. How many feet long is the piece of ribbon?

$\boxed{\phantom{xxxxxxxxxxxxxxxxxx}}$

## Example

❷ **Converting Metric Units** Convert 400 centimeters to meters.

Multiply the given measure by a ratio of equivalent measurements.
Write the new unit, meter, in the numerator.

**Step 1** First, write a ratio of equivalent measurements. Write the new unit, meter, in the numerator.

$$\frac{1\ \boxed{\phantom{xx}}}{\boxed{\phantom{xx}}\ \text{centimeters}}$$

400 cm = $\boxed{\phantom{xx}}$

**Step 2** Multiply the given measure by the ratio.

$$400\ \text{cm} = 400\ \text{cm} \times \frac{1\ \text{m}}{100\ \text{cm}}$$

$$= \boxed{\phantom{xx}}$$

## Quick Check

**2.** Convert 2,500 grams to kilograms.

$$\boxed{\phantom{xxxxxxxxxxxxxxxxxxxxxxxxxxxxxxxxx}}$$

## Example

❸ **Using More Than One Ratio** Marlis walks 600 feet in 8 seconds.
At this rate how many seconds does it take Marlis to walk 1,000 yards?

**Step 1** Use a ratio to find the number of feet in 1,000 yards. Use feet in the numerator.

$$1,000\ \text{yards} = 1,000\ \text{yards} \times \frac{\boxed{\phantom{x}}\ \text{feet}}{\boxed{\phantom{x}}\ \text{yard}}$$

$$= \boxed{\phantom{xx}}$$

**Step 2** Use Marlis' walking rate to find the number of seconds she needs to walk 1,000 yards. Use seconds in the numerator.

$$3,000\ \text{feet} = 3,000\ \text{feet} \times \frac{8\ \text{seconds}}{600\ \text{feet}}$$

$$= \boxed{\phantom{xx}}$$

It will take Marlis $\boxed{\phantom{xxx}}$ to walk 1,000 yards.

## Quick Check

**3.** Art drinks 2 quarts of milk every 3 days. How many days will it take him to drink 3 gallons of milk?

$$\boxed{\phantom{xxxxxxxxxxxxxxxxxxxxxxxxxxxxxxxxx}}$$

# Lesson 5-5
**Understanding Percents**

| Lesson Objective | Common Core State Standard |
|---|---|
| To model percents and to write percents using equivalent ratios | Ratios and Proportional Relationships: 6.RP.3.c |

## Vocabulary

A percent is _____

_____

## Examples

❶ **Using Models with Percents** In a floor plan of a 10 × 10 room, a chair takes up 4 spaces. Write the ratio and percent of the chair space to the total floor space.

There are ☐ grid spaces for the chair. Write as a ratio to the total number

of grid spaces, ☐ . Then write it as a percent.

❷ **Using Models with Percents** Model 82% in a 10 × 10 grid.

Shade ☐ of the 100 grid spaces.

❸ **Finding Percents Using Models** What percent does the shaded area represent?

$$\frac{\square}{\square} = \frac{\square}{100} = \square \%$$

Daily Notetaking Guide

**④ Using Equivalent Ratios** Write each ratio as a percent.

**a.** $\frac{3}{10}$

$$\frac{3}{10} = \frac{3 \cdot \boxed{\phantom{x}}}{10 \cdot \boxed{\phantom{x}}}$$ ← **Multiply to get a denominator of 100.** →

$$= \frac{\boxed{\phantom{x}}}{100}$$ ← **Simplify.** →

$$= \boxed{\phantom{x}}\%$$ ← **Write as a percent.** →

**b.** $\frac{4}{5}$

$$\frac{4}{5} = \frac{4 \cdot \boxed{\phantom{x}}}{5 \cdot \boxed{\phantom{x}}}$$

$$= \frac{\boxed{\phantom{x}}}{100}$$

$$= \boxed{\phantom{x}}\%$$

## Quick Check

**1.** Write a ratio and a percent to represent the unused floor space.

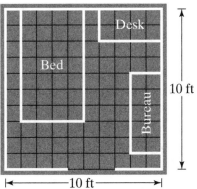

10 ft

10 ft

**2.** Model 80% on a 10 × 10 grid.

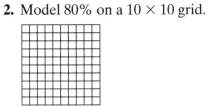

**3.** Write a ratio and a percent for each shaded area.

**a.**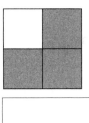

**b.**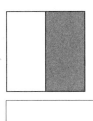

**c.**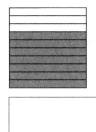

**4.** A tennis team played a total of 25 games and won 20 of them. What percent of the games did the team win?

# Lesson 5-6                                     Percents, Fractions, and Decimals

**Lesson Objective**

To find equivalent forms of fractions, decimals, and percents

## Examples

**❶ Representing Percents** Write 8% as a fraction. Write your answer in simplest form.

$$8\% = \dfrac{8}{\boxed{\phantom{00}}} \qquad \leftarrow \text{ } \textbf{Write the percent as a fraction with a denominator of 100.}$$

$$= \dfrac{\boxed{\phantom{0}}}{\boxed{\phantom{00}}} \qquad \leftarrow \text{ } \textbf{Write the fraction in simplest form.}$$

**❷ Writing a Percent as a Decimal** Write each percent as a decimal.

**a.** 87%                                           **b.** 9%

 $87\% = \dfrac{87}{\boxed{\phantom{00}}} \leftarrow$ **Write each percent as a fraction with a denominator of** $\boxed{\phantom{00}}$. $\rightarrow$  $9\% = \dfrac{9}{\boxed{\phantom{00}}}$

 $= \boxed{\phantom{00}} \leftarrow$ **Write each fraction as a decimal.** $\rightarrow$ $= \boxed{\phantom{00}}$

## Quick Check

**1. a.** Write 55% as a fraction.

**b.** Write 4% as a fraction.

**2. a.** Write 25% as a decimal.

**b.** Write 2% as a decimal.

Name _____ Class _____ Date _____

## Examples

❸ **Writing a Decimal as a Percent** Write 0.16 decimal as a percent.

$0.16 = \dfrac{\boxed{\phantom{0}}}{100} = \boxed{\phantom{00}}\%$ ← **Write the decimal as a fraction with a denominator of** $\boxed{\phantom{00}}$.

❹ **Writing a Decimal as a Percent** Write $\dfrac{7}{20}$ as a percent.

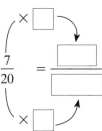

$\dfrac{7}{20} =$  ← **Find the fraction with a denominator of** $\boxed{\phantom{00}}$ **equal to** $\dfrac{7}{20}$.

$\dfrac{7}{20} = \dfrac{35}{100} = \boxed{\phantom{00}}\%$ ← **Write using a percent symbol.**

## Quick Check

**3.** Write each decimal as a percent.

**a.** 0.52

**b.** 0.05

**c.** 0.5

**4.** According to a news article, 1 of every 20 neurosurgeons in the United States is a woman. Write the fraction $\dfrac{1}{20}$ as a percent.

Name _____ Class _____ Date _____

# Lesson 5-7                                          Finding the Percent of a Number

| Lesson Objective | Common Core State Standard |
|---|---|
| To use percents to find part of a whole | Ratios and Proportional Relationships: 6.RP.3.c |

## Examples

**①  Using a Model**  Find 60% of 45.

The bar model shows the total and the percent of the total.

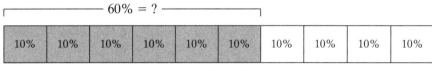

10 parts = ☐

1 part = 45 ÷ 10 = ☐

60% is ☐ parts and ☐ × ☐ = ☐

60% of 45 is ☐ .

**②  Using a Decimal**  Find 88% of 250.

88% = ☐                              ← **Write 88% as a decimal.**

☐ × 250 = ☐                          ← **Multiply.**

So, 88% of 250 is ☐ .

## Quick Check

**1.** You buy a $40 shirt on sale at 20% off. Find 20% of $40.

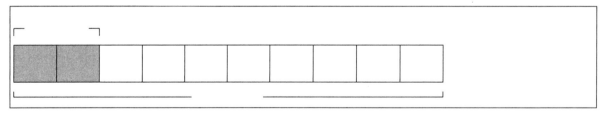

**2. a.** Find 12% of 91.                    **b.** Find 18% of 121.

Name _____ Class _____ Date _____

## Example

❸ **Using Mental Math** Use mental math to find 75% of 80.

**What you think**

$75\% = \dfrac{3}{4}$ $\qquad$ $\dfrac{3}{4} \times 80 = \boxed{\phantom{00}}$ $\qquad$ 75% of 80 is $\boxed{\phantom{00}}$.

**Why it works**

$75\% = \dfrac{75}{\boxed{\phantom{00}}}$

 $\leftarrow$ **Write 75% as a fraction in simplest form.**

$\dfrac{3}{4} \times 80 = \dfrac{3}{4} \times \dfrac{\boxed{\phantom{00}}}{\boxed{\phantom{0}}}$ $\qquad \leftarrow$ **Multiply $\frac{3}{4}$ by 80. Rewrite 80 as $\dfrac{\boxed{\phantom{00}}}{\boxed{\phantom{0}}}$.**

$= \dfrac{\boxed{\phantom{00}}}{\boxed{\phantom{0}}}$ $\qquad \leftarrow$ **Simplify.**

$= \boxed{\phantom{00}}$ $\qquad \leftarrow$ **Divide.**

## Quick Check

**3.** Use mental math to find 75% of 12.

# Lesson 5-8

**Finding the Whole**

| Lesson Objective | Common Core State Standard |
|---|---|
| To solve problems involving finding the whole, given a part and the percent | Ratio and Proportional Relationships: 6.RP.3.c |

## Examples

**❶ Using Equivalent Ratios** There are 18 students in sixth grade who ride the bus to school. This is 40% of all the students in sixth grade. How many students are in sixth grade?

**(A)** 40 students   **(B)** 45 students   **(C)** 58 students   **(D)** 63 students

**Step 1** Write the fraction for 40% in simplest form.

$$40\% = \frac{40}{100} = \frac{\boxed{\phantom{0}}}{\boxed{\phantom{0}}}$$

**Step 2** Make a table of equivalent ratios to find the whole.

$$2 \times 9$$

| | | | |
|---|---|---|---|
| Part | 40 | 2 | 18 |
| Whole | 100 | | |

$$5 \times 9$$

There are $\boxed{\phantom{0}}$ sixth grade students in school. The correct answer is choice $\boxed{\phantom{0}}$.

**❷ Using an Equation** There are 350 people attending a concert in an auditorium. If 70% of the seats are filled, how many seats are in the auditorium?

First, write a fraction in simplest form for 70%.       $70\% = \dfrac{\boxed{\phantom{0}}}{100} = \dfrac{\boxed{\phantom{0}}}{\boxed{\phantom{0}}}$

Complete the diagram to see how the whole, the part, and the percent are related.

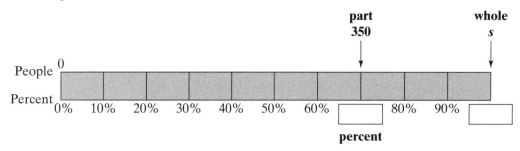

Write an equation. Solve to find the whole, $s$.

$$350 = \frac{7}{\boxed{\phantom{0}}} s \qquad \leftarrow \text{ Write the equation. Think: 350 is } \frac{7}{10} \text{ of what number?}$$

$$\frac{\boxed{\phantom{0}}}{\boxed{\phantom{0}}} \cdot 350 = \frac{\boxed{\phantom{0}}}{\boxed{\phantom{0}}} \cdot \frac{7}{10} s \qquad \leftarrow \text{ Multiply each side by } \frac{10}{7}, \text{ the reciprocal of } \frac{7}{10}.$$

$$\boxed{\phantom{0}} = 1 \cdot s \qquad \leftarrow \text{ Multiply.}$$

$$\boxed{\phantom{0}} = s$$

There are $\boxed{\phantom{0}}$ seats in the auditorium.

## Quick Check

**1.** Michael won 35 chess games. This is 70% of the games he played. How many games did he play? Make a table of equivalent ratios to help you.

**2.** Jordan has walked 6 miles this month. This is 20% of the distance she usually walks in a month. How many miles does she usually walk?

## Example

❸ **Using Mental Math** There are 14 roses in the vase of flowers. This is 50% of the flowers in the vase. How many flowers are in the vase?

**Think**

The fraction in simplest form for 50% is $\dfrac{\boxed{\phantom{0}}}{\boxed{\phantom{0}}}$.

Since $\frac{1}{2}$ of the number is 14, I can multiply 14 by $\boxed{\phantom{0}}$ to find the number.  $14 \times \boxed{\phantom{0}} = \boxed{\phantom{0}}$
There are $\boxed{\phantom{0}}$ flowers in the vase.

## Quick Check

**3.** Six students in a class received a perfect score on a spelling test. If this is 25% of the class, how many are in the class? Use mental math to solve this problem.

# Lesson 6-1

**Exploring Integers**

| Lesson Objective | Common Core State Standards |
|---|---|
| To use integers, opposites, and absolute values to represent real-world situations | The Number System: 6.NS.5, 6.NS.6, 6.NS.6.a, 6.NS.6.c, 6.NS.7.c |

## Vocabulary

Two numbers are opposites if _____

_____

Integers are _____

_____

The absolute value of a number is _____

_____

## Examples

❶ **Representing Situations with Integers** You are six spaces behind your opponent in a board game. What integer represents your situation?

[  ]  ← **An integer less than 0 is represented as** [          ].

❷ **Identifying Opposites** Write the opposite of 6.

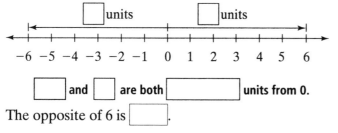

[  ] and [  ] are both [       ] units from 0.

The opposite of 6 is [    ].

## Quick Check

**1.** The lowest elevation in New Orleans, Louisiana, is 8 feet below sea level. Use an integer to represent this elevation. What does zero represent?

[                                    ]

**2.** Write the opposite of −5.

[                                    ]

## Example

❸ **Finding Absolute Value** A student withdraws $19 from a savings account. This can be represented by −19. Find |−19| and explain its meaning.

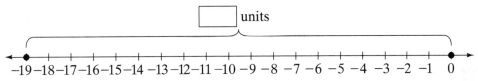

Since −19 is [    ] units from 0, |−19| = [    ].

|−19| represents [                              ].

## Quick Check

3. A bird dives down 12 feet.

   **a.** Write an integer for this situation.

   [                                                              ]

   **b.** Explain the meaning of the absolute value of the integer.

   [                                                              ]

# Lesson 6-2

**Comparing and Ordering Integers**

| Lesson Objective | Common Core State Standard |
|---|---|
| To compare and order integers | The Number System: 6.NS.7.a |

## Examples

**❶ Comparing Integers**

   **a.** Compare $-12$ and $-10$.

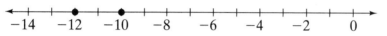

   ← Graph $-12$ and $-10$ on the same number line.

   Since $-12$ is to the [ ] of $-10$ on the number line, $-12$ [ ] $-10$, or $-10$ [ ] $-12$.

   **b.** Compare $3$ and $-5$.

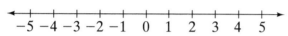

   ← Graph $3$ and $-5$ on the same number line.

   Since $3$ is to the [ ] of $-5$ on the number line, $3$ [ ] $-5$, or $-5$ [ ] $3$.

**❷ Ordering Integers**

   **a.** Order from least to greatest: $16, -2, -35, 68, -10$. Use five as the number line interval.

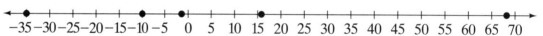

   In order from least to greatest, the numbers are

   [ ] , [ ] , [ ] , [ ] , [ ] .

   **b.** Order from least to greatest: $4, 0, -3, 1, -2$.

   Use one as the number line interval.

   In order from least to greatest, the numbers are

   [ ] , [ ] , [ ] , [ ] , [ ] .

Daily Notetaking Guide

Name _____ Class _____ Date _____

## Quick Check

**1.** Compare using $<$ or $>$ .

   **a.** $5 \ \boxed{\phantom{x}} -3$

   **b.** $-12 \ \boxed{\phantom{x}} \ 9$

**2.** Order these scores from least to greatest: $-25, 100, -50, 75.$

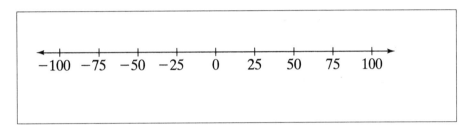

Name _____ Class _____ Date _____

# Lesson 6-3

**Rational Numbers**

| Lesson Objective | Common Core State Standards |
|---|---|
| To show that numbers are rational and to plot rational numbers on a number line | The Number System: 6.NS.5, 6.NS.6, 6.NS.6.c, 6.NS.7.b |

## Vocabulary

A rational number is _____

_____

## Examples

**❶ Showing That Numbers Are Rational** Show that each number is a rational number by writing it as a quotient of two integers.

**a.** $\frac{2}{3}$

$\frac{2}{3}$ is a [＿＿＿]. It is rational.

**b.** $-7$

$-7$ is an integer and can be written as [＿＿＿]. It is rational.

**c.** $-3\frac{4}{5}$

$-3\frac{4}{5}$ can be written as [＿＿＿]. It is rational.

**d.** 15.36

15.36 can be written as [＿＿＿＿]. It is [＿＿＿].

**❷ Plotting Fractions on a Number Line** Plot $-\frac{2}{6}$ and $\frac{1}{6}$ on a number line.

The denominator of each fraction is [＿]. Divide your number line in [＿＿＿]. Label the sixths.

For positive numbers, count [＿＿＿] from 0. Find and plot a point at [＿＿].

For negative numbers, count [＿＿＿] from 0. Find and plot a point at [＿＿].

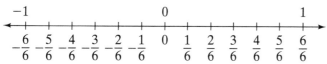

$$
\begin{array}{c}
-1 \qquad\qquad 0 \qquad\qquad 1 \\
-\frac{6}{6}\ -\frac{5}{6}\ -\frac{4}{6}\ -\frac{3}{6}\ -\frac{2}{6}\ -\frac{1}{6}\ 0\ \frac{1}{6}\ \frac{2}{6}\ \frac{3}{6}\ \frac{4}{6}\ \frac{5}{6}\ \frac{6}{6}
\end{array}
$$

## Quick Check

**1.** Show that each number is a rational number by writing it as a quotient of two integers.

**a.** $-6.4$ [＿＿＿] **b.** 9 [＿＿＿] **c.** $-\frac{5}{7}$ [＿＿＿] **d.** $-0.75$ [＿＿＿]

**2.** Plot each fraction on a number line.

**a.** $-\frac{5}{3}$

**b.** $\frac{3}{8}$

## Example

**❸ Plotting Decimals on a Number Line** Guy owes his sister $1.40.
This debt is represented by $-1.4$. Plot the decimal on a number line.

The smallest place value in $-1.4$ is [ ]. Divide your number
line into [ ]. Label the tenths.

For negative numbers, count [ ] from 0. Find and plot a point at [ ].

## Quick Check

**3.** Plot each decimal on a number line.

    **a.** $-0.3$                  **b.** $1.52$

## Example

**❹ Plotting on a Vertical Number Line** Plot –2 on a vertical number line.

Draw a vertical number line. Label the integers.

Count [ ] from 0 to find [ ]. Plot a point at $-2$.

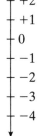

## Quick Check

**4.** Plot each rational number on a vertical number line.

    **a.** 6                  **b.** $-3.85$

 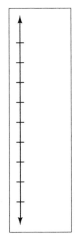

## Lesson 6-4

Comparing and Ordering Rational Numbers

| Lesson Objective | Common Core State Standards |
|---|---|
| To compare and order rational numbers | The Number System: 6.NS.5, 6.NS.6, 6.NS.6.c, 6.NS.7.a, 6.NS.7.b |

### Examples

**❶ Comparing Decimals** Compare $-11.6$ and $-11.75$.

Plot both negative decimals on the same number line. Divide the number

line into [        ]. Locate $-11.75$ halfway between [        ] and [        ].

Compare the locations of the points. Since [        ] is to the left of

[        ] on the number line, [        ] is less than [        ].

$-11.6$ [        ] $-11.75$

**❷ Comparing Fractions** Compare $-\dfrac{1}{6}$ and $-\dfrac{3}{8}$.

Because your denominators are [  ] and [  ], divide your number line

into [        ] and also into [        ]. Plot both fractions.

```
                        -3/6                    0
  -1                                            
◄──┼──┼──┼──┼──┼──┼──┼──┼──┼──┼──┼──┼──►
  -1                    -4/8                    0
```

Compare the locations of the points. Since $-\dfrac{1}{6}$ is to the [        ] of $-\dfrac{3}{8}$ on

the number line, $-\dfrac{1}{6}$ is [        ] than $-\dfrac{3}{8}$.

$-\dfrac{3}{8}$ [  ] $-\dfrac{1}{6}$

### Quick Check

Compare using $<$, $=$, or $>$.

**1. a.** $-12.05$ [  ] $-12.5$  **b.** $-12.98$ [  ] $-12.89$

**2. a.** $-\dfrac{5}{8}$ [  ] $-\dfrac{1}{2}$  **b.** $-4\dfrac{7}{12}$ [  ] $-4\dfrac{2}{3}$

## Examples

❸ **Comparing Decimals and Fractions** Two cities are below sea level. City A has an elevation of $-1\frac{3}{4}$ feet. City B has an elevation of $-1.9$ feet. Which city has a lower elevation?

Locate each elevation on the same number line. The denominator is

[ ] and the decimal is to the [ ] place. Mark off [ ]

and [ ] to plot the numbers.

$-2$            $-1\frac{2}{4}$            $-1$

$-2.0$            $-1.5$            $-1.0$

Then compare the locations of the points. $-1.9$ [ ] $-1\frac{3}{4}$

City B has a [ ] elevation than City A.

❹ **Ordering Rational Numbers** On Monday, the temperature was $-0.4°C$. On Tuesday, the temperature was $-1\frac{1}{4}$ °C. It was $-2°C$ on Wednesday, $2.5°C$ on Thursday, and $1\frac{1}{2}$ °C on Friday. Write the temperatures in order from least to greatest.

**Step 1:** Draw a number line from [ ] to [ ] and divide it into halves. Plot each temperature on a number line. Locate numbers on or in between the labels.

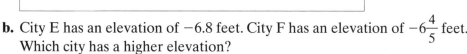

$-2$      $-1$      $0$      $1$      $2$      $3$

**Step 2:** Compare the locations of the points. The least number is on the [ ].

The temperatures from least to greatest are: _____

## Quick Check

3. Solve each problem.

   **a.** City C has an elevation of $-1.24$ feet. City D has an elevation of $-1\frac{3}{10}$ feet. Which city has a higher elevation?

   [ ]

   **b.** City E has an elevation of $-6.8$ feet. City F has an elevation of $-6\frac{4}{5}$ feet. Which city has a higher elevation?

   [ ]

4. Order the temperatures from least to greatest. $-6.45°C$, $-6\frac{3}{4}°C$, $6.2°C$, $-6.3°C$, $-6\frac{1}{2}°C$

   [ ]

# Lesson 6-5                                                      Inequalities

| Lesson Objective | Common Core State Standards |
|---|---|
| To express and identify solutions of inequalities | Expressions and Equations: 6.EE.5, 6.EE.6, 6.EE.8<br>The Number System: 6.NS.7.d |

## Vocabulary

An inequality is _____

_____

| Symbol | Meaning |
|---|---|
| < | is [____] than |
| > | is [____] than |
| ≤ | is [____] than or [____] to |
| ≥ | is [____] than or [____] to |
| ≠ | is [____] equal to |

The graph of an inequality shows _____

_____

A solution of an inequality is _____

_____

## Example

❶ **Writing an Inequality** Maria threw the softball more than 90 feet.
Write an inequality that represents the distance.

**Words**

| distance Maria threw the softball | is more than | 90 feet |

Let [____] = the distance Maria threw the softball.

**Inequality**

[____]    [____]    [____]

The inequality is [____].

## Quick Check

1. Skydivers jump from an altitude of 14,500 feet or less. Write an inequality to express the altitude from which skydivers jump.

_____

Name _____ Class _____ Date _____

## Examples

❷ **Graphing Inequalities** Write the inequality for the situation. Then graph the inequality.

**a.** Everyone in our class is 10 years old or older.

Let $a$ = the age of a person in our class, $a$ ☐ 10.

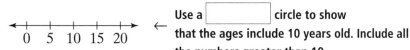

← Use a ☐ circle to show that the ages include 10 years old. Include all the numbers greater than 10.

**b.** The temperature is 6 degrees below zero or colder.

Let $t$ = the temperature, $t$ ☐ −6.

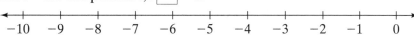

❸ **Identifying Solutions of an Inequality** In order to get a bulk discount, a company must order at least 15 computers. Company X ordered 17 new computers. Do they qualify for the discounted rate?

**Words**    ☐ order ☐    ☐ is at least ☐    ☐ 15 computers ☐

Let $c$ = computers in the order

**Inequality**    $c$    ☐  ☐

Decide whether the inequality is true or false for Company X.

$17 \geq 15$ ☐

Company X ☐ qualify for the discounted rate.

## Quick Check

**2.** You spend at least 2 hours studying. Write the inequality for the situation. Then graph the inequality.

```



```

**3.** You must be at least 48 inches tall to ride a certain roller coaster. Ian is 3 ft 11 in. tall. Is Ian tall enough to ride the roller coaster?

```



```

# Lesson 6-6

Solving One-Step Inequalities

| Lesson Objective | Common Core State Standard |
|---|---|
| To solve one-step inequalities by adding or subtracting | Expressions and Equations: 6.EE.5 |

## Examples

❶ **Solving Inequalities** Solve $f - 4 \geq 8$.

$$f - 4 \geq 8$$

$$f - 4 + \boxed{\phantom{x}} \geq 8 + \boxed{\phantom{x}} \quad \leftarrow \quad \textbf{Add} \boxed{\phantom{x}} \textbf{ to each side to undo the } \boxed{\phantom{xxxxxxxx}}.$$

$$f \geq \boxed{\phantom{x}} \quad \leftarrow \quad \textbf{Simplify.}$$

❷ **Solving Inequalities** Solve $p + 16 < 34$.

$$p + 16 < 34$$

$$p + 16 - \boxed{\phantom{x}} < 34 - \boxed{\phantom{x}} \quad \leftarrow \quad \textbf{Subtract} \boxed{\phantom{x}} \textbf{ from each side to undo the } \boxed{\phantom{xxxxx}}.$$

$$p < \boxed{\phantom{x}} \quad \leftarrow \quad \textbf{Simplify.}$$

## Quick Check

**1.** Solve $u - 6 \leq 3$.

**2.** Solve $z + 15 > 24$.

Name _____ Class _____ Date _____

## Example

❸ **Saving Money** Missy wants to save at least $150 this month. She has saved $112 so far. Write and solve an inequality to find how much more money she would like to save this month (*d*).

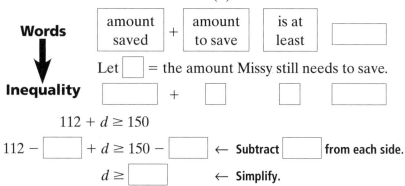

**Words**

| amount saved | + | amount to save | is at least | ☐ |

Let ☐ = the amount Missy still needs to save.

**Inequality**     ☐  +  ☐     ☐     ☐

$$112 + d \geq 150$$

$$112 - \boxed{\phantom{x}} + d \geq 150 - \boxed{\phantom{x}}$$   ← **Subtract** ☐ **from each side.**

$$d \geq \boxed{\phantom{x}}$$   ← **Simplify.**

Missy would like to save at least ☐ more this month.

## Quick Check

3. A restaurant can serve a maximum of 115 people. There are now 97 people dining in the restaurant. Write and solve an inequality to find how many more people can be served.

# Lesson 7-1

**Points in the Coordinate Plane**

| Lesson Objective | Common Core Standards |
|---|---|
| To name and graph points on a coordinate plane | The Number System: 6.NS.6, 6.NS.6.c, 6.NS.8 |

## Vocabulary

The coordinate plane is _____

_____

The plane is divided into four regions,
called ☐ .

The origin is _____

_____

An ordered pair is _____

_____

_____

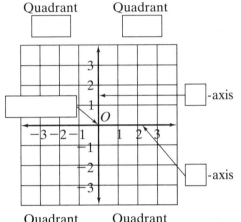

## Example

**1** **Naming Coordinates** Find the coordinates of point A.

Point A is ☐ units to the ☐ of the y-axis.

The x-coordinate is ☐ .

Point A is ☐ units below the x-axis. The y-coordinate

is ☐ .

The coordinates of point A are ☐ .

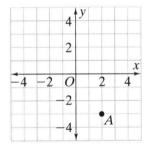

## Quick Check

**1.** Find the coordinates of each point in the coordinate plane.

**a.** B ☐

**b.** D ☐

**c.** E ☐

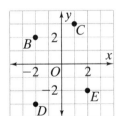

Name _____ Class _____ Date _____

## Examples

❷ **Graphing Ordered Pairs** Graph point $X(-1, -3)$ on a coordinate plane.

**Step 1**

Start at the [       ].

**Step 2**

Move [   ] unit to the [       ].

**Step 3**

Move [   ] units [       ].

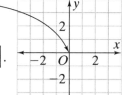

❸ **Using Map Coordinates** Use the coordinate grid. If you travel 2 units down and 3 units right from $B$, what are the coordinates of your location?

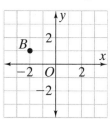

You are at [       ].

## Quick Check

2. Graph these points on the coordinate plane:

   **a.** $A\ (2.8, 4.25)$

   **b.** $B\left(-3, 2\frac{3}{4}\right)$

   **c.** $C\ (-4, -4)$

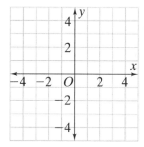

3. Use the map at the right. Suppose you leave the library and walk 5 blocks east and then 2 blocks south.

   **a.** At which building do you arrive?

   [                                                    ]

   **b.** What are the coordinates of the building?

   [                                                    ]

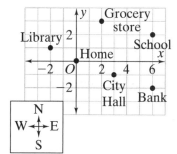

Name _____ Class _____ Date _____

# Lesson 7-2

**Polygons in the Coordinate Plane**

| Lesson Objective | Common Core Standards |
|---|---|
| To graph polygons in a coordinate plane | The Number System: 6.NS.6.b, 6.NS.8<br>Geometry: 6.G.3 |

## Vocabulary / Key Concepts / Example

A [          ] line is perfectly flat. The _____
of every point on a horizontal line are the same.

A [          ] line is straight up and down. The _____
of every point on a horizontal line are the same.

The distance between two points on a horizontal line is

_____

The distance between two points on a vertical line is

_____

## Example

❶ **Finding Distances** Find the distance from $M$ to $N$.

$M$ is located at [          ].

$N$ is located at [          ].

$M$ and $N$ have the same _____, so they are on
the same _____ line.

Find the _____ of the difference
of the _____.

$MN = |\ \square\ - (\ \square\ )| = |\ \square\ | = \square$

The distance between $M$ and $N$ is $\square$.

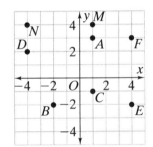

## Quick Check

1. Find the distance between the points.

   **a.** $A$ and $C$        **b.** $E$ and $B$        **c.** $F$ and $A$

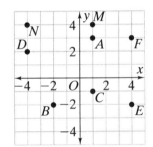

## Example

❷ **Drawing Polygons** An architect uses a rectangle that has a diagonal with coordinates $(-10, -5)$ and $(10, 9)$ to represent a house on a blue print. What is the perimeter of the house? The scale represents yards.

**Step 1** Plot the points. Find the coordinates of the other diagonal.

_____ and _____

**Step 2** Connect the points to make a rectangle.

**Step 3** Find the length of each side.

**Side 1:** $|10 - (-10)| = |20| = 20$

**Side 2:** $|9 - (-5)| = |14| = 14$

**Side 3:** $|\boxed{\phantom{xx}} - \boxed{\phantom{xx}}| = |\boxed{\phantom{xx}}| = \boxed{\phantom{xx}}$

**Side 4:** $|\boxed{\phantom{xx}} - \boxed{\phantom{x}}| = |\boxed{\phantom{xx}}| = \boxed{\phantom{xx}}$

**Step 4** Add the distances.

_____ + _____ + _____ + _____ = _____

The perimeter of the house is _____.

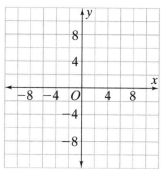

## Quick Check

**2.** The designer uses a rectangle with coordinates $(3, -3), (5, -3), (5, -5)$, and $(3, -5)$ to represent a flower garden. What is the perimeter of the flower garden? Each unit of length represents one meter.

## Example

❸ **Reflecting Points** How is the point $(-1, 3)$ related to the point $(1, 3)$?

The _____ for each point is the same, _____.

The _____, _____ and _____, differ by _____.

The point is reflected across the _____.

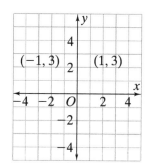

## Quick Check

**3.** How is the point $(2, 5)$ related to the point $(2, -5)$?

# Lesson 7-3 Functions

| Lesson Objective | Common Core Standard |
|---|---|
| To make a function table and to write an equation | Expressions and Equations: 6.EE.9 |

## Vocabulary / Key Concepts / Example

A _____ is a rule that assigns exactly one output value to each input value.

The input value is also called the _____.
In a table, it is the _____ column.

The output value is called the _____ because it

_____. In a table it is the _____ column.

## Example

❶ **Completing a Function Table** Complete the function table if the rule is
Output = Input ÷ (3).

| Input | Output |
|---|---|
| 9 | 3 |
| 3 | 1 |
| 12 | |
| 15 | |

← Divide 9 by ☐ . Place 3 in the Output column.
← Divide 3 by ☐ . Place 1 in the Output column.
← Divide 12 by ☐ . Place ☐ in the Output column.
← Divide 15 by ☐ . Place ☐ in the Output column.

## Quick Check

1. Complete the function table for each rule.
   **a.** Output = Input ÷ 4

   | Input | Output |
   |---|---|
   | 16 | |
   | 24 | |
   | 36 | |

   **b.** Output = Input − 8

   | Input | Output |
   |---|---|
   | 15 | |
   | 10 | |
   | 8 | |

## Example

❷ **Identifying Independent and Dependent Variables** Identify the independent and dependent variable.
*the height of a child and the age of a girl*

Does the height of a girl depend on her age? _____

Does the age of a girl depend on her height? _____

Think: Which makes more sense?

As the girl gets taller, her age changes.
OR
As the girl gets older, her height changes.

As a girl gets _____, her _____ changes.

Because _____ depends on _____, height is the _____ variable and age is the _____ variable.

## Quick Check

**2.** Identify the independent variable and dependent variable.
*the time spent studying and the test score*

_____

_____

## Example

❸ **Writing Equations for Functions** The sixth grade class is selling posters as a fundraiser. They record their daily sales and income in a table.

| Posters | Income |
|---------|--------|
| 15 | 120 |
| 24 | 192 |
| 41 | 328 |
| 68 | 544 |

Write an equation for the amount of income the class gets from its sale of posters.

The income *depends* on _____.

The income is _____ times the number of posters sold.

income = 8 · _____

$y =$ _____

## Quick Check

**3.** The 8th grade class decides to sell hoodies.

Write an equation for the amount of income the class gets from its sale of hoodies.

| Number/ Hoodies | Income |
|-----------------|--------|
| 14 | 280 |
| 20 | 400 |
| 36 | 720 |
| 49 | 980 |

# Lesson 7-4                                           Graphing Functions

| Lesson Objective | Common Core Standard |
|---|---|
| To graph functions using data in a table | Expressions and Equations: 6.EE.9 |

## Vocabulary

A linear function is _____

_____

## Examples

**1** **Graphing a Function from a Table** Graph points from the function table to determine if the function is linear.

| Input | Output |
|---|---|
| 9 | 3 |
| 3 | 1 |
| 12 | 4 |
| 15 | 6 |

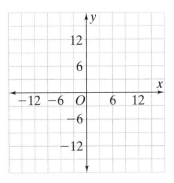

Is the function linear? _____

**2** **Graphing a Function** Make a table and graph some points of the function $y = 2x$.

| Input (x) | Output (y) |
|---|---|
| 4 | 8 |
| 3 |  |
| 2 |  |
| 1 |  |
| 0 | 0 |

← 2(4) = 8

← 2(3) = ☐

← 2(☐) = ☐

← 2(☐) = ☐

← 2(0) = 0

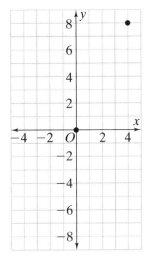

**❸** Henry receives $8.00 per hour for babysitting two children. The function $e = 8h$ shows how the earnings $e$ relate to the number of hours $h$ that Henry babysits. Make a table and graph the function.

| Hours | Earnings ($) |
|-------|--------------|
| 1 | 8 |
| 2 | |
| 3 | |
| 4 | |

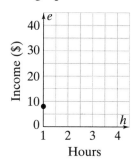

## Quick Check

**1.** Use a graph to determine if the function table represents a linear function.

| x | y |
|---|---|
| 4 | 7 |
| 3 | 5 |
| 2 | 4 |
| 1 | 1 |

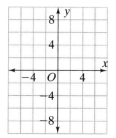

Is the graph linear? _____

**2.** Make a table and graph some points of the function $y = x - 3$.

| Input (x) | Output (y) |
|-----------|------------|
| 7 | |
| 6 | |
| 5 | |
| 4 | |
| 3 | |

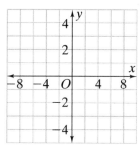

**3.** A car is driven at a steady rate of 45 miles per hour. The function $d = 45t$ shows how time $t$ relates to distance $d$. Make a table and graph the function.

| Time (hours) | Distance (miles) |
|--------------|------------------|
| 0 | |
| 1 | |
| 2 | |
| 3 | |
| 4 | |
| 5 | |

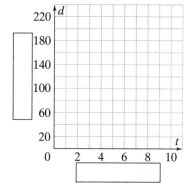

# Lesson 7-5

**Functions in the Real World**

| Lesson Objective | Common Core Standard |
|---|---|
| To use equations, tables, and graphs to represent real-world function situations | Expressions and Equations: 6.EE.9 |

## Example

❶ **Using a Table** Caroline makes $9 per hour while working at a department store. Make a table showing the relationship between hours worked and amount earned. How much will she make in a 37-hour week?

**Step 1:** Determine the independent and dependent variables.

The amount she earns depends on _____, so _____ is the dependent variable and _____ is the independent variable.

**Step 2:** Then, make a _____ of possible amounts that she earns.

Choose some values for the number of hours worked, including 37. Then, find the amount she earned for each value. To do this, multiply the number of hours by _____.

| Hours | $ Earned |
|---|---|
| 8 | |
| 23 | |
| 37 | |
| 40 | |

**Step 3:** Read the table. If Caroline works 37 hours, she earns _____.

## Quick Check

1. Helen is a manager at a pet store. She earns $12 per hour. Make a table showing the relationship between hours worked and amount earned. How much does Helen earn if she works 40 hours?

Name _____ Class _____ Date _____

## Examples

❷ **Using a Graph** A train travels at 40 miles per hour. Make a graph showing the relationship between time and distance. How far does it travel in 7 hours?

**Step 1:** Make a graph for the situation. Graph three points and connect them.

In 0 hours, the train goes _____ miles.
The point is _____.

In 1 hour, the train goes _____ miles.
The point is _____.

In 5 hours, the train goes _____ miles.
The point is _____.

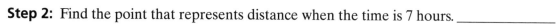

**Step 2:** Find the point that represents distance when the time is 7 hours. _____

In 7 hours, this train traveled _____

❸ **Using an Equation** In a card game, you get 10 points for every hand that you win. Write an equation showing the relationship between the number of hands and the number of points. How many points do you get if you win 7 hands?

**Step 1:** Write an equation.

The independent variable ($x$) is

_____,

and the dependent variable ($y$) is

_____.

$y = $ _____

**Step 2:** Substitute _____ for $x$, and simplify.

$y = 10($_____$) = $ _____ ← **Substitute**

You would get _____ points.

## Quick Check

2. Allen drives his car on vacation. He drives at 55 miles per hour. How far does Allen travel in 3 hours?

3. Josh buys tickets to a baseball game. Each ticket costs $8.75. Write an equation showing the relationship between tickets purchased and cost. How much will it cost Josh to buy 4 tickets?

# Lesson 8-1

**Areas of Parallelograms and Triangles**

| Lesson Objective | Common Core State Standard |
|---|---|
| To solve problems involving areas of parallelograms, triangles, and complex figures | Geometry: 6.G.1 |

## Vocabulary and Key Concepts

**Area of a Parallelogram**

$A = \boxed{\phantom{x}} \times \boxed{\phantom{x}}$

**Area of a Triangle**

$A = \frac{1}{2}\boxed{\phantom{x}} \times \boxed{\phantom{x}}$

The $\boxed{\phantom{xxxxx}}$ of a parallelogram can be any side of a parallelogram.

The height of a parallelogram is _____

Any side of a triangle can be the $\boxed{\phantom{xxxx}}$ of a triangle.

The height of a triangle is _____

_____

## Example

**❶ Finding the Area of a Parallelogram** Find the area of the parallelogram.

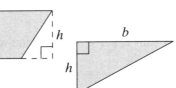

5 in.

3.3 in.

8 in.

$A = \boxed{\phantom{x}} \times \boxed{\phantom{x}}$  ← Use the formula for the area of a parallelogram.

$= \boxed{\phantom{x}} \times \boxed{\phantom{xx}}$  ← Substitute $\boxed{\phantom{x}}$ for *b* and $\boxed{\phantom{x}}$ for *h*.

$= \boxed{\phantom{xx}}$  ← Simplify.

The area of the parallelogram is $\boxed{\phantom{xxxx}}$ square inches.

## Quick Check

**1.** Find the area of a parallelogram with $b = 14$ m and $h = 5$ m.

$\boxed{\phantom{xxxxxxxxxxxxxxxxxxxxxx}}$

Name _____ Class _____ Date _____

## Examples

**➋ Finding the Area of a Triangle** A park is a triangular plot of land. The triangle has a base of 214 m and a height of 70 m. Find its area.

$A = \frac{1}{2}\boxed{\phantom{x}} \times \boxed{\phantom{x}}$     ← **Use the formula for the area of a triangle.**

$= \frac{1}{2} \times \boxed{\phantom{xxx}} \times \boxed{\phantom{xxx}}$     ← **Substitute** $\boxed{\phantom{xxx}}$ **for** *b* **and** $\boxed{\phantom{xxx}}$ **for** *h*.

$= \boxed{\phantom{xxx}}$     ← **Simplify.**

The area of the triangle is $\boxed{\phantom{xxxxx}}$ square meters.

**➌ Finding the Area of a Complex Figure** Find the area of the figure.

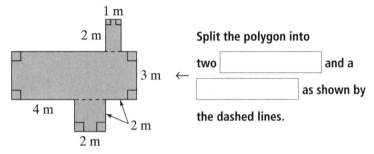

Split the polygon into

two $\boxed{\phantom{xxxxxxx}}$ and a

$\boxed{\phantom{xxxxxxx}}$ as shown by

the dashed lines.

Area of the smaller rectangle: $\boxed{\phantom{x}} \times \boxed{\phantom{x}} = \boxed{\phantom{x}}$, or $\boxed{\phantom{x}}$ m²

Area of the larger rectangle: $\boxed{\phantom{x}} \times \boxed{\phantom{x}} = \boxed{\phantom{x}}$, or $\boxed{\phantom{x}}$ m²  ← **Find the area of each polygon.**

Area of the square: $\boxed{\phantom{x}} \times \boxed{\phantom{x}} = \boxed{\phantom{x}}$, or $\boxed{\phantom{x}}$ m²

The total area is $\boxed{\phantom{x}} + \boxed{\phantom{x}} + \boxed{\phantom{x}}$, or $\boxed{\phantom{x}}$ square meters.

## Quick Check

**2.** An obtuse triangle has a base of 30 meters and a height of 17.3 meters. Find the triangle's area.

$\boxed{\phantom{xxxxxxxxxxxxxxxxxxxxxxxxxxxxxxxxxxxxx}}$

**3.** Find the area of the figure below.

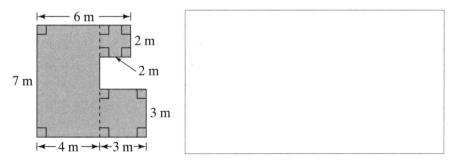

# Lesson 8-2

**Areas of Polygons**

| Lesson Objective | Common Core State Standard |
|---|---|
| To compose and decompose polygons to solve problems involving area | Geometry: 6.G.1 |

## Vocabulary

Compose means _____

Decompose means _____

## Example

**1** **Making Simpler Shapes** Pam drew this diagram of a deck she's going to build. What is the area of the deck?

**A.** 36.8 square feet          **C.** 57.2 square feet

**B.** 48.2 square feet          **D.** 66.4 square feet

The deck is in the shape of a [＿＿＿＿＿].

Think of the pentagon as a [＿＿＿＿＿] and a [＿＿＿＿＿]

that share an edge.

To find the area of the deck, find the sum of the areas of the rectangle and the triangle.

| **Rectangle** | **Triangle** |
|---|---|
| $A = l \times w$ | $A = \frac{1}{2} \times b \times h$ |
| $= \boxed{\phantom{x}} \times \boxed{\phantom{x}}$ | $= \frac{1}{2} \times \boxed{\phantom{x}} \times \boxed{\phantom{x}}$ |
| $= \boxed{\phantom{x}}$ | $= \boxed{\phantom{x}}$ |

Sum of the areas: $\boxed{\phantom{x}}$ + $\boxed{\phantom{x}}$ = $\boxed{\phantom{x}}$

The total area is $\boxed{\phantom{x}}$ square meters. The correct answer choice is choice $\boxed{\phantom{x}}$.

## Quick Check

**1.** Find the area of the deck at the right.

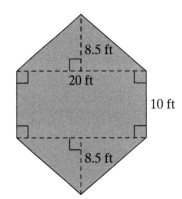

**Example**

❷ **Composing a Polygon to Find Area** Keith drew a diagram of the two sections of his garden. Find the total area of his garden.

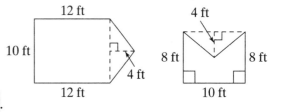

Compose the two polygons into one [      ].

Find the area of the new rectangle.

$A = b \times h$

$= \left(\boxed{\phantom{xx}} + \boxed{\phantom{xx}}\right) \times \boxed{\phantom{xx}} = \boxed{\phantom{xx}} \times \boxed{\phantom{xx}} = \boxed{\phantom{xx}}$

The total area of Keith's garden is [      ] square feet.

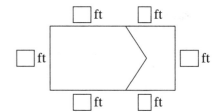

**Quick Check**

2. Tyler's garden has the two sections shown. Find the total area of Tyler's garden.

[                                        ]

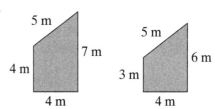

**Example**

❸ **Decomposing a Polygon to Find Area** Find the area of the polygon.

Decompose the polygon into two [            ] and a [            ].

Area of smaller rectangle: $b \times h = \boxed{\phantom{x}} \times \boxed{\phantom{x}}$, or $\boxed{\phantom{x}}$ cm²

Area of larger rectangle: $b \times h = \boxed{\phantom{x}} \times \boxed{\phantom{x}}$, or $\boxed{\phantom{x}}$ cm²

Area of triangle: $\frac{1}{2} \times b \times h = \frac{1}{2} \times \boxed{\phantom{x}} \times \boxed{\phantom{x}}$, or $\boxed{\phantom{x}}$ cm²

The total area is $\boxed{\phantom{x}} + \boxed{\phantom{x}} + \boxed{\phantom{x}}$, or $\boxed{\phantom{x}}$ cm².

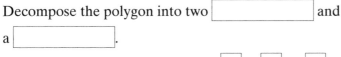

**Quick Check**

3. Find the area of the figure at the right.

[                                        ]

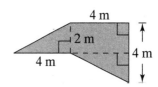

# Lesson 8-3

**Three-Dimensional Figures and Spatial Reasoning**

**Lesson Objective**

To identify three-dimensional figures

## Vocabulary

A three-dimensional figure is _____

_____

A prism is _____

_____

A cube is _____

_____

 A pyramid is _____

_____

A cylinder is _____

_____

 A cone is _____

_____

A sphere is _____

_____

The flat surfaces of three-dimensional figures

are called [        ].

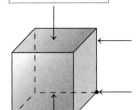 An [        ] is a segment where two faces meet.

A [        ] is a point where two or more edges meet.

When you draw three-dimensional figures, use dashed lines to
indicate "hidden" edges.

## Examples

**❶ Naming Prisms** Name the prism.

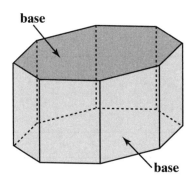

Each base is an [          ]. The figure is an [          ] prism.

**❷ Identifying Three-Dimensional Figures** Name the three-dimensional figure shown.

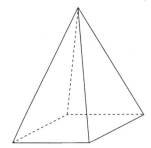

The figure is a [          ] with a [          ]

for a base. The figure is a [              ].

## Quick Check

1. Name each prism.

**a.**

**b.**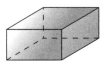

**c.**

[                ]     [                ]     [                ]

2. Name the three-dimensional figures below.

[                ]     [                ]

# Lesson 8-4

**Surface Areas of Prisms and Pyramids**

| Lesson Objective | Common Core State Standard |
|---|---|
| To use nets and to find the surface areas of prisms and pyramids | Geometry: 6.G.4 |

## Vocabulary

A net is _____

_____

Surface area is _____

_____

## Example

❶ **Drawing a Net** Draw a net for the hexagonal prism.

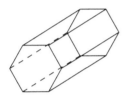

**Step 1** Draw one ⬜ . ────────────►

**Step 2** Draw one ⬜ that connects the two bases.

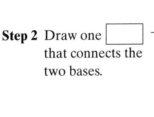

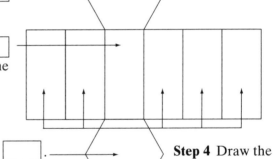

**Step 3** Draw the other ⬜ . ────────────►    **Step 4** Draw the remaining ⬜ .

## Quick Check

**1.** Draw a net for a cube.

## Examples

❷ **Finding the Surface Area of a Prism** Find the surface area of the pizza box.

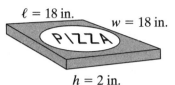

$\ell = 18$ in.
$w = 18$ in.
$h = 2$ in.

**Step 1** Draw and label a net for the prism.

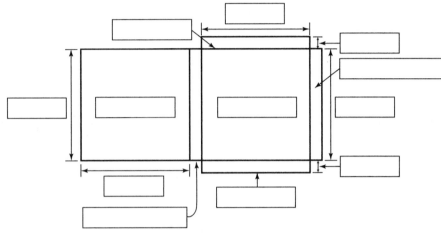

**Step 2** Find and add the areas of all the rectangles.

| Back | Top | Left | Bottom | Right | Front |
|------|-----|------|--------|-------|-------|

☐ × ☐ + ☐ × ☐ + ☐ × ☐ + ☐ × ☐ + ☐ × ☐ + ☐ × ☐

= ☐ + ☐ + ☐ + ☐ + ☐ + ☐ = ☐

The surface area of the pizza box is ☐ square inches.

❸ **Finding the Surface Area of a Pyramid** Find the surface area of the square pyramid at the right.

Find and add the areas of the ☐ and the ☐.

Since the base is a ☐, the triangular faces are ☐.

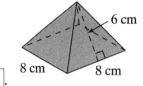

6 cm
8 cm   8 cm

| Square | Triangle | Triangle | Triangle | Triangle |
|--------|----------|----------|----------|----------|

☐ × ☐ + $\frac{1}{2}$(☐ × ☐) + $\frac{1}{2}$(☐ × ☐) + $\frac{1}{2}$(☐ × ☐) + $\frac{1}{2}$(☐ × ☐)

= ☐ + ☐ + ☐ + ☐ + ☐

= ☐

The surface area of the pyramid is ☐ square centimeters.

## Quick Check

**2.** Find the surface area of the prism.

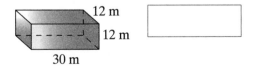

12 m
12 m
30 m

**3.** Find the surface area of the square pyramid.

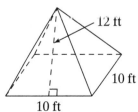

12 ft
10 ft
10 ft

# Lesson 8-5

**Volumes of Rectangular Prisms**

| Lesson Objective | Common Core State Standard |
|---|---|
| To find the volume of rectangular prisms with fractional edge lengths | Geometry: 6.G.2 |

## Vocabulary and Key Concepts

**Volume of a Prism**

Volume = Area of Base × Height

$V = \boxed{\phantom{x}} \times \boxed{\phantom{x}}$

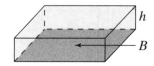

Volume is _____

_____

## Examples

❶ **Counting Cubes to Find Volume** Find the volume of the rectangular prism shown.

**Step 1:** Choose an appropriate cube. Two of the mixed numbers have fractions with denominators of $\boxed{\phantom{x}}$. Use a $\boxed{\phantom{x}}$-unit cube.

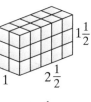
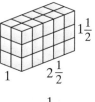

**Step 2:** Count the number of cubes in the prism.

$2\frac{1}{2} = \boxed{\phantom{x}}$ or $\boxed{\phantom{x}} \times \frac{1}{2}$  ← There are $\boxed{\phantom{x}}$ cubes across the front.

$1 = \boxed{\phantom{x}}$ or $\boxed{\phantom{x}} \times \frac{1}{2}$  ← There are $\boxed{\phantom{x}}$ cubes along the side.

$1\frac{1}{2} = \boxed{\phantom{x}}$ or $\boxed{\phantom{x}} \times \frac{1}{2}$  ← There are $\boxed{\phantom{x}}$ cubes up.

So the prism has a total of $\boxed{\phantom{x}} \times \boxed{\phantom{x}} \times \boxed{\phantom{x}}$, or $\boxed{\phantom{x}}$ cubes.

**Step 3:** The volume of one cube is $\boxed{\phantom{x}} \times \boxed{\phantom{x}} \times \boxed{\phantom{x}}$, or $\boxed{\phantom{x}}$ cubic unit.

**Step 4:** Multiply the number of cubes by the volume of each cube.

$\boxed{\phantom{x}} \times \boxed{\phantom{x}} = \boxed{\phantom{x}} = \boxed{\phantom{x}}$

The volume of the prism is $\boxed{\phantom{x}}$ cubic units.

**❷ Finding the Volume of a Prism** Find the volume of the storage container shown.

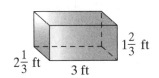

$2\frac{1}{3}$ ft   3 ft   $1\frac{2}{3}$ ft

**Method 1** Count the cubes.

Choose an appropriate sized cube. Two of the mixed numbers have fractions with denominators of ☐. Use a ☐-unit cube.

$3 = \dfrac{\boxed{\phantom{x}}}{3}$    ← There are ☐ cubes across the front.

$2\frac{1}{3} = \dfrac{\boxed{\phantom{x}}}{3}$    ← There are ☐ cubes along the side.

$1\frac{2}{3} = \dfrac{\boxed{\phantom{x}}}{3}$    ← There are ☐ cubes up.

So the prism has a total of ☐ × ☐ × ☐, or ☐ cubes.

The volume of a $\frac{1}{3}$-foot cube is ☐ × ☐ × ☐, or ☐ cubic foot.

315 × ☐ = ☐ = ☐ = ☐

The volume of the prism is ☐ cubic feet.

**Method 2** Use a formula.

$V = l \times w \times h$    ← Use the formula for the volume of a rectangular prism.

$= \boxed{\phantom{x}} \times \boxed{\phantom{x}} \times \boxed{\phantom{x}}$    ← Substitute ☐ for *l*, ☐ for *w*, and ☐ for *h*.

$= \boxed{\phantom{x}} \times \boxed{\phantom{x}} \times \boxed{\phantom{x}}$    ← Multiply.

$= \boxed{\phantom{x}} = \boxed{\phantom{x}}$

The volume is ☐ cubic feet, or ☐ ft³.

## Quick Check

**1.** Choose an appropriate sized cube and then count the cubes to find the volume of the prism.

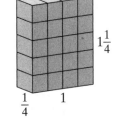

$1\frac{1}{4}$   $\frac{1}{4}$   1

**2.** Find the volume of a rectangular prism with a length of $8\frac{1}{5}$ meters, a width of 7 meters, and a height of $10\frac{2}{5}$ meters.

# Lesson 9-1

**Finding the Mean**

| Lesson Objective | Common Core Standards |
|---|---|
| To find and analyze the mean of a data set using models and calculations | Statistics and Probability: 6.SP.3, 6.SP.5, 6.SP.5.c |

## Vocabulary

The [____] is the sum of a set of data divided by the number of data items.

An outlier is _____

## Example

**①  Using a Model to Find the Mean** In five days Rebecca spent $3, $4, $2, $1, and $5. Find the mean amount of money spent.

Shade in the cubes to model the situation.

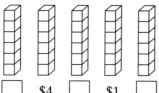

← Shade the cubes to model the amount of money spent each day.

There are [____] shaded cubes altogether.

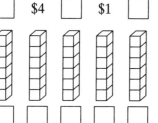

← Next, shade in the correct number of cubes so that the height of each stack is the same.

## Quick Check

**1.** Use a model to find the mean of 3, 6, 3, 4, 2, and 6.

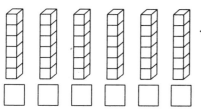

← Shade the cubes to model the amount of money spent each day.

There are [____] shaded cubes altogether.

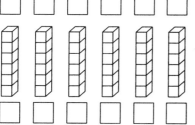

← Next, shade in the correct number of cubes so that the height of each stack is the same.

Name _____ Class _____ Date _____

## Examples

❷ **Calculating the Mean** Find the mean test score of 78, 85, 94, 88, and 91.

$78 + 85 + 94 + 88 + 91 =$ [ ]    ← **Add the test scores.**

$\dfrac{[\quad]}{[\quad]} = [\quad]$    ← **Divide by the number of tests.**

The mean test score is [ ].

**Check for Reasonableness** The mean is between the lowest value, [ ],

and the greatest value, [ ]. So the answer [ ] is reasonable.

❸ **Analyzing the Mean** Identify the outlier in the data set 64, 66, 61, 91, 68 and 59. Find the mean with and without the outlier. What effect does the outlier have on the mean?

The outlier is [ ].

Calculate the mean with the outlier.

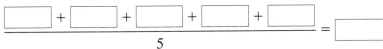

$\dfrac{64 + 66 + 61 + [\quad] + [\quad] + [\quad]}{6} \approx [\quad]$

Calculate the mean *without* the outlier.

$\dfrac{[\quad] + [\quad] + [\quad] + [\quad] + [\quad]}{5} = [\quad]$

The outlier increases the value of the mean by about [ ].

## Quick Check

2. You play a word game. Your scores are 12, 23, 13, 32, and 30. Find your mean score.

[                                                              ]

3. You keep track of the number of hours you baby-sit for six days: 1.25, 1.50, 1.50, 1.75, 2.0, 5.5. What effect does the outlier have on the mean?

[                                                              ]

Name _____ Class _____ Date _____

# Lesson 9-2

**Median and Mode**

| Lesson Objective | Common Core Standards |
|---|---|
| To find and analyze the median and mode of a data set | Statistics and Probability: 6.SP.3, 6.SP.5, 6.SP.5.c |

## Vocabulary

The median is _____

The mode is _____

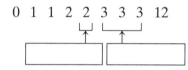

## Example

1. **Finding the Median** A bird-watcher keeps a count of the number of birds she sees each week. The results are 23, 35, 27, 55, 41, 23, 45, and 69. Find the median number of birds.

$$23, 23, 27, 35, 41, 45, 55, 69 \qquad \leftarrow \text{ Order the data.}$$

$$23, 23, 27, 35, 41, 45, 55, 69 \qquad \leftarrow \text{ Since there are 8 items (an even number), use the } \boxed{\phantom{xx}} \text{ values.}$$

$$\frac{\boxed{\phantom{x}} + \boxed{\phantom{x}}}{2} = \frac{\boxed{\phantom{x}}}{2} = \boxed{\phantom{x}} \qquad \leftarrow \text{ Find the mean of } \boxed{\phantom{x}} \text{ and } \boxed{\phantom{x}}.$$

The median number of birds is $\boxed{\phantom{xx}}$.

## Quick Check

1. Weekly sales of comics at a store are 39, 19, 28, 9, 32, 35, and 17 comics. What is the median number of comics sold?

Name _____ Class _____ Date _____

## Examples

❷ **Finding the Mode** The list shows the favorite colors of 12 children. Find the mode.

blue, red, blue, yellow, yellow, blue, red, blue, yellow, blue, red, yellow

Group the data.

    blue, blue, blue, blue, blue
    red, red, red
    yellow, yellow, yellow, yellow

⬚ occurs the most. It is the ⬚ .

❸ **Analyzing Data** The ages of everyone at a family reunion are listed. Find the mean, median, and mode. Which one best describes the typical age of the family members at the reunion?

22, 100, 26, 4, 30, 33, 21, 44, 47, 83, 47

mean $\dfrac{22 + 100 + 26 + 4 + 30 + 33 + 21 + 44 + 47 + 83 + 47}{\boxed{\phantom{XX}}} = \dfrac{\boxed{\phantom{XX}}}{\boxed{\phantom{XX}}} \approx \boxed{\phantom{XXX}}$

median   4, 21, 22, 26, 30, 33, 44, 47, 47, 83, 100: ⬚

mode   ⬚

The ⬚ and the ⬚ are only close to some of the data points.

The mean best describes the typical age of the family members at the reunion.

## Quick Check

2. The list shows the favorite lunches of 15 students. How many students would have to switch from hamburger to taco as their favorite lunch for taco to be the only mode?

hamburger, pizza, taco, pizza, spaghetti, taco, spaghetti, hamburger, hamburger, pizza, taco, pizza, pizza, spaghetti, taco

3. The top five women's 1-meter diving scores are 288.75, 261.83, 254.85, 254.1, and 246.8. Does the mean, median, or mode best describe these data? Explain.

# Lesson 9-3

**Frequency Tables and Dot Plots**

| Lesson Objective | Common Core Standard |
|---|---|
| To analyze a set of data by finding the range and by making frequency tables and dot plots | Statistics and Probability: 6.SP.4 |

## Vocabulary

A frequency table is _____

_____

A dot plot _____

_____

The range of a data set is _____

## Example

❶ **Frequency Table** The favorite lunch choices of ten students are: pizza, pizza, chicken, hamburger, chicken, pizza, chicken, pizza, pizza, pizza. Organize the data in a frequency table. Find the mode.

**Favorite Lunch**

| Lunch | Tally | Freq. |
|---|---|---|
| hamburger | | | |
| pizza | | |
| | | |

Make a tally mark for each lunch item chosen.

The number of tally marks in each row is the [          ].

Since the most students selected [          ] as their favorite

lunch item, the mode is [          ].

## Quick Check

**1.** The first initials of the names of 15 students are listed below.

A  J  B  K  L  C  K  D  L  S  T  D  V  P  L

Organize the data in a frequency table. Find the mode.

| Initial | A | B | C | D | J | K | L | P | S | T | V |
|---|---|---|---|---|---|---|---|---|---|---|---|
| Tally | | | | | | | | | | | |
| Frequency | | | | | | | | | | | |

The mode is [   ].

Name _____ Class _____ Date _____

### Examples

❷ **Using a Dot Plot** Make a dot plot to display the dinner hour for seven families:

5:00  7:00  6:00  6:00  8:00  7:00  6:00

**Dinner Hours**

5  6

← Each • represents one family.

← The scale of a graph includes all of the data values. The scale is ☐ to ☐ in this line plot.

❸ **Finding the Range** Find the range of the data in Example 2.

☐ − 5 = ☐   ← Subtract the least from the greatest value.

The range of dinner times is ☐ hours.

### Quick Check

**2.** Use a dot plot to interpret the number of sales calls made each hour:

2, 3, 0, 7, 1, 1, 9, 8, 2, 8, 1, 2, 8, 7, 1, 8, 6, 1.

| **Number of Phone Calls** |
|---|
|  |

0   1   2   3   4   5   6   7   8   9
Phone Calls

**3.** The numbers of pottery items made by students are 36, 21, 9, 34, 36, 10, 4, 35, 30, 7, 5, and 10. Find the range of the data.

# Lesson 9-4

**Box-and-Whisker Plots**

| Lesson Objective | Common Core Standards |
|---|---|
| To analyze a set of data by creating a box-and-whisker plot | Statistics and Probability: 6.SP.4, 6.SP.5.a, 6.SP.5.b |

## Vocabulary

A box-and-whisker plot is _____

_____

The lower quartile is _____

The upper quartile is _____

## Example

① **Constructing a Box-and-Whisker Plot**  A school principal recorded the following number of students absent each day: 5, 3, 0, 9, 6, 2, 10. Construct a box-and-whisker plot to represent the data.

In the boxes below, list the data values in order and label the five key values.

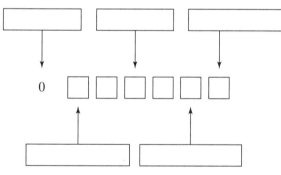

Draw a number line from 1 to 10.

Draw a box from the lower quartile ☐ to the upper quartile

☐. Draw a vertical line at the median ☐. Draw whiskers connecting

the box to the least ☐ and greatest ☐ values.

Name _____ Class _____ Date _____

## Quick Check

1. A girls' basketball team had the following scores: 7, 10, 16, 18, 20, 22, 22, 25, 30, 37, 43. The basketball team scored 40 points in a playoff game. Add the value 40 to the list of data. What are the five key values for a box-and-whisker plot that includes this game?

<br><br><br>

## Example

❷ **Analyzing a Box-and-Whisker Plot** Olivia studied the prices for women's flip-flop sandals at different stores. She made the box-and-whisker plot below. Label the number line with the unit of measurement.

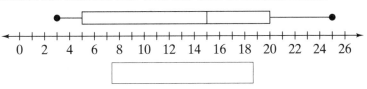

The lower quartile is [    ]. The upper quartile is [    ].

The fraction of the sandal prices that are between these values is [        ].

## Quick Check

2. The box-and-whisker plot represents the number of minutes it takes 10 students to get to school. What is the unit of measurement for this set of data? What fraction of the students get to school in less than 20 minutes?

**Time it Takes to Get to School**

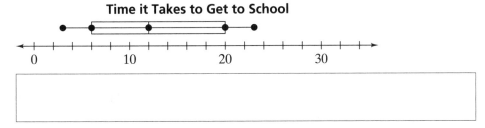

<br><br>

Name _____ Class _____ Date _____

# Lesson 9-5
**Histograms**

| Lesson Objective | Common Core Standards |
|---|---|
| To construct and interpret a histogram | Statistics and Probability: 6.SP.4, 6.SP.5, 6.SP.5.b, 6.SP.5.c |

## Vocabulary

A histogram is _____

_____

## Example

**1  Interpreting a Histogram** The frequency table shows the number of books students read during the summer.

| Number of Books Read | | | | | |
|---|---|---|---|---|---|
| Interval | 1–3 | 4–6 | 7–9 | 10–12 | 13–15 |
| Frequency | 2 | 5 | 8 | 2 | 1 |

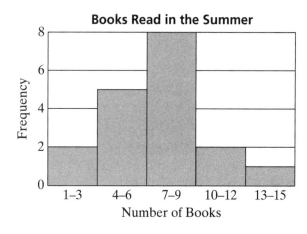

The interval tells how the ☐.

There are ☐ intervals for this data.

The ☐ tells the number of students whose answers were in each interval.

Add the frequencies to find the total number of observations of students.

☐

The number of students who reported that they read fewer than 7 books is ☐.

The fewest students reported that they read ☐ books.

## Quick Check

1. Interpret the histogram to answer.

   **a.** Which interval had the greatest number of customer responses?

   ☐

   **b.** Did most customers spend less than 30 minutes or more than 30 minutes on shopping sites?

   ☐

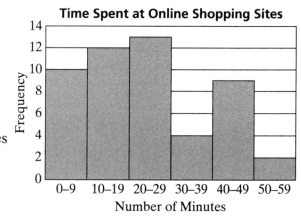

Name _____ Class _____ Date _____

## Example

❷ **Constructing a Histogram** Charlie asked his friends and relatives the value of the loose change they had in their pockets or purse. The frequency table shows the result.

| Interval | Frequency |
|----------|-----------|
| 0–$0.24 | 3 |
| $0.25–$0.49 | 2 |
| $0.50–$0.74 | 7 |
| $0.75–$0.99 | 3 |
| $1.00–$1.24 | 5 |
| $1.25–$1.49 | 1 |

The frequencies vary from ☐ to ☐

Choose a vertical scale from 0 to ☐.

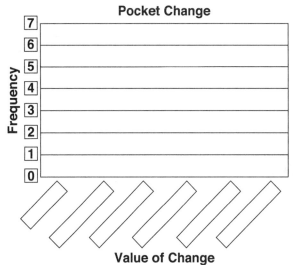

Label the intervals on the *x*-axis.

Draw a bar for each interval.

## Quick Check

**2.** Which histogram matches the data in the table?

| Interval | Frequency |
|----------|-----------|
| 0–19 | 10 |
| 20–29 | 2 |
| 30–39 | 6 |
| 40–49 | 8 |

**A**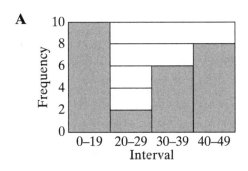

**B**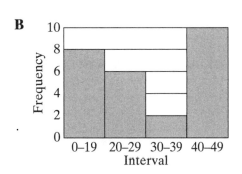

# Lesson 9-6

Variability of Data

| Lesson Objective | Common Core Standards |
|---|---|
| To find and use measures of variability to describe and compare data sets | Statistics and Probability: 6.SP.2, 6.SP.3, 6.SP.5.c |

## Vocabulary

A measure of center is _____

A measure of variability is _____

The mean absolute deviation (MAD) is _____

The interquartile range (IQR) measures _____

## Example

**1** **Using Variability of Data: Mean Absolute Deviation** The table shows the number of minutes ten students spent talking to their friends on the phone in a day. Find the mean absolute deviation.

**Step 1:** Find the mean number of minutes for all the students. Record the mean in the table below.

**Step 2:** Find the distance between each student's number of minutes and the mean. Write each distance as a positive number.

| Minutes on the Phone with Friends | | | | | | | | | | |
|---|---|---|---|---|---|---|---|---|---|---|
| **Student** | 1 | 2 | 3 | 4 | 5 | 6 | 7 | 8 | 9 | 10 |
| **Number of Minutes** | 15 | 35 | 55 | 45 | 60 | 20 | 30 | 25 | 45 | 20 |
| **Mean** | | | | | | | | | | |
| **Distance from Mean** | | | | | | | | | | |

**Step 3:** Calculate the mean of all the distances in the bottom row.

Name _____ Class _____ Date _____

## Example

❷ **Using Variability of Data: Interquartile Range** Describe the variability of the talking on the phone data in Example 1 in a different way.

Another way to describe the variability is to find the interquartile range for the data.

Order the data to determine the median, the [＿＿＿＿＿＿], and the [＿＿＿＿＿＿].

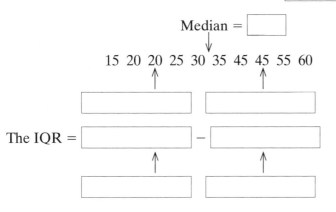

Median = [＿＿]

15  20  20  25  30  35  45  45  55  60

The IQR = [＿＿＿＿＿] − [＿＿＿＿＿]

You can say that the interquartile range of the data values is [＿＿].

## Quick Check

**1.** A scientist investigated the yield of his Big Boy tomato plants. The table shows his data.

| Plant | 1 | 2 | 3 | 4 | 5 | 6 | 7 | 8 | 9 | 10 |
|---|---|---|---|---|---|---|---|---|---|---|
| Number of Tomatoes | 17 | 22 | 16 | 45 | 18 | 24 | 30 | 22 | 27 | 19 |
| Mean | 24 | 24 | 24 | 24 | 24 | 24 | 24 | 24 | 24 | 24 |
| Distance from Mean | 7 | 2 | 8 | 21 | 6 | 0 | 6 | 2 | 3 | 5 |

The mean average deviation of the data above is 6.

Suppose that Plant 1 grows 5 more tomatoes for a total of 22 instead of 17.

**a.** What is the new mean absolute deviation for the data? _____

**b.** What does the change in MAD for the new data set tell you about the data set? Explain.

_____

_____

**2.** Suppose that two more Big Boy tomato plants produced 20 and 25 tomatoes.

**a.** What is the interquartile range for the 12 data values?

[＿＿＿＿＿＿＿＿＿＿＿＿＿＿＿＿]

**b.** How does this result affect your conclusion about the middle range of the data?

[＿＿＿＿＿＿＿＿＿＿＿＿＿＿＿＿]

# Lesson 9-7

**Shape of Distributions**

| Lesson Objective | Common Core Standards |
|---|---|
| To relate the shape of a data display to how the data is distributed | Statistics and Probability: 6.SP.2, 6.SP.5.d |

## Vocabulary and Key Concepts

A _____ is several data points that lie _____ within a small interval.

A _____ in an ordered set of data is a value that is _____ the values on either side.

A gap is _____.

Symmetry in data is a _____ that has _____.

## Example

❶ Describe the shape of each distribution using the terms *gap*, *peak*, and *symmetry*.

**a.** Dot plot: no ☐☐☐☐ , no ☐☐☐☐ ,

gap between ☐☐☐☐

**b.** Box-and-whisker plot: clustered around the

☐☐☐☐ no ☐☐☐☐

**c.** Histogram: no ☐☐☐☐ , no ☐☐☐☐ ,

☐☐☐☐ between ☐☐☐☐

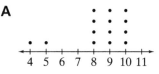

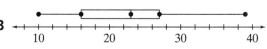

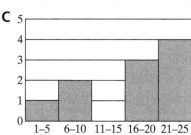

## Quick Check

**1. a.** Match the shape of each distribution with the description that best fits it.

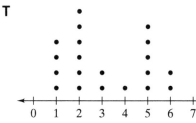

**x.** a gap and 2 peaks
**y.** cluster and a gap
**z.** no gap, and 2 peaks

**b.** How would your description of the dot plot T change if the value 4 were removed from the data?

_____

Name _____ Class _____ Date _____

## Example

❷ **Relating Distribution Shape to Measures** What can the shape of this dot plot tell you about its measures of center and variability?

The distribution is almost [        ].

Except for the [        ], the data are

clustered around a [        ], which is

also the [        ] and the [        ].

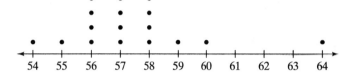

The [        ] will be a greater number because of the outlier. The IQR

will be [        ] because the middle half of the data is close together.

The [        ] will be somewhat greater because it is affected by the outlier.

## Quick Check

2. Compare the dot plot on the left to the one on the right.

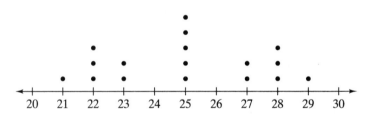 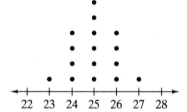

**a.** What similarities and differences are there between the two dot plots?

**b.** What do your observations tell you about the variability and center of the dot plot on the left?

**c.** What if the dot plot on the left had 6 more dots at 21 and 29? How would your answer change?

# Lesson 9-8

| Lesson Objective | Common Core Standards |
|---|---|
| To identify a statistical question and to recognize and remove bias from statistical questions | Statistics and Probability: 6.SP.1, 6.SP.2 |

## Vocabulary

A statistical question is _____

_____

_____

## Example

**1** **Identifying Statistical Questions** Tell whether the question is a statistical question. If it is, identify possible answers. If not, explain why not.

**a.** What is the temperature at which water freezes in degrees Fahrenheit?

This ☐ a statistical question because ☐ answer:

☐ A statistical question might ask a group of people: At what outdoor temperature do you feel it is necessary to put on a jacket?

**b.** What is the favorite sport for the sixth graders in your school to watch?

This ☐ a statistical question because ☐

depending on whom you ask. Possible favorites: ☐.

**c.** How many pairs of shoes do I own?

This ☐ a statistical question. There is ☐ factual answer.

A statistical question might ask 20 different people in a show store: How many pairs of shoes do you own?

Name _____ Class _____ Date _____

## Quick Check

1. Tell whether the question is a statistical question. If it is, identify possible answers. If not, explain why not.

   **a.** How many students are taller than 6 feet?

   ┌─────────────────────────────────────────────────────────┐
   │                                                           │
   │                                                           │
   └─────────────────────────────────────────────────────────┘

   **b.** What size shoe do you wear?

   ┌─────────────────────────────────────────────────────────┐
   │                                                           │
   │                                                           │
   │                                                           │
   └─────────────────────────────────────────────────────────┘

## Example

❷ **Identifying Bias** Stephie and John wanted to find out about favorite seasons. Which question is likely to give biased results? Why?

- Stephie's question: Which is your favorite season: freezing winter, summer, mild spring, or fall?
- John's question: Which is you favorite season: winter, spring, summer, or fall?

[          ] question is biased. The words in the question could influence the answers.

The word [                    ], could make people avoid that answer.

The word [                ], could make people choose that answer.

## Quick Check

2. Determine if the survey question is biased and explain your answer. If it is biased, rewrite the question so it is unbiased.

   **a.** Rolondo wrote the survey question: Do you prefer delicious sweet red grapes or bitter strawberries?

   ┌─────────────────────────────────────────────────────────┐
   │                                                           │
   │                                                           │
   │                                                           │
   └─────────────────────────────────────────────────────────┘

   **b.** Eliana wants to find out which internet service people in her area people think is best. She asks: Which is the fastest internet service in your area?

   ┌─────────────────────────────────────────────────────────┐
   │                                                           │
   │                                                           │
   │                                                           │
   └─────────────────────────────────────────────────────────┘

## A Note to the Student:

This section of your workbook contains a series of pages that support your mathematics understandings for each chapter and lesson presented in your student edition.

- Practice pages provide additional practice for every lesson.

- Guided Problem Solving pages lead you through a step-by-step solution to an application problem in each lesson.

- Vocabulary pages contain a variety of activities to increase your reading and math understanding, ranging from graphic organizers to vocabulary review puzzles.

Practice • Guided Problem Solving • Vocabulary

# Practice 1-1 ................................................ Properties of Numbers

**Name each property of addition or multiplication used below.**

**1.** $(6 + 3) + 21 = 6 + (3 + 21)$

_____

_____

**2.** $13 \times 1 = 13$

_____

_____

**3.** $8 + 20 + 12 = 8 + 12 + 20$

_____

_____

**4.** $5 \times 2 \times 11 = 2 \times 11 \times 5$

_____

_____

**Use mental math to find each sum or product.**

**5.** $53 + 12 + 7$

_____

**6.** $2 \times 53 \times 5$

_____

**7.** $8 + 0 + 6$

_____

**8.** $(19 + 22) + 8$

_____

**9.** $5 \times (13 \times 20)$

_____

**10.** $40 \times 31 \times 25$

_____

**11.** $25 + (13 + 5)$

_____

**12.** $7 \times 25 \times (1 \times 8)$

_____

**13.** $7 + 14 + (23 + 6)$

_____

**14.** $4 \times (25 \times 17)$

_____

**15.** $43 + 4 + (13 + 3)$

_____

**16.** $5 \times 1 \times 13 \times 20$

_____

**Solve.**

**17.** Roshonda's garden produced 25 carrots, 127 blackberries, and 5 pumpkins. What was the total number of fruits and vegetables produced by Roshonda's garden? Use mental math to find the solution.

_____

**18.** Michael washes the Gomez family's cars once a month. They pay him $25 every 3 months for his work. At this rate, how much money will Michael earn in one year?

_____

# 1-1 • Guided Problem Solving

**GPS** **Student Page 7, Exercise 32:**

**Art Class** In a student art contest there are 14 drawings, 22 sculptures, and some paintings. There are 18 more paintings than sculptures. What is the total number of art pieces?

## Understand

1. What are you being asked to do?

   _____

2. Circle the information you will need to solve this problem.

3. Estimate what you expect the answer to be.

   _____

## Plan and Carry Out

4. How many drawings are there? _____

5. How many sculptures are there? _____

6. How many more paintings are there than sculptures? _____

7. What will you have to do to find the number of paintings?

   _____

8. How many paintings are there? _____

9. What is the total number of art pieces in the contest?

   _____

## Check

10. Is your answer close to your original estimate? Why or why not?

    _____

## Solve Another Problem

11. Janelle has 10 marbles. Ralph has 13 marbles, and Jennifer has 17 more marbles than Ralph has. What is the total number of marbles Janelle, Ralph, and Jennifer have?

    _____

# Practice 1-2

Order of Operations

**Which operation would you perform first in each expression?**

**1.** $4 + 6 \times 9$

**2.** $(7 - 5) \times 3$

**3.** $14 \div 2 \times 3$

_____

_____

_____

**4.** $18 - 5 + 3$

**5.** $5 \times 2 + 6$

**6.** $(9 + 14) - 8 \div 2$

_____

_____

_____

**Find the value of each expression.**

**7.** $8 - 3 \times 1 + 5$

**8.** $(43 - 16) \times 5$

**9.** $14 \times 6 \div 3$

_____

_____

_____

**10.** $100 \div (63 - 43)$

**11.** $9 \times (3 \times 5)$

**12.** $7 \times (8 + 6)$

_____

_____

_____

**13.** $15 - (5 + 7)$

**14.** $(12 - 9) \times (6 + 1)$

**15.** $(9 - 3) \times 2$

_____

_____

_____

**16.** $8 - 3 \times 2 + 7$

**17.** $(9 - 4) \times 6$

**18.** $(35 - 5) \times 3$

_____

_____

_____

**19.** $4 + (20 \div 4) - 2$

**20.** $9 - (2 \times 3) \div 2$

**21.** $55 + 10 - 7 \times 6$

_____

_____

_____

**22.** $7 \times (10 - 2) \div 4$

**23.** $(16 + 2) \div 9 + 9$

**24.** $1 \times 2 + 8 \div 4 \times 5$

_____

_____

_____

**Insert parentheses to make each statement true.**

**25.** $6 + 7 \times 4 - 2 = 26$

**26.** $14 - 5 \div 3 = 3$

_____

_____

**27.** $27 \div 4 + 5 - 1 = 2$

**28.** $6 \times 7 + 2 - 1 = 53$

_____

_____

**Write a mathematical expression and solve.**

**29.** Haircuts for boys cost $7. Haircuts for men cost $10. If 20 boys and 20 men went to the barber yesterday, how much did the barber earn?

_____

# 1-2 • Guided Problem Solving

**GPS** **Student Page 11, Exercise 34:**

**Coins** There are 300 coins of the same type in two stacks. One stack is 380 millimeters tall. The other is 220 millimeters tall. Find the thickness of one coin.

## Understand

1. What are you being asked to find?

   _____

2. What will you need to know to find this information?

   _____

3. What operations will you have to perform to answer the question?

   _____

## Plan and Carry Out

4. How will you find the total height of the 300 coins?

   _____

5. What is the total height of the 300 coins? _____

6. Will you have to multiply or divide to find the height of one coin?

   _____

7. How thick is one coin? _____

## Check

8. Based on your answer, how tall is a stack of 300 coins?

   _____

9. Does this match the height given in the problem? _____

## Solve Another Problem

10. Georgia walks 325 meters to an intersection, and then another 125 meters to the store. If she spends a total of 9 minutes walking, how many meters does she walk in one minute?

    _____

# Practice 1-3 ............................ **Understanding Decimals**

**Write each decimal in words.**

**1.** 213.23

_____
_____
_____
_____

**2.** 7,430.25

_____
_____
_____
_____

**3.** 81.8887

_____
_____
_____
_____

**4.** 12.873

_____
_____
_____
_____

**5.** 8.0552

_____
_____
_____
_____

**6.** 0.00065

_____
_____
_____
_____

**Write each decimal in standard form and in expanded form.**

**7.** three tenths

_____

**8.** eight tenths

_____

**9.** two hundredths

_____

**10.** forty hundredths

_____

**What is the value of the digit 7 in each number?**

**11.** 0.7

_____

**12.** 4.00712

_____

**13.** 2.179

_____

**14.** 1.8887

_____

**15.** 15.002237

_____

**16.** 27.002

_____

**Round each decimal to the underlined place.**

**17.** 28,467.0$\underline{8}$9

_____

**18.** 348.92$\underline{9}$71

_____

**19.** 72.$\underline{1}$4

_____

**20.** 22.985$\underline{5}$3

_____

**21.** 19.82$\underline{5}$49

_____

**22.** 1.999$\underline{2}$8

_____

# 1-3 • Guided Problem Solving

**GPS** Student Page 17, Exercise 43:

Artists use a ratio called the Golden Mean to describe a person's height. Your height from the floor to your waist is usually six hundred eighteen thousandths of your total height. Round this number to the nearest hundredth.

## Understand

1. Is the number more or less than 1? Explain.

   _____

   _____

2. The word *thousandths* represents how many decimal places to the right of the decimal point?

   _____

## Plan and Carry Out

3. Write six hundred eighteen thousandths in standard form.

   _____

4. What digit is in the hundredths place?

   _____

5. What digit is to the right of the hundredths place?

   _____

6. Based on the number above, should you round up or down?

   _____

7. Round this number to the nearest hundredth.

   _____

## Check

8. Did you round up or down? Why?

   _____

   _____

## Solve Another Problem

9. Liz has a height of five feet and two and forty-five hundredths of an inch. Round Liz's height to the nearest inch.

   _____

# Practice 1-4 ....................................... Adding and Subtracting Decimals

**First estimate. Then find each sum or difference.**

**1.** $0.6 + 5.8$      **2.** $2.1 + 3.4$      **3.** $3.4 - 0.972$      **4.** $3.1 - 2.076$

_____     _____     _____     _____

**5.** $8.13 - 2.716$      **6.** $5.91 + 2.38$      **7.** $3.086 + 6.152$      **8.** $4.7 - 1.9$

_____     _____     _____     _____

**9.** $9.3 - 3.9$      **10.** $5.2 - 1.86$      **11.** $15.98 + 26.37$      **12.** $9.27 + 15.006$

_____     _____     _____     _____

**13.** $5.9 - 2.803$      **14.** $15.7 - 8.923$      **15.** $4.19 - 2.016$      **16.** $14.75 - 6.9264$

_____     _____     _____     _____

**Use front-end estimation to estimate each sum.**

**17.** $12 + 0.25 + 4.75$      **18.** $18.5 + 0.25 + 0.25$      **19.** $17 + 23 + 10.6$

_____     _____     _____

**20.** $11.3 + 5.7$      **21.** $5 + 6.2 + 4.05$      **22.** $50.6 + 10.4 + 20$

_____     _____     _____

**23.** $2.1 + 0.6 + 0.3$      **24.** $14.3 + 16$      **25.** $4.9 + 0.6 + 4$

_____     _____     _____

**Use the table at the right for Exercises 26–28.**

**26.** Find the sum of the decimals given in the chart. What is the meaning of this sum?

_____

_____

**27.** What part of the hourly work force is aged 25–44?

_____

**28.** Which three age groups combined represent one-fourth of the hourly work force?

_____

_____

**Ages of Workers Earning Hourly Pay**

| Age of Workers | Part of Work Force |
|---|---|
| 16–19 | 0.08 |
| 20–24 | 0.15 |
| 25–34 | 0.29 |
| 35–44 | 0.24 |
| 45–54 | 0.14 |
| 55–64 | 0.08 |
| 65 & over | 0.02 |

# 1-4 • Guided Problem Solving

**GPS** **Student Page 22, Exercise 33:**

**Population** In 2000, the New England states had a total population of about 13.92 million. Find the population of Maine.

| State | Population |
|---|---|
| Connecticut | 3.41 million |
| Maine | ■ |
| Massachusetts | 6.35 million |
| New Hampshire | 1.24 million |
| Rhode Island | 1.05 million |
| Vermont | 0.61 million |

## Understand

1. What are you being asked to do?

   _____

2. How will you use the total population of the New England states to answer the question?

   _____

## Plan and Carry Out

3. Find the sum of the populations of the other states.

   _____

4. What is the total population of all the New England states?

   _____

5. Write an expression to find the population of Maine.

   _____

6. Evaluate the expression to find the population of Maine.

   _____

7. Find the population of Maine.

   _____

## Check

8. How can you check your answer?

   _____

   _____

## Solve Another Problem

9. You and a friend calculate your grade for a class. You have an 83.5 and your friend has an 85.65. Who has the higher grade? How much higher is it?

   _____

# Practice 1-5

**Multiplying Decimals**

**Place the decimal point in each product.**

**1.** $4.3 \times 2.9 = 1247$

**2.** $0.279 \times 53 = 14787$

**3.** $4.09 \times 3.96 = 161964$

_____

_____

_____

**4.** $5.90 \times 6.3 = 3717$

**5.** $0.74 \times 83 = 6142$

**6.** $2.06 \times 15.9 = 32754$

_____

_____

_____

**Find each product.**

**7.** $43.59 \times 0.1$

**8.** $246 \times 0.01$

**9.** $\begin{array}{r} 5.342 \\ \times \quad 13 \\ \hline \end{array}$

_____

_____

_____

**10.** $\begin{array}{r} 0.19 \\ \times 0.05 \\ \hline \end{array}$

**11.** $\begin{array}{r} 240 \\ \times 0.02 \\ \hline \end{array}$

**12.** $\begin{array}{r} 43.79 \\ \times \quad 42 \\ \hline \end{array}$

_____

_____

_____

**Write a multiplication statement you could use for each situation.**

**13.** A pen costs $.59. How much would a dozen pens cost?

_____

**14.** A mint costs $.02. How much would a roll of 10 mints cost?

_____

**15.** An orange costs $.09. How much would 2 dozen oranges cost?

_____

**Find each product. Tell whether you would use mental math, paper and pencil, or a calculator.**

**16.** $19(0.35)$

**17.** $30 \times 0.1$

**18.** $22.62 \times 1.08$

_____

_____

_____

_____

_____

_____

Name _____ Class _____ Date _____

# 1-5 • Guided Problem Solving

**GPS** Student Page 28, Exercise 36:

**Nutrition** There is 0.2 gram of calcium in 1 serving of cheddar cheese. How much calcium is in 3.25 servings of cheddar cheese?

## Understand

1. What is being compared in the exercise?

_____

_____

_____

2. What are you being asked to do?

_____

_____

3. Will you multiply or divide to determine the answer? Explain.

_____

_____

_____

## Plan and Carry Out

4. How much calcium is in one serving? _____

5. How many servings do you want? _____

6. Write an expression to answer the exercise. _____

7. How many grams of calcium are in 3.25 servings of cheddar cheese? _____

## Check

8. Should there be more or less than 0.2 gram of calcium in 3.25 servings of cheddar cheese? Explain.

_____

## Solve Another Problem

9. There is 0.5 gram of fat in one serving of a breakfast cereal. How many grams of fat are in 4.25 servings?

_____

# Practice 1-6 ......................................................... Dividing Decimals

**Draw a model to find each quotient.**

1. $0.4 \div 0.08$ _____

2. $0.8 \div 0.4$ _____

3. $0.9 \div 0.15$ _____

**Find each quotient.**

4. $1.8 \div 6$

_____

5. $16\overline{)3.2}$

_____

6. $17\overline{)5.1}$

_____

7. $9\overline{)21.6}$

_____

8. $15\overline{)123}$

_____

9. $108 \div 5$

_____

10. $50\overline{)17.5}$

_____

11. $14\overline{)889}$

_____

12. $5\overline{)316}$

_____

**Solve.**

13. A package of 25 mechanical pencils costs $5.75. How much does each pencil cost?

_____

14. A sales clerk is placing books side by side on a shelf. She has 12 copies of the same book. If the books cover 27.6 in. of the shelf, how thick is each book?

_____

15. The salt content in the Caspian Sea is 0.13 kg for every liter of water. How many kg of salt are in 70 liters?

_____

**Find each quotient.**

16. $0.4 \div 0.02$

_____

17. $3.9 \div 0.05$

_____

18. $0.2\overline{)26}$

_____

19. $0.68 \div 0.2$

_____

20. $0.02\overline{)0.06}$

_____

21. $0.09\overline{)0.108}$

_____

# 1-6 • Guided Problem Solving

**GPS** Student Page 34, Exercise 29:

**School Supplies** A stack of paper measures 0.9 centimeter thick. Each piece of paper is 0.01 centimeter thick.

    **a.** How many pieces of paper are in the stack?

    **b.** Could each of 25 students get three pieces of paper?

## Understand

  **1.** Circle the information you will need to solve.

  **2.** What are you being asked to do in part (a)?

    _____

  **3.** What are you being asked to do in part (b)?

    _____

    _____

## Plan and Carry Out

  **4.** How thick is one piece of paper? _____

  **5.** How thick is the stack of paper? _____

  **6.** Do you multiply or divide to answer part (a)? _____

  **7.** Write an expression to answer part (a). _____

  **8.** How many pieces of paper are in the stack? _____

  **9.** How many pieces of paper are needed for each of 25 students to get three pieces of paper?

    _____

  **10.** Is there enough paper? _____

## Check

  **11.** Why is the number of pieces of paper 100 times more than the height of the stack of paper?

    _____

## Solve Another Problem

  **12.** A stack of baseball cards measures 5.4 centimeters thick. Each baseball card is 0.1 centimeter thick. How many baseball cards are in the stack?

    _____

Name _____ Class _____ Date _____

# 1A: Graphic Organizer

**Study Skill** As you read over the material in the chapter, keep a paper and pencil handy to write down notes and questions that you have. As with any new textbook, take a few minutes to explore the general contents of the book.

**Write your answers.**

1. How many chapters are in the text? _____

2. Where is the index located? _____

3. How many lessons are there in Chapter 1? _____

4. What is the topic of the Test-Taking Strategies page in Chapter 1?

   _____

5. Complete the graphic organizer below as you work through the chapter.
   • In the center, write the title of the chapter.
   • When you begin a lesson, write the lesson name in a rectangle.
   • When you complete a lesson, write a skill or key concept in an oval linked to that lesson block.
   • When you complete the chapter, use this graphic organizer to help you review.

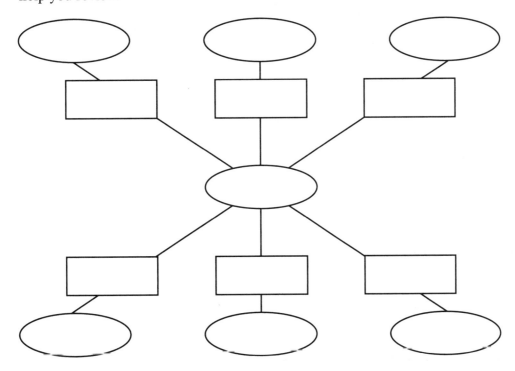

# 1B: Reading Comprehension

**For use after Lesson 1-2**

**Study Skill** Write assignments down; do not rely on your memory.

**Read the paragraph and answer the questions that follow.**

> A beaver can grow to be up to 76.2 centimeters long and stand 30.5 centimeters high. Beavers have large, flat tails that average about 25.4 centimeters long and have several uses. The tail can serve as a warning signal when slapped against the water. A beaver also uses its tail to navigate through the water while swimming or to stand on its hind legs. Beavers also have two front teeth on their upper and lower jaws. These teeth are primarily used for cutting down trees to build dams. Typically, a beaver cuts down trees up to 20 centimeters in diameter, but has been known to cut down trees as large as 75 centimeters in diameter.

1. What is the paragraph about?

   _____

2. How large can a beaver grow?

   _____

3. How long is the average beaver's tail?

   _____

4. How many numbers in the paragraph are lengths?

   _____

5. What unit of length is used?

   _____

6. Use expanded form to write the maximum length of a beaver in centimeters.

   _____

7. What are the uses of a beaver's tail?

   _____

   _____

   _____

8. **High-Use Academic Words** In the paragraph, what does *typically* mean?

   **a.** usually                    **b.** rarely

Name _____ Class _____ Date _____

# 1C: Reading/Writing Math Symbols  For use after Lesson 1-3

**Study Skill** When you take notes, it helps if you learn to use abbreviations and symbols to represent words. For instance, @ means *at*, # means *number*, w/ means *with* and = means *equal*.

**Match the symbol in Column A with its meaning in Column B.**

**Column A**                                      **Column B**

1.  +                                             **A.** dollar

2.  =                                             **B.** plus

3.  $                                             **C.** times

4.  ×                                             **D.** divided by

5.  ÷                                             **E.** is equal to

6.  −                                             **F.** minus

**Write each mathematical statement in word form.**

7.  $3.1 = 3 + 0.1$ _____

8.  $\$4 + \$7 = \$11$ _____

9.  $5 \div 2 = 2.5$ _____

10. $4 \times 2$ _____

11. $3 + 10$ _____

12. $6 - 1 = 5$ _____

**Write a mathematical statement for each word description.**

13. The sum of seven plus nine is sixteen. _____

14. Seven plus six equals thirteen. _____

15. Fourteen minus eight equals six. _____

16. Eight divided by four equals two. _____

17. Twenty is two times ten. _____

18. The product of four and five is twenty. _____

# 1D: Visual Vocabulary Practice

**For use after Lesson 1-3**

**Study Skill** When learning a new word, it helps to know if it is a name or action.

**Concept List**

Commutative Property of Addition        Identity Property of Addition

Associative Property of Addition        Identity Property of Multiplication

Commutative Property of Multiplication        standard form

Associative Property of Multiplication        expanded form

order of operations

**Write the concept that best describes each exercise. Choose from the concept list above.**

| 1.<br><br>$70 + 5 + 0.2 + 0.04$<br><br>_____ | 2.<br><br>$0 + 2 = 2$<br><br>_____ | 3.<br><br>$2 + 4 = 4 + 2$<br><br>_____ |
|---|---|---|
| 4.<br><br>$(3 + 2) \times 1 = (3 + 2)$<br><br>_____ | 5.<br><br>$4 + 12 \div (8 - 2)$<br>$= 4 + 12 \div 6$<br>$= 4 + 2$<br>$= 6$<br><br>_____ | 6.<br><br>$(9 + 3) + 7 = 9 + (3 + 7)$<br><br>_____ |
| 7.<br><br>$(15 - 3)7 = 7(15 - 3)$<br><br>_____ | 8.<br><br>$75.24$<br><br>_____ | 9.<br><br>$2 \times (3 \times 4) = (2 \times 3) \times 4$<br><br>_____ |

Name _____ Class _____ Date _____

# 1E: Vocabulary Check

**Study Skill** Strengthen your vocabulary. Use these pages and add cues and summaries by applying the Cornell Notetaking style.

**Write the definition for each word or term at the right. To check your work, fold the paper back along the dotted line to see the correct answers.**

Associative Property
of Addition

_____

_____

_____

Commutative Property
of Addition

_____

_____

expression

_____

_____

_____

Commutative Property
of Multiplication

_____

_____

Identity Property
of Multiplication

_____

_____

_____

## 1E: Vocabulary Check (continued)          For use after Lesson 1-4

Write the vocabulary word or term for each definition. To check your
work, fold the paper forward along the dotted line to see the correct
answers.

Changing the grouping of the
addends does not change the sum.

_____

Changing the order of the
addends does not change the sum.

_____

a mathematical phrase containing
numbers and operation symbols

_____

Changing the order of the factors
does not change the product.

_____

The product of 1 and 13 is 13.

_____

# 1F: Vocabulary Review

**Study Skill** Review your class notes as soon as possible. This will help you identify any concepts in which you need additional explanation.

**Match the term in Column A with its definition or example in Column B.**

| Column A | Column B |
|---|---|
| **1.** Identity Property of Multiplication | **A.** adding the "front-end" digits and adjusting the sum |
| **2.** place value | **B.** $7 + (3 + 9) = (7 + 3) + 9$ |
| **3.** compatible numbers | **C.** numbers that are easy to compute mentally |
| **4.** front-end estimation | **D.** $6 + 8 = 8 + 6$ |
| **5.** Associative Property of Addition | **E.** $8.3 \times 1 = 8.3$ |
| **6.** Commutative Property of Addition | **F.** value of a digit based on its location in a particular number |

**Match the term in Column A with its definition or example in Column B.**

| Column A | Column B |
|---|---|
| **7.** Identity Property of Addition | **G.** $8 \cdot 4 = 4 \cdot 8$ |
| **8.** Associative Property of Multiplication | **H.** sum that shows the place and value of each digit |
| **9.** Commutative Property of Multiplication | **I.** a number written using digits |
| **10.** expanded form | **J.** mathematical phrase containing numbers and operations |
| **11.** standard form | **K.** $8(7 \cdot 9) = (8 \cdot 7)9$ |
| **12.** expression | **L.** $4 + 0 = 4$ |

Vocabulary and Study Skills

Name _____ Class _____ Date _____

# Practice 2-1 • • • • • • • • • • • • • • • • • • • • • • • • • • • • • • • • • • **Variables and Expressions**

**Write an algebraic expression for each model. Squares represent ones.**
**Shaded rectangles represent variables.**

**1.** ☐ ☐ ▨ ▨
   ☐
_____

**2.** ▨ ▨ ▨ ☐ ☐ ☐
         ☐ ☐ ☐
_____

**3.** ▨ ▨ ☐ ☐ ☐
         ☐ ☐
_____

**Evaluate each expression.**

**4.** $56 \div b$ for $b = 7$
_____

**5.** $3m$ for $m = 9$
_____

**6.** $v + 16$ for $v = 9$
_____

**7.** $2t - 8$ for $t = 21$
_____

**8.** $2(4e)$ for $e = 5$
_____

**9.** $12 - 2g$ for $g = 3$
_____

**10.** $3pq$ for $p = 3$
and $q = 5$
_____

**11.** $9r + 16$ for $r = 8$
_____

**12.** $s(58 + t)$ for $s = 2$
and $t = 7$
_____

**13.** $24 - 4t$ for $t = 4$
_____

**14.** $3v + 5k$ for $v = 3$
and $k = 6$
_____

**15.** $5d - (h + 9)$ for $d = 3$
and $h = 5$
_____

**Copy and complete each table.**

**16.**

| x | x + 7 |
|---|---|
| 2 | 9 |
| 5 | 12 |
| 8 | |
| 11 | |
| | 21 |

**17.**

| x | 5x |
|---|---|
| 3 | |
| 6 | |
| 9 | |
| 12 | |
| | 75 |

**18.**

| x | 125 − x |
|---|---|
| 15 | |
| 30 | |
| 45 | |
| 60 | |
| | 50 |

**19.**

| x | 6x + 5 |
|---|---|
| 2 | |
| 4 | |
| | 41 |
| 8 | |
| 10 | |

**20.** A cellular phone company charges a $49.99 monthly fee for 600 free minutes. Each additional minute costs $.35. This month you used 750 minutes. How much do you owe?

_____

Name _____ Class _____ Date _____

# 2-1 • Guided Problem Solving

GPS **Student Page 50, Exercise 28:**

**Dogs** A dog walker charges $10 to walk a large dog and $6 to walk a small dog. She uses $10d + 6s$ to calculate her earnings, where $d$ is the number of large dogs and $s$ is the number of small dogs. How much does she earn for walking each group?

   **a.** 4 large and 2 small dogs

   **b.** 6 small dogs

## Understand

**1.** What are you being asked to do?

_____

_____

## Plan and Carry Out

**2.** What is the expression for calculating the dog walker's earnings?

_____

**3.** What do you replace $d$ and $s$ with in part (a)? _____

**4.** Replace $d$ and $s$ with the values and simplify the expression.

_____

**5.** How much does she earn to walk 4 large dogs and 2 small dogs?

_____

**6.** Repeat Steps 3–5 to determine the dog walker's earnings for

walking 6 small dogs. _____

## Check

**7.** How can you check your answer? Use your method to see if your answer is correct.

_____

_____

## Solve Another Problem

**8.** The sum of the interior angles of a polygon can be found using the formula $S = (N - 2) \times 180°$, where $N$ is the number of sides of the polygon. What is the sum of the interior angles of a polygon with 8 sides?

_____

Name _____ Class _____ Date _____

# Practice 2-2                                    **Writing Algebraic Expressions**

**Write two word phrases for each algebraic expression.**

**1.** $5m$

_____

_____

_____

**2.** $8 + b$

_____

_____

_____

**3.** $q \div 15$

_____

_____

_____

**4.** $c - 10$

_____

_____

_____

**5.** $18 \div a$

_____

_____

_____

**6.** $27 - m$

_____

_____

_____

**7.** You buy 5 bags of peanuts to share with your friends. Each bag contains $p$ ounces of peanuts. How many ounces of peanuts did you buy? Draw a model for this situation. Then write an expression to describe the relationship.

_____

**8.** Write an expression to describe the relationship of the data in the table.

| $n$ | ▢ |
|---|---|
| 15 | 19 |
| 20 | 24 |
| 25 | 29 |

_____

**Write an algebraic expression for each word phrase.**

**9.** nine less than $t$

_____

**10.** eleven more than a number

_____

**11.** the quotient of 700 and a number

_____

**12.** two times the number of windows

_____

**13.** $b$ divided by seven

_____

**14.** 81 increased by $n$

_____

**15.** twelve times the number of muffin pans

_____

**16.** $15 times the number of hours

_____

**17.** 8 less than the product of $k$ and 3

_____

# 2-2 • Guided Problem Solving

**GPS** Student Page 56, Exercise 28

**Painting** Customers in a paint store use the table at the right to decide how much paint they need.

   **a.** Write an expression for the number of gallons of paint needed for an area of $A$ square feet.

   **b.** Paint costs $17.95 per gallon. Write an expression for the cost of the paint needed for an area of $A$ square feet.

| Area sq. ft. | Gallons |
|---|---|
| 400 | 1 |
| 800 | 2 |
| 2,000 | 5 |
| 3,200 | 8 |

## Understand

1. What are you being asked to do?

_____

_____

2. Circle the information you will need to solve the problem.

## Plan and Carry Out

3. How much does paint cost per gallon?

_____

4. Write an expression for the number of gallons of paint needed for an area of $A$ square feet.

_____

5. Write an expression to find the cost of the paint needed for an area of $A$ square feet.

_____

## Check

6. Use your expression to find out how much it would cost a customer to paint an area of 2,000 square feet. Does your answer make sense?

_____

## Solve Another Problem

7. Anna and Tom are window washers. They are working on a house that has $r$ rooms, with 4 windows in each room. They have 2 windows left to wash before the job is complete. Write an expression for the number of windows they have already washed.

_____

# Practice 2-3
**Using Number Sense to Solve One-Step Equations**

**Find the missing number that makes the equation true.**

**1.** $7 + \boxed{\phantom{x}} = 12$

**2.** $\boxed{\phantom{x}} \times 5 = 30$

**3.** $13 - \boxed{\phantom{x}} = 4$

_____  _____  _____

**Tell whether each equation is true or false.**

**4.** $12 + 10 = 10 + 12$

**5.** $31 + 4 = 41 + 3$

**6.** $3.5 \times 1 = 1$

_____  _____  _____

**7.** $(3 \times 5) \times 4 = 3 \times (5 \times 4)$

**8.** $(7 \times 2) + 6 = 7 \times (2 + 6)$

**9.** $0 \times a = a$

_____  _____  _____

**Solve each equation. Use either mental math or the strategy *Guess, Check*, and *Revise*.**

**10.** $8b = 72$

**11.** $n + 14 = 45$

**12.** $h - 3.6 = 8$

_____  _____  _____

**13.** $w \div 12 = 3$

**14.** $53 = z - 19$

**15.** $86 = 29 + y$

_____  _____  _____

**16.** $153 = 9k$

**17.** $4 = m \div 24$

**18.** $c + 14.7 = 29.8$

_____  _____  _____

**19.** The winners of a slam dunk basketball competition receive T-shirts. The coach spends $50.40 on shirts for the entire team. Each T-shirt costs $4.20. Solve the equation $(4.20)n = 50.40$ to find the number of team members.

_____

_____

Name _____ Class _____ Date _____

# 2-3 • Guided Problem Solving

**GPS** Student Page 61, Exercise 29

You have *c* pounds of cashews and 2.7 pounds of peanuts. You have 6 pounds of nuts altogether. Solve the equation $c + 2.7 = 6$ to find how many pounds of cashews you have.

## Understand

1. What are you being asked to do?

   _____

   _____

2. How can mental math help you to solve this problem?

   _____

   _____

## Plan and Carry Out

3. What does the equation $c + 2.7 = 6$ mean?

   _____

   _____

4. What is $6 - 2.7$? _____

5. How many pounds of cashews do you have?

   _____

## Check

6. Explain how you can check your answer. Then check your answer.

   _____

   _____

## Solve Another Problem

7. At a school, there are 60 teachers for 1,500 students. Each teacher has the same number of students. Use the equation $60n = 1{,}500$ to find how many students each teacher has.

   _____

# Practice 2-4

**Solve each equation. Check the solution. Remember, you can draw a diagram to help you solve an equation.**

**1.** $38 + b = 42$
　　　
**2.** $n + 14 = 73$
　　　
**3.** $h + 3.6 = 8.6$

_____　　_____　　_____

**4.** $12.4 = 9 + t$
　　　
**5.** $m + 7.3 = 9.1$
　　　
**6.** $5.62 + p = 5.99$

_____　　_____　　_____

**Write and solve an equation. Then check each solution.**

**7.** The height of the male giraffe in one zoo is 17.3 feet. The male is 3.2 feet taller than the female giraffe. How tall is the female giraffe?

_____

_____

_____

**8.** The top three best-selling record albums of all time are Michael Jackson's *Thriller* (24 million copies), Fleetwood Mac's *Rumours* (17 million copies), and Boston's *Boston* (*b* million copies). The three albums sold a combined total of 56 million copies. How many copies of *Boston* were sold?

_____

_____

_____

**Solve each equation. Then check the solution.**

**9.** $a + 22 = 120$
　　　
**10.** $10 = e + 2.7$
　　　
**11.** $3.89 + x = 5.2$

_____　　_____　　_____

_____　　_____　　_____

# 2-4 • Guided Problem Solving

## GPS Student Page 67, Exercise 21

**Music** You add a 4-minute song to your digital music player. The player now has 2 hours of music. Use an equation to find how much music was on the player before you added the song.

### Understand

1. What are you being asked to do? _____

   _____

2. What will the variable represent in the equation? _____

   _____

3. Circle the information you will need to solve.

### Plan and Carry Out

4. How long was the song that you added? _____

5. Write an expression for the length of the song you added plus the amount of music that was on the player before you added the new song. Choose any variable for the amount of music that was on the player. _____

6. How much music (in minutes) was on the player after you

   added the song? _____

7. Write an equation comparing the amounts in Steps 5 and 6.

   _____

8. What do you do to both sides of the equation to isolate the variable?

   _____

9. Solve the equation.

   _____

10. How much music was on the player before you added the song?

    _____

### Check

11. Explain how you can check your answer. Then check your answer.

    _____

### Solve Another Problem

12. The book *A Tree Grows in Brooklyn* has 420 pages. It is 206 pages longer than *The Catcher in the Rye*. Use an equation to find the number of pages in *The Catcher in the Rye*.

    _____

Guided Problem Solving

# Practice 2-5

**Solving Subtraction Equations**

**Solve each equation. Then check the solution. Remember, you can draw a diagram to help you solve an equation.**

**1.** $x - 10 = 89$

**2.** $14 = y - 15$

**3.** $a - 10 = 3.4$

**4.** $12.3 = b - 7$

**5.** $n - 2.7 = 8.3$

**6.** $3.12 = d - 6.88$

**Write and solve an equation. Then check each solution.**

**7.** The owner of a used music store bought a compact disc for $4.70. When she sold it, her profit was $4.75. What was the selling price?

**8.** Yesterday, Stephanie spent $38.72 on new shoes and $23.19 on computer software. When she was finished, she had $31.18. How much money did she have before she went shopping?

**Solve each equation. Then check the solution.**

**9.** $x - 7 = 77$

**10.** $3.1 = r - 7.5$

**11.** $k - 5.13 = 2.9$

# 2-5 • Guided Problem Solving

**GPS** **Student Page 70, Exercise 20:**

You buy several posters. The total cost is $18.95. You have $7.05 left after you pay. Write and solve an equation to find how much money you had before this purchase.

## Understand

1. What are you being asked to do?

   _____

2. What will the variable represent in the equation?

   _____

3. Circle the information you will need to solve.

## Plan and Carry Out

4. How much did you pay for the posters? _____

5. Write an expression for the amount of money you had before the purchase minus the amount you paid for the posters. Choose any variable for the amount of money you had.

   _____

6. How much money did you have left after the purchase?

   _____

7. Write an equation comparing the amounts in Steps 5 and 6.

   _____

8. What do you do to both sides of the equation to isolate the variable?

   _____

9. Solve the equation.

   _____

   _____

10. How much money did you have before the purchase?

    _____

## Check

11. Check your answer by substituting the result in step 10 into the equation you wrote in step 7. Does it check?

    _____

## Solve Another Problem

12. Jim has saved $78. This is $23 less than his sister has saved. Write and solve an equation to find how much his sister has saved.

    _____

# Practice 2-6
**Solving Multiplication and Division Equations**

**State whether the number given is a solution to the equation.**

1. $8c = 80; c = 10$   2. $b \div 7 = 8; b = 56$   3. $9m = 108; m = 12$   4. $y \div 9 = 17; y = 163$

_____   _____   _____   _____

5. $9r = 72; r = 7$   6. $14b = 56; b = 4$   7. $48 = y \div 4; y = 12$   8. $32 = y \div 8; y = 256$

_____   _____   _____   _____

9. $17a = 41; a = 3$   10. $w \div 21 = 17; w = 357$   11. $21c = 189; c = 8$   12. $52 = y \div 6; y = 302$

_____   _____   _____   _____

**Solve each equation. Then check each solution.**

13. $905 = 5a$   14. $6v = 792$   15. $12 = y \div 12$   16. $b \div 18 = 21$

_____   _____   _____   _____

17. $80 = 16b$   18. $19m = 266$   19. $d \div 1,000 = 10$   20. $g \div 52 = 18$

_____   _____   _____   _____

21. $672 = 21f$   22. $z \div 27 = 63$   23. $43h = 817$   24. $58 = j \div 71$

_____   _____   _____   _____

**Write and solve an equation for each situation.**
**Then check the solution.**

25. Lea drove 420 miles and used 20 gallons of gas. How many miles per gallon did her car get?

_____

26. Ty bought 5 folders that cost $3 each. How much did he spend on folders?

_____

27. Julia wants to buy copies of a book to give as presents. How many books can she buy if they are on sale for $12 each, and she has $100 to spend?

_____

28. Virginia bought 18 packs of envelopes for $2 each and 15 packs of Thank You cards for $4 each. If she gives the cashier $100, how much change should she receive?

_____

# 2-6 • Guided Problem Solving

### GPS Student Page 76, Exercise 29

**Biology** An elephant's height is about 5.5 times the length of her hind footprint. Use an equation to find the approximate height of an elephant whose hind footprint is 1.5 feet long.

## Understand

1. What are you being asked to do?

   _____

   _____

   _____

2. Circle the information you will need to solve.

3. The phrase "*5.5 times*" tells you to perform what operation?

   _____

## Plan and Carry Out

4. What is the length of the hind footprint of this particular adult female elephant? _____

5. Write an expression to represent the phrase "*5.5 times the length of the hind footprint.*"

   _____

6. Write an equation for the height of the elephant. _____

7. What is the height of the elephant? _____

## Check

8. Explain how you can check your answer. Does your answer check?

   _____

   _____

## Solve Another Problem

9. Angela makes 1.75 times the amount of money that Janet makes. If Janet makes $38,200, how much does Angela make? Write and solve an equation.

   _____

# 2A:  Graphic Organizer

**For use before Lesson 2-1**

**Study Skill**  Read over the lesson before you come to class. Reading ahead of time will help you to grasp new concepts quicker.

**Write your answers.**

1. What is the chapter title? _____

2. How many lessons are there in this chapter? _____

3. What is the topic of the Test-Taking Strategies page? _____

4. Complete the graphic organizer below as you work through the chapter.
   - In the center, write the title of the chapter.
   - When you begin a lesson, write the lesson name in a rectangle.
   - When you complete a lesson, write a skill or key concept in an oval linked to that lesson block.
   - When you complete the chapter, use this graphic organizer to help you review.

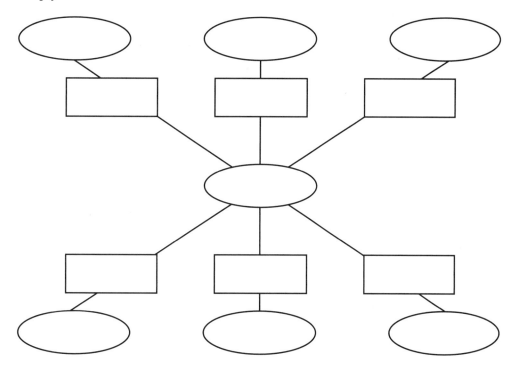

# 2B: Reading Comprehension

**Study Skill** Practice storing and recalling information while it is still fresh in your mind.

**Read the paragraph and answer the questions.**

On July 3, 2002, the major league record for the most home runs hit in one day was set topping by 5 the previous record of 57 set on April 7, 2000. Fifty-three different players contributed to this milestone. A game between Detroit and Chicago added twelve home runs. San Francisco and Colorado added 10 more. Around the league, an amazing four grand slams were also hit. But this was not the only record broken on that day. Nine different players hit more than one home run in a game.

1. What is the paragraph about?

   _____

2. On what date did the new record occur?

   _____

3. How many numbers are written in word form, and what are they?

   _____

4. Identify the smallest number in the paragraph.

   _____

5. How many home runs is the new record?

   _____

6. How many of the home runs were not grand slams?

   _____

7. What is the total number of home runs hit during the Detroit-Chicago and San Francisco-Colorado games?

   _____

8. **High-Use Academic Words** In Exercise 4, what does the word *identify* mean?

   **a.** to show that you recognize something　　**b.** to place in some order

# 2C: Reading/Writing Math Symbols

**For use after Lesson 2-2**

**Study Skill** Bring all necessary tools with you to class. Never go to class unprepared.

**Match the phrase in Column A with its expression in Column B.**

| Column A | Column B |
|---|---|
| **1.** 4 increased by a number | **A.** $4 - n$ |
| **2.** a number divided by 4 | **B.** $4 + n$ |
| **3.** a number subtracted from 4 | **C.** $n \div 4$ |
| **4.** 4 multiplied by a number | **D.** $n - 4$ |
| **5.** 4 less than a number | **E.** $4n$ |

| Column A | Column B |
|---|---|
| **6.** the difference of 6 and a number | **A.** $n \div 6$ |
| **7.** the product of 6 and a number | **B.** $6n$ |
| **8.** the sum of a number and 6 | **C.** $6 - n$ |
| **9.** 6 divided into a number | **D.** $n - 6$ |
| **10.** 6 less than a number | **E.** $6 + n$ |

| Column A | Column B |
|---|---|
| **11.** the quotient of 12 and a number | **A.** $12 \div n$ |
| **12.** a number times 12 | **B.** $n - 12$ |
| **13.** 12 decreased by a number | **C.** $n + 12$ |
| **14.** the total of 12 and a number | **D.** $12 - n$ |
| **15.** 12 subtracted from a number | **E.** $12n$ |

Vocabulary and Study Skills

Name ____________________ Class ____________ Date ____________

# 2D: Visual Vocabulary Practice

**For use after Lesson 2-3**

*High-Use Academic Words*

**Study Skill** If a word is not in the glossary, use a dictionary to find its meaning.

**Concept List**

| | | |
|---|---|---|
| solve | compare | define |
| order | organize | sum |
| table | estimate | evaluate |

**Write the concept that best describes each exercise. Choose from the concept list above.**

**1.**

$$x - 1 = 9$$
$$x - 1 + 1 = 9 + 1$$
$$x = 10$$

____________

**2.**

$$4 + 6 + 11 + 2 = 23$$

____________

**3.**

**2004 Olympic Medal Totals**

| Country | Number |
|---|---|
| Russia | 38 |
| U.S.A. | 29 |
| China | 14 |

____________

**4.**

An equation is a mathematical sentence that has an equal sign.

____________

**5.**

2, 1.85, 3.2, 1.6, 3.27
becomes
1.6, 1.85, 2, 3.2, 3.27

____________

**6.**

$$3.05 < 3.5$$

____________

**7.**

$$59 \div 3.1 \approx 60 \div 3$$

____________

**8.**

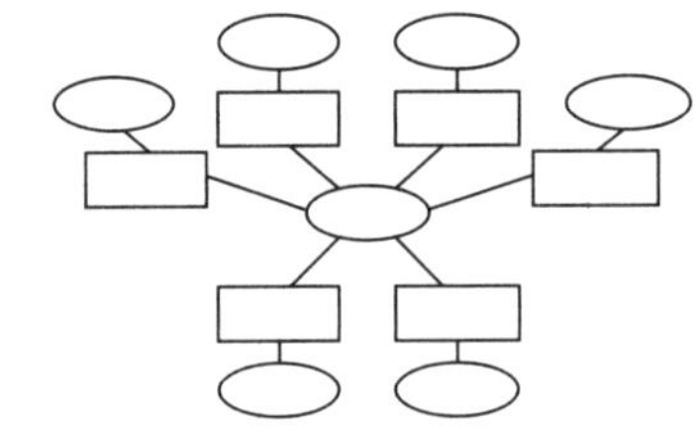

____________

**9.**

$2z - 4$ for $z = 13$

____________

# 2E: Vocabulary Check

**Study Skill** Strengthen your vocabulary. Use these pages and add cues and summaries by applying the Cornell Notetaking style.

**Write the definition for each word or term at the right. To check your work, fold the paper back along the dotted line to see the correct answers.**

_____

_____

_____

equation

_____

_____

_____

inverse operations

_____

_____

_____

variable

_____

_____

_____

numerical expression

_____

_____

_____

open sentence

# 2E: Vocabulary Check (continued)

**For use after Lesson 2-4**

**Write the vocabulary word or term for each definition. To check your work, fold the paper forward along the dotted line to see the correct answers.**

a mathematical sentence with an equal sign

_____

operations that undo each other

_____

a letter that stands for a number

_____

an expression with only numbers and operation symbols

_____

an equation with one or more variables

_____

# 2F: Vocabulary Review Puzzle

**For use with the Chapter Review**

**Study Skill** Follow directions carefully.

Complete the crossword puzzle. For help, use the glossary in your textbook.

## ACROSS

**2.** 12 + (3 + 9) = (12 + 3) + 9 is an example of this property

**5.** kind of expression that has no variable

**7.** find the value of an expression

**8.** kind of expression that has at least one variable

**9.** mathematical phrase containing numbers and operations

**10.** a symbol that stands for an unknown number

**11.** mathematical sentence that contains an equal sign

## DOWN

**1.** 100 + 32 = 32 + 100 is an example of this property

**3.** number that makes an equation true

**4.** operations that undo one another

**6.** property that allows adding the same thing to both sides of an equation

# Practice 3-1 ................................ Divisibility and Mental Math

**Is the first number divisible by the second? Use mental math.**

1. 475 by 5 _____

2. 5,296 by 3 _____

3. 843 by 2 _____

4. 456,790 by 5 _____

5. 3,460 by 2 _____

6. 4,197 by 3 _____

**Test each number for divisibility by 2, 3, 5, 9, or 10.**

7. 126

8. 257

9. 430

10. 535

_____

_____

_____

_____

11. 745

12. 896

13. 729

14. 945

_____

_____

_____

_____

15. 4,580

16. 6,331

17. 7,952

18. 8,000

_____

_____

_____

_____

19. 19,450

20. 21,789

21. 43,785

22. 28,751

_____

_____

_____

_____

**Find the digit that makes each number divisible by 9.**

23. 54,78☐

24. 42,☐97

25. 83,2☐4

**Name the numbers that are divisible by the numbers given.**

26. numbers between 10 and 20, divisible by 2, 3, and 9

_____

27. numbers between 590 and 610, divisible by 2, 3, 5, and 10

_____

28. There are 159 students to be grouped into relay teams. Each team is to have the same number of students. Can each team have 3, 5, or 6 students?

_____

# 3-1 • Guided Problem Solving

**GPS** Student Page 89, Exercise 31:

**Money** Elissa and eight friends have lunch at a restaurant. The bill is $56.61. Can the friends split the bill into nine equal shares? Use the divisibility rule for 9 to explain your answer.

## Understand

1. What are you being asked to do?

   _____

   _____

2. What do you have to use to explain your answer?

   _____

3. What is the divisibility rule for 9?

   _____

   _____

## Plan and Carry Out

4. How much is the bill? _____

5. What are the digits? _____

6. What is the sum of the digits? _____

7. Does 9 divide evenly into the sum? _____

8. Can the friends split the bill into nine equal shares? _____

## Check

9. How can you check that your answer is correct?

   _____

   _____

## Solve Another Problem

10. Melissa, Dyanna, and Cristina are counselors at a summer camp. They want to divide the campers evenly among them. If there are 137 campers, use the rule for divisibility by 3 to determine if this is possible.

    _____

# Practice 3-2 ................................................ Exponents

**Write each expression using an exponent. Name the base and the exponent.**

**1.** $3 \times 3 \times 3 \times 3$

**2.** $7 \times 7 \times 7 \times 7 \times 7 \times 7$

**3.** $9 \times 9 \times 9$

_____

_____

_____

_____

_____

_____

**Write each number in expanded form using powers of 10.**

**4.** 98,364

**5.** 20,351,401

**6.** 875,020

_____

_____

_____

_____

_____

_____

_____

_____

_____

**Simplify each expression.**

**7.** $9^2$

**8.** $6^4$

**9.** $5^3$

_____

_____

_____

**10.** $156 + (256 \div 8^2)$

**11.** $32 + 64 + 2^3$

**12.** $53 + 64 \div 2^3$

_____

_____

_____

**13.** $(3 \times 4)^2$

**14.** $60 \div (8 + 7) + 11$

**15.** $2^2 \times 5^2 + 106$

_____

_____

_____

**16.** $4 + 7 \times 2^3$

**17.** $60 + (5 \times 4^3) + 22 \times 55$

**18.** $7^2 + 4$

_____

_____

_____

**19.** $7^2 - 7 \times 2$

**20.** $48 \div 4 \times 5 - 2 \times 5$

**21.** $(4^2 - 4) \times 10$

_____

_____

_____

**22.** $(4 + 3) \times (2 + 1)$

**23.** $2^4 \times 2^5$

**24.** $12 \times (30 + 37)$

_____

_____

_____

**25.** $(3 + 2) \times (6^2 - 7)$

**26.** $5 \times (9 + 4) + 362 \div 2$

**27.** $3^4 + 405 \div 81$

_____

_____

_____

## 3-2 • Guided Problem Solving

### GPS Student Page 139, Exercise 33:

**Biology** A single-celled organism splits in two after one hour. Each new cell also splits in two after one hour. How many cells will there be after eight hours? Write your answer using an exponent.

### Understand

1. What are you being asked to do?

   _____

2. Explain what it means to write a number with an exponent.

   _____

   _____

### Plan and Carry Out

3. How many cells are there after 3 hours?
   Write the number using an exponent.

   _____

4. How many cells are there after 4 hours?
   Write the number using an exponent.

   _____

5. How many cells are there after 6 hours?
   Write the number using an exponent.

   _____

6. How many cells are there after 8 hours?
   Write the number using an exponent.

   _____

### Check

7. Why is the exponent 8?

   _____

### Solve Another Problem

8. Scientists recently discovered a type of cell that divides into 3 different cells after one hour. Each of those 3 cells divides into 3 different cells after a second hour. If this pattern continues, how many cells are there after 4 hours? Write the number using an exponent.

   _____

Name _____ Class _____ Date _____

# Practice 3-3

**Prime Numbers and Prime Factorization**

**1.** Make a list of all the prime numbers from 50 through 75. _____

**Tell whether each number is prime or composite.**

**2.** 53        **3.** 86        **4.** 95        **5.** 17

_____     _____     _____     _____

**6.** 24        **7.** 27        **8.** 31        **9.** 51

_____     _____     _____     _____

**10.** 103        **11.** 47        **12.** 93        **13.** 56

_____     _____     _____     _____

**Complete each factor tree.**

**14.**       **15.**      **16.** 84

**Find the prime factorization of each number.**

**17.** 58

_____

**18.** 72

_____

**19.** 40

_____

**20.** 30

_____

**21.** 144

_____

**22.** 310

_____

**Find the number with the given prime factorization.**

**23.** $2 \times 2 \times 5 \times 7 \times 11$       **24.** $2 \times 3 \times 5 \times 7 \times 11$

_____       _____

**25.** $2 \times 2 \times 13 \times 17$       **26.** $7 \times 11 \times 13 \times 17$

_____       _____

**27.** There are 32 students in a class. How many ways can the class be divided into groups with equal numbers of students? What are they?

_____

Name _____ Class _____ Date _____

# 3-3 • Guided Problem Solving

**GPS** Student Page 97, Exercise 30:

**Parades** A group has 36 ceremonial guards. When they march, they form rows of equal numbers of guards. What numbers of rows can they make? How many guards will be in each row?

## Understand

1. What are you being asked to do?

_____

_____

2. What do you have to know to do this problem?

_____

3. Without solving, how can you tell how many answers there are to this question?

_____

## Plan and Carry Out

4. List the factors of 36.

_____

5. What are the possible numbers of rows?

_____

6. For each number of rows, how many guards are in each row?

_____

_____

## Check

7. How can you check your answer?

_____

_____

## Solve Another Problem

8. Louise is planting 30 bunches of pansies in her garden. She wants to put them in rows of equal numbers of bunches. What numbers of rows can they make? How many bunches will be in each row?

_____

# Practice 3-4 ......................................... Greatest Common Factor

**List the factors to find the GCF of each set of numbers.**

**1.** 8, 12          **2.** 18, 27          **3.** 15, 23          **4.** 17, 34

_____    _____    _____    _____

**5.** 24, 12         **6.** 18, 24          **7.** 5, 25           **8.** 20, 25

_____    _____    _____    _____

**Use a division ladder to find the GCF of each set of numbers.**

**9.** 10, 15         **10.** 25, 75         **11.** 14, 21         **12.** 18, 57

_____    _____    _____    _____

**13.** 32, 24, 40    **14.** 25, 60, 75     **15.** 12, 35, 15     **16.** 15, 35, 20

_____    _____    _____    _____

**Use factor trees to find the GCF of each set of numbers.**

**17.** 28, 24              **18.** 27, 36              **19.** 15, 305

_____         _____         _____

**20.** 57, 27              **21.** 24, 48              **22.** 56, 35

_____         _____         _____

**23.** 75, 200             **24.** 90, 160             **25.** 72, 108

_____         _____         _____

**Solve.**

**26.** The GCF of two numbers is 850. Neither number is divisible by the other. What is the smallest that these two numbers could be?

_____

**27.** The GCF of two numbers is 479. One number is even and the other number is odd. Neither number is divisible by the other. What is the smallest that these two numbers could be?

_____

# 3-4 • Guided Problem Solving

## GPS Student Page 102, Exercise 30:

Three friends pool their money to buy baseball cards. Brand A has 8 cards in each pack, Brand B has 12 cards, and Brand C has 15 cards. If they want to split each pack of cards equally, which two brands should they buy? Explain.

### Understand

**1.** What does *split each pack of cards equally* mean?

_____

### Plan and Carry Out

**2.** How many cards will they have if they buy Brand A and Brand B?

_____

**3.** Is the number you found in Step 2 divisible by 3? Why or why not?

_____

**4.** How many cards will they have if they buy Brand A and Brand C?

_____

**5.** How many cards will they have if they buy Brand B and Brand C?

_____

**6.** Which of the answers to Steps 4 and 5 is divisible by 3? _____

**7.** Which two brands should they buy?

_____

### Check

**8.** Explain your decision.

_____

### Solve Another Problem

**9.** Carrie is lining up 45 students in the drill team and 25 students in the color guard. She wants each row to have the same number of students in both groups. How many rows are there, and how many students are in each row?

_____

_____

Name _____ Class _____ Date _____

# Practice 3-5

Least Common Multiple

**List multiples to find the LCM of each set of numbers.**

**1.** 5, 10

_____

**2.** 2, 3

_____

**3.** 6, 8

_____

**4.** 8, 10

_____

**5.** 5, 6

_____

**6.** 12, 15

_____

**7.** 9, 15

_____

**8.** 6, 15

_____

**9.** 6, 9

_____

**10.** 3, 5

_____

**11.** 4, 5

_____

**12.** 9, 21

_____

**13.** 4, 6, 8

_____

**14.** 6, 8, 12

_____

**15.** 4, 9, 12

_____

**16.** 6, 12, 15

_____

**17.** 8, 12, 15

_____

**18.** 2, 4, 5

_____

**Use prime factorizations to find the LCM of each set of numbers.**

**19.** 18, 21

_____

**20.** 15, 21

_____

**21.** 18, 24

_____

**22.** 15, 30

_____

**23.** 24, 30

_____

**24.** 24, 72

_____

**25.** 8, 42

_____

**26.** 16, 42

_____

**27.** 8, 56

_____

**28.** 8, 30

_____

**29.** 16, 30

_____

**30.** 18, 30

_____

**31.** 12, 24, 16

_____

**32.** 8, 16, 20

_____

**33.** 12, 16, 20

_____

**34.** At a store, hot dogs come in packages of eight and hot dog buns come
in packages of twelve. What is the least number of packages of
each type that you can buy and have no hot dogs or buns left over?

_____

# 3-5 • Guided Problem Solving

**GPS** **Student Page 105, Exercise 29:**

**Business** During a promotion, a music store gives a free CD to every fifteenth customer and a free DVD to every fortieth customer. Which customer will be the first to get both gifts?

## Understand

1. Circle the information you will need to solve.

2. What are you being asked to do?

   _____

   _____

## Plan and Carry Out

3. Which customers will receive a free CD?

   _____

   _____

4. Which customers will receive a free DVD?

   _____

5. Which customer will be the first to get both gifts?

   _____

## Check

6. Explain how you can check your answer.

   _____

   _____

## Solve Another Problem

7. Emanuel, Michelle, and Kim volunteer at the swimming pool. Emanuel works every 5 days. Michelle works every 6 days. Kim works every 15 days. They are working together today. How many days will it be until the next time they work together?

   _____

   _____

   _____

   _____

# Practice 3-6

**Use the Distributive Property to write an equivalent expression for each of the following.**

**1.** $6(x + 7)$

**2.** $8(7 + 9p)$

**3.** $4(3h + 5 + 6k)$

**4.** $(5n + 12) \times 4$

**5.** $6(7c + 4d + 11)$

**6.** $(8x + 5y) \times 3$

**Factor each expression. Check your solution.**

**7.** $27 + 33$

**8.** $30 + 72$

**9.** $45 + 55 + 20$

**10.** $12 + 56$

**11.** $56 + 120$

**12.** $27 + 63 + 54$

**13.** $4x + 18$

**14.** $65 + 15x$

**15.** $15b + 24c + 33$

**16.** $24h + 36$

**17.** $54 + 72y$

**18.** $36x + 16y + 28$

**19.** The auditorium at the School for the Arts has 7 rows of seats, and each row has 102 seats in it. Use the Distributive Property to find the number of seats in the auditorium.

_____

**20.** A movie theater charges $5.50 for a student ticket. Use the Distributive Property to find the cost for 8 students.

_____

**21.** Samantha has saved $35 from doing chores around the house. She buys 5 packs of gum and 8 packs of erasers from the school store. Use the Distributive Property to find how much Samantha spent at the school store. How much change should she receive from the cashier?

| Item | Cost per pack |
|------|------|
| Pencils | $3.00 |
| Erasers | $1.75 |
| Gum | $2.50 |
| Taffy | $2.00 |

_____

# 3-6 • Guided Problem Solving

**GPS** **Student Page 111, Exercise 44:**

**Gardening** Your school's ecology club plants 8 rows of trees in a vacant lot. Each row has 27 trees. Find the total number of trees that the ecology club plants.

## Understand

**1.** What are you being asked to do?

_____

**2.** Circle the information you will need to solve.

## Plan and Carry Out

**3.** How many rows of trees are there?

_____

**4.** How many trees are there in each row?

_____

**5.** Write an expression for the total number of trees.

_____

**6.** Use the Distributive Property to simplify the expression.

_____

**7.** How many trees are there total?

_____

## Check

**8.** Explain how you can check your answer. Does your answer check?

_____

_____

## Solve Another Problem

**9.** Alyce is tiling her living room. There are 29 rows of tiles, with 9 tiles in each row. How many tiles are there total?

_____

# Practice 3-7 · · · · · · · · · · · · · · · · · · · · · · · · · · · · · · · Simplifying Algebraic Expressions

**Find an equivalent expression for each expression by simplifying.**

**1.** $8x + (6x + y)$

_____

**2.** $(3x - 5y) + 7y$

_____

**3.** $22m + 6n + (4m - 8)$

_____

**4.** $14k + (8 - k + h)$

_____

**5.** $7 + m + (6m - 3)$

_____

**6.** $(18x - 3) + (4y + 12)$

_____

**7.** $9 - 4b + (8 + 7b + 5c)$

_____

**8.** $9f + (16f + 3 - f)$

_____

**9.** $10 - 25x + 12 + 26x$

_____

**10.** $3y + (7x + 6y + z - 9)$

_____

**11.** $(5c - 2b) + (7 + 9c)$

_____

**12.** $8 + 7h + (6 - 5h + 3k)$

_____

**13.** The diagram shows the shape of a city plaza with its dimensions labeled. What is the perimeter of the plaza?

_____

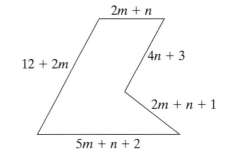

**14.** The diagram shows the floor plan of an apartment with its dimensions labeled. What is the perimeter of the apartment?

_____

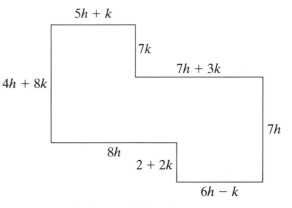

Name _____ Class _____ Date _____

# 3-7 • Guided Problem Solving

**GPS** Student Page 116, Exercise 21:

**Algebra** Three consecutive even numbers can be represented by the expressions $2n, 2n + 2$, and $2n + 4$, where $n$ is a whole number. Write the shortest expression you can to represent the sum of the three consecutive even numbers.

## Understand

1. What are you being asked to do?

   _____

   _____

2. Which part of the question indicates that you need to simplify an algebraic expression in order to solve this problem?

   _____

   _____

3. Do you need to add, subtract, multiply, or divide? How do you know?

   _____

## Plan and Carry Out

4. Summarize the steps you need to take to solve this problem.

   _____

   _____

5. Without doing any calculations, write an expression for the sum of the three consecutive numbers.

   _____

6. Write the expression after combining like terms and simplifying.

   _____

## Check

7. Explain how you can check your answer.

   _____

   _____

## Solve Another Problem

8. Four consecutive multiples of 3 can be represented by the expressions $3n, 3n + 3, 3n + 6$, and $3n + 9$, where $n$ is a whole number. Write the shortest expression you can to represent the sum of the four consecutive multiples of 3.

   _____

Guided Problem Solving

# 3A: Graphic Organizer

For use before Lesson 3-1

**Study Skill** As you read over the material in the chapter, keep a paper and pencil handy to write down notes and questions that you have.

**Write your answers.**

1. What is the chapter title? _____

2. How many lessons are there in this chapter? _____

3. What is the topic of the Test-Taking Strategies page? _____

4. Complete the graphic organizer below as you work through the chapter.
   - In the center, write the title of the chapter.
   - When you begin a lesson, write the lesson name in a rectangle.
   - When you complete a lesson, write a skill or key concept in an oval linked to that lesson block.
   - When you complete the chapter, use this graphic organizer to help you review.

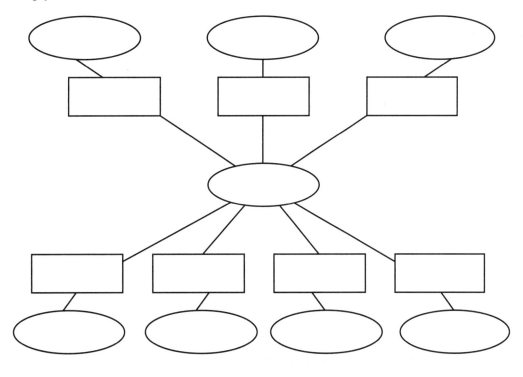

# 3B: Reading Comprehension

**Study Skill** Read aloud or recite when you are learning. Reciting a rule or a formula may help you remember and recall it.

**Read the following and answer the questions.**

The following is the ingredient list for peanut butter cookies. This recipe makes 36 cookies.

**Use the table below to answer the questions.**

| Peanut Butter Cookies | |
|---|---|
| $1\frac{1}{4}$ cup brown sugar | $\frac{3}{4}$ cup peanut butter |
| $\frac{1}{2}$ cup shortening | 3 tablespoons milk |
| 2 teaspoons vanilla | 2 eggs |
| $1\frac{3}{4}$ cup flour | $\frac{3}{4}$ teaspoon salt |
| $\frac{3}{4}$ teaspoon baking soda | 1 cup roasted peanuts |

1. What does the list of ingredients make? _____

2. What is the greatest measured quantity in the ingredient list? _____

3. What is the smallest measured quantity in the ingredient list? _____

4. What fraction of a cup of milk does the recipe call for? (There are 16 tablespoons in a cup.) _____

5. How many cups of peanuts and peanut butter does the recipe use all together? _____

6. If you double the recipe, how many cups of shortening would you need? _____

7. How many dozen cookies does the recipe make? (There are 12 cookies in a dozen.)

   _____

8. Suppose you wanted to make 24 cookies. What fraction of the recipe should you make?

   _____

9. **High-Use Academic Words** In the study skill given at the top of the page, what does it mean to *recall*?

   **a.** to bring back to mind          **b.** to change something

Vocabulary and Study Skills

# 3C: Reading/Writing Math Symbols

**For use after Lesson 3-2**

**Study Skill** After completing homework, take a break. Then spend some time checking each exercise.

**Write the following statements using mathematical symbols.**

**1.** the quantity of a number plus 4

_____

**2.** the quantity of a number plus three, increased by 2

_____

**3.** three more than the quantity $n$ plus five

_____

**4.** the quantity $n$ plus 10, decreased by three squared

_____

**5.** six decreased by the quantity of a number increased by 2

_____

**6.** four to the third power plus the quantity $n$ decreased by 3

_____

**7.** eight squared decreased by the quantity of the sum of a number and 4

_____

**8.** six cubed decreased by the quantity of the difference of a number and 1

_____

**Write the meaning in words of each mathematical expression.**

**9.** $(n - 5)$

_____

**10.** $(n + 3) + 1$

_____

**11.** $2 + (n + 10)$

_____

**12.** $5^2 + (n - 6)$

_____

**13.** $(n + 7) - 6$

_____

**14.** $(n + 3) + 4^3$

_____

**15.** $10^2 - (n + 2)$

_____

# 3D: Visual Vocabulary Practice

**Study Skill** When a math exercise is difficult, try to determine what makes it difficult. Is it a word that you don't understand? Are the numbers difficult to use?

**Concept List**

| | |
|---|---|
| factor | base |
| prime factorization | greatest common factor |
| coefficient | least common multiple |
| equivalent expressions | exponent |

**Write the concept that best describes each exercise. Choose from the concept list above.**

| 1. $8$ in $8^4$ | 2. The number 4 represents this for the numbers 28 and 48. | 3. $4$ in $8^4$ |
|---|---|---|
| **4.** The number 120 represents this for the numbers 24 and 30. | **5.** $90 = 2 \times 3^2 \times 5$ | **6.** $24x + 16y$ and $8(3x + 2y)$ |
| **7.** $4$ in $(2 + 1 \times 3)^4$ | **8.** $5$ or $7$ in $5 \times 7 = 35$ | **9.** $9$ in $9x$ |

# 3E: Vocabulary Check

**For use after Lesson 3-5**

**Study Skill** Strengthen your vocabulary. Use these pages and add cues and summaries by applying the Cornell Notetaking style.

**Write the definition for each word or term at the right. To check your work, fold the paper back along the dotted line to see the correct answers.**

common factor

_____

_____

_____

term

_____

_____

_____

prime number

_____

_____

_____

composite number

_____

_____

_____

prime factorization

_____

_____

_____

# 3E: Vocabulary Check (continued)

**For use after Lesson 3-5**

**Write the vocabulary word or term for each definition. To check your work, fold the paper forward along the dotted line to see the correct answers.**

a factor that two or more numbers share

_____

a number, a variable, or the product of a number and one or more variables

_____

a whole number whose only factors are 1 and the number itself

_____

a whole number greater than 1 with more than 2 factors

_____

a product of prime numbers

_____

# 3F: Vocabulary Review Puzzle

**For use with the Chapter Review**

**Study Skill** Combine clue words and pictures to prompt your memory.

**Use the word list below to find hidden words in the puzzle. Once you have found a word, draw a circle around it and cross the word off in the word list. Words can be displayed forwards, backwards, up, down, or diagonally but they are always in a straight line.**

| | | | |
|---|---|---|---|
| divisible | prime factor | Distributive Property | factor tree |
| multiple | composite number | equivalent | simplest form |
| term | base | least common multiple | |
| factor | power | common factor | |

```
A Z E L P I T L U M N O M M O C T S A E L
C E B A S E W X T Y N U Z N A O G P H O E
O J V G R O T C A F N O M M O C S Q A P Q
M W A G H M L L I F H P F D O P O W E R U
P H P O W E R H E M N O B Q E R Y F Z I I
O I B P E L B I S I V I D C M X A F B M V
S K K G L L C R M E N D B I W C D A P E A
I X J K T S F J L U Q R X V T I V C D F L
T I Y W T D X P K R M E A O P U Y T O A E
E J Z U A E I F G Q D L R F A J E O G C N
N I V M R E T F L N Z T Q B C C T R Z T T
U B L X L K W M U I R D K X E Y Z N C O F
M W K U F E C M J E P A H S V B S T U R R
B N M V V O B U E X T J H M R W W N X A A
E U O I N E S D Z Y M U L T I P L E Q G C
R Y L Q R T P M R O F T S E L P M I S Y T
D I S T R I B U T I V E P R O P E R T Y I
K S I R B M T B Q A H O F M D G F H N I O
D A U C E W E N D O Z P V L Q L X A J C N
J T G U H S V G E P I C W R X M Z Y B K S
```

# Practice 4-1

**Multiplying Fractions and Mixed Numbers**

**Draw a model to find each product.**

1. $\frac{1}{6} \times \frac{3}{4}$

_____

2. $\frac{2}{5} \times \frac{1}{2}$

_____

**Find each product.**

3. $\frac{3}{5}$ of 10

_____

4. $\frac{1}{4}$ of 12

_____

5. $\frac{2}{3}$ of 6

_____

6. $\frac{1}{2} \times \frac{5}{6}$

_____

7. $\frac{3}{4} \times \frac{7}{8}$

_____

8. $\frac{2}{5} \times \frac{7}{11}$

_____

9. $2\frac{5}{6} \cdot 1\frac{3}{4}$

_____

10. $3\frac{3}{8} \cdot 7\frac{1}{4}$

_____

11. $5\frac{3}{8} \times 2\frac{7}{8}$

_____

12. $2\frac{3}{8} \cdot 4\frac{4}{5}$

_____

13. $6\frac{7}{12} \times 5\frac{9}{10}$

_____

14. $7\frac{1}{3} \times 10\frac{11}{12}$

_____

15. $12\frac{1}{4} \times 3\frac{3}{4}$

_____

16. $8\frac{1}{6} \cdot 2\frac{1}{4}$

_____

17. $15\frac{2}{3} \cdot 5\frac{5}{7}$

_____

18. What product does the model represent?

_____

**Solve.**

19. A kitten eats $\frac{1}{4}$ cup of cat food. Another cat in the same household eats 6 times as much. How much food does the cat eat?

_____

20. Ken used a piece of lumber to build a bookshelf. If he made three shelves that are each $2\frac{1}{2}$ ft long, how long was the piece of lumber?

_____

# 4-1 • Guided Problem Solving

**GPS** **Student Page 131, Exercise 25a:**

A mother is $1\frac{3}{8}$ times as tall as her daughter. The girl is $1\frac{1}{3}$ times as tall as her brother. The mother is how many times as tall as her son?

## Understand

1. What are you being asked to do?

   _____

2. What do you do first when you multiply mixed numbers?

   _____

## Plan and Carry Out

3. Write an equation for the sentence "A mother is $1\frac{3}{8}$ times as tall as her daughter," where $m$ represents the height of the mother and $d$ represents the height of the daughter.

   _____

4. Write an equation for the sentence "The girl is $1\frac{1}{3}$ times as tall as her brother," where $d$ represents the height of the girl and $b$ represents the height of the brother.

   _____

5. Substitute the expression for $d$ from Step 4 for $d$ in the equation you wrote in Step 3. _____

6. Simplify by multiplying the two mixed numbers. _____

7. The mother is how many times as tall as her son? _____

## Check

8. Divide $1\frac{5}{6}$ by either $1\frac{3}{8}$ or $1\frac{1}{3}$.

   _____

## Solve Another Problem

9. Nora is building a birdhouse. The height of the birdhouse is $2\frac{1}{2}$ times the length of the birdhouse. If the length is $8\frac{2}{3}$ in., how tall is the birdhouse?

   _____

Name _____ Class _____ Date _____

# Practice 4-2

**Use circle models to find each quotient.**

**1.** $2 \div \frac{1}{3}$ _____

**2.** $4 \div \frac{1}{2}$ _____

**3.** $5 \div \frac{1}{4}$ _____

**4.** $7 \div \frac{1}{5}$ _____

**5.** $5 \div \frac{1}{6}$ _____

**6.** $3 \div \frac{1}{8}$ _____

**Use a model to find each quotient.**

**7.** $1\frac{1}{2} \div \frac{1}{6}$ _____

**8.** $2\frac{3}{4} \div \frac{1}{8}$ _____

**9.** $1\frac{1}{3} \div \frac{1}{12}$ _____

**10.** $1\frac{3}{5} \div \frac{1}{10}$ _____

**11.** $2\frac{1}{4} \div \frac{1}{8}$ _____

**12.** $1\frac{2}{3} \div \frac{1}{9}$ _____

**13.** Suppose you have 4 large cheese quesadillas to divide into eighths at a party. Write the division expression you want to solve. Then use a model to find into how many eighths you can cut the quesadillas.

_____

**14.** You have $2\frac{3}{4}$ units of tape to wrap packages. Use a model to find how many quarter length units you can cut from the tape. Then write the division problem shown in the model.

_____

# 4-2 • Guided Problem Solving

**GPS** **Student Page 140, Exercise 24:**

Use a model to find the quotient $3 \div \frac{3}{4}$.

## *Understand*

1. What are you being asked to find?

   _____

2. What operation do you use to find a quotient?

   _____

## *Plan and Carry Out*

3. What is the dividend of this division problem _____

4. What is the divisor? _____

5. Draw a model to represent $3 \div \frac{3}{4}$.

6. What is the quotient $3 \div \frac{3}{4}$? _____

## *Check*

7. What related multiplication sentence does your model show?

   _____

8. How does the Multiplication Property of Equality relate the multiplication sentence in Exercise 7 to the answer to the problem? Explain.

   _____

   _____

   _____

## Solve Another Problem

9. Use a model to find the quotient $4 \div \frac{2}{3}$.

   _____

## Practice 4-3

**Write the reciprocal of each number.**

**1.** $\frac{7}{10}$ _____    **2.** $4$ _____    **3.** $\frac{1}{3}$ _____    **4.** $\frac{1}{12}$ _____

**5.** Draw a diagram to show how many $\frac{3}{4}$-foot pieces of string can be cut from a piece of string $4\frac{1}{2}$ feet long.

**Find each quotient.**

**6.** $\frac{3}{10} \div \frac{4}{5}$ _____    **7.** $\frac{3}{8} \div 3$ _____    **8.** $\frac{1}{3} \div \frac{2}{7}$ _____

**9.** $\frac{1}{4} \div \frac{1}{4}$ _____    **10.** $\frac{7}{8} \div \frac{2}{7}$ _____    **11.** $\frac{1}{4} \div \frac{1}{8}$ _____

**12.** $\frac{1}{2} \div \frac{2}{5}$ _____    **13.** $\frac{8}{9} \div \frac{1}{2}$ _____    **14.** $3 \div \frac{3}{8}$ _____

**Solve.**

**15.** How many $\frac{3}{4}$-cup servings are there in a 6-cup package of rice?

_____

**16.** George cut 5 oranges into quarters. How many slices of orange did he have?

_____

**17.** Maureen, Frank, Tashia, Zane, Eric, and Wesley are addressing envelopes for volunteer work at a local charity. They were given $\frac{3}{4}$ of an entire mailing to address to be evenly divided among six of them. What fraction of the entire mailing does each person address?

_____

**18.** Study the tangram pieces at the right. If the entire square is 1, find the fractional value of each piece. You can copy the tangram and cut the pieces to compare them.

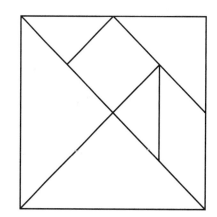

# 4-3 • Guided Problem Solving

**GPS** Student Page 139, Exercise 30:

**Baking** A recipe for a loaf of banana bread requires $\frac{2}{3}$ cup of vegetable oil. You have 3 cups of oil. How many loaves of banana bread can you make with the oil?

## Understand

1. What are you being asked to do?

   _____

   _____

2. Explain how to divide fractions.

   _____

   _____

## Plan and Carry Out

3. What number are you dividing by? Why?

   _____

4. How many cups of oil are available
   to make the banana bread? _____

5. What number are you dividing? Why?

   _____

6. Write a division expression to solve the problem. _____

7. Re-write the expression using multiplication. _____

8. Evaluate the expression. _____

9. How many loaves of banana bread can
   you make with the oil? _____

## Check

10. Multiply $\frac{2}{3} \times 4\frac{1}{2}$. Does your answer check? _____

## Solve Another Problem

11. Greg bought 24 bags of mulch for the planters in his front yard. If each
    planter uses $\frac{3}{4}$ bag, how many planters can he fill with mulch?

    _____

# Practice 4-4

**Dividing Mixed Numbers**

**Estimate each quotient.**

**1.** $\frac{4}{5} \div \frac{7}{8}$

**2.** $2\frac{4}{7} \div \frac{5}{6}$

**3.** $12\frac{3}{8} \div 3\frac{3}{4}$

_____

_____

_____

**4.** $\frac{1}{8} \div \frac{11}{12}$

**5.** $17\frac{11}{13} \div 2\frac{7}{9}$

**6.** $51\frac{1}{5} \div 4\frac{9}{10}$

_____

_____

_____

**7.** $4 \div 1\frac{8}{11}$

**8.** $21\frac{2}{3} \div \frac{15}{17}$

**9.** $32\frac{5}{8} \div 2\frac{6}{11}$

_____

_____

_____

**Find each quotient.**

**10.** $1\frac{4}{5} \div \frac{1}{3}$

**11.** $1\frac{2}{3} \div \frac{1}{8}$

**12.** $3\frac{4}{7} \div 3\frac{1}{2}$

_____

_____

_____

**13.** $\frac{2}{5} \div 4\frac{3}{5}$

**14.** $4\frac{1}{8} \div \frac{3}{7}$

**15.** $2\frac{4}{5} \div 4\frac{3}{4}$

_____

_____

_____

**16.** $1\frac{5}{7} \div 1\frac{2}{3}$

**17.** $\frac{1}{3} \div 2\frac{1}{6}$

**18.** $1\frac{4}{9} \div \frac{6}{7}$

_____

_____

_____

**19.** $\frac{1}{2} \div 3\frac{1}{4}$

**20.** $4\frac{2}{7} \div 1\frac{1}{6}$

**21.** $\frac{4}{5} \div 3\frac{2}{5}$

_____

_____

_____

**22.** $\frac{1}{4} \div 1\frac{5}{9}$

**23.** $1\frac{3}{4} \div \frac{1}{5}$

**24.** $4\frac{2}{7} \div 1\frac{1}{2}$

_____

_____

_____

**25.** $1\frac{1}{2} \div 1\frac{2}{3}$

**26.** $1\frac{5}{8} \div \frac{5}{9}$

**27.** $1\frac{3}{5} \div \frac{1}{3}$

_____

_____

_____

**Anna bought a strip of fabric 10 yards long. She needs a $1\frac{1}{3}$-yard piece to make a pillow.**

**28.** How many pillows can Anna make?

_____

**29.** Anna decides to make smaller pillows using $\frac{2}{3}$-yard pieces. How many small pillows can she make?

_____

**30.** A bulletin board is 56 inches wide and 36 inches high. How many $3\frac{1}{2}$-inch columns can be created?

_____

Name _____ Class _____ Date _____

# 4-4 • Guided Problem Solving

**Construction** An attic ceiling 24 feet wide needs insulation. Each strip of insulation is $1\frac{1}{3}$ feet wide. Estimate the number of insulation strips that are needed.

## Understand

**1.** What are you being asked to do?

_____

_____

**2.** Which number(s) will you round to estimate?

_____

## Plan and Carry Out

**3.** To what number do you round $1\frac{1}{3}$?

_____

**4.** Divide 24 by the rounded number. What is the result?

_____

**5.** Approximately how many strips do you need?

_____

## Check

**6.** How do you check your answer?

_____

_____

## Solve Another Problem

**7.** A closet bar is $8\frac{3}{4}$ inches long. If a standard shirt is $1\frac{1}{2}$ inches wide, estimate how many shirts can you hang on the bar?

_____

# Practice 4-5

**Equations With Fractions**

**Solve each equation using mental math. Write your solution in simplest form.**

**1.** $\frac{5}{17} + x = \frac{8}{17}$

_____

**2.** $\frac{2}{7} + x = \frac{5}{7}$

_____

**3.** $x - \frac{1}{2} = 10\frac{1}{10}$

_____

**4.** $5\frac{7}{8} - x = \frac{13}{16}$

_____

**Solve each equation. Check the solution.**

**5.** $\frac{n}{4} = \frac{1}{2}$

$n =$ _____

**6.** $\frac{x}{7} = 6$

$x =$ _____

**7.** $\frac{y}{19} = 3$

$y =$ _____

**8.** $\frac{3}{7}q = \frac{3}{8}$

$q =$ _____

**9.** $\frac{5}{14}c = \frac{1}{2}$

$c =$ _____

**10.** $\frac{3}{2}b = \frac{6}{7}$

$b =$ _____

**Write and solve an equation for each situation.**

**11.** Lori and Fraz ate $\frac{7}{12}$ of a vegetable pizza. If Lori ate $\frac{1}{3}$ of the pizza, how much of it did Fraz eat?

_____

**12.** Last year, Wyatt weighed $74\frac{1}{8}$ pounds at football camp. When he weighed in this year, he was $4\frac{5}{12}$ pounds heavier. How much does Wyatt currently weigh?

_____

**13.** The largest U.S. standard postage stamp ever issued has a width of about 1 inch, which was $\frac{3}{4}$ of the height of the stamp. Write and solve an equation to find the height of the stamp.

_____

**14.** Candace said, "I'm thinking of a fraction. If I divide it by $\frac{1}{2}$, I get $\frac{3}{11}$." What fraction was Candace thinking of?

_____

# 4-5 • Guided Problem Solving

**GPS** Student Page 150, Exercise 26:

**Shopping** The price of a shirt is $\frac{5}{6}$ of the price of a pair of pants. The shirt costs $12.50. How much do the pants cost?

## Understand

1. What are you being asked to do?

   _____

2. Define a variable to represent the unknown.

   _____

3. Fill in the boxes with the correct information.

   ☐ · ☐ = ☐

## Plan and Carry Out

4. Write an expression for the phrase
   "$\frac{5}{6}$ the price of the pants" if the pants cost $p$ dollars. _____

5. How much does the shirt cost? _____

6. Write an equation to solve the problem. _____

7. What do you do to both sides of the
   equation to solve for $p$? _____

8. Solve the equation. _____

9. How much did the pants cost? _____

## Check

10. Determine if 12.50 is $\frac{5}{6}$ of 15.

    _____

## Solve Another Problem

11. Lupe and Carlos are $\frac{1}{4}$ of the way done painting their new house. So
    far they have used $6\frac{2}{3}$ cans of paint. How many cans of paint will they
    use to paint the entire house?

    _____

# 4A: Graphic Organizer

**Study Skill** As you read over the material in the chapter, keep a paper and pencil handy to write down notes and questions that you have.

**Write your answers.**

1. What is the chapter title? _____

2. How many lessons are there in this chapter? _____

3. What is the topic of the Test-Taking Strategies page?

   _____

4. Complete the graphic organizer below as you work through the chapter.

   • In the center, write the title of the chapter.

   • When you begin a lesson, write the lesson name in a rectangle.

   • When you complete a lesson, write a skill or key concept in an circle linked to that lesson block.

   • When you complete the chapter, use this graphic organizer to help you review.

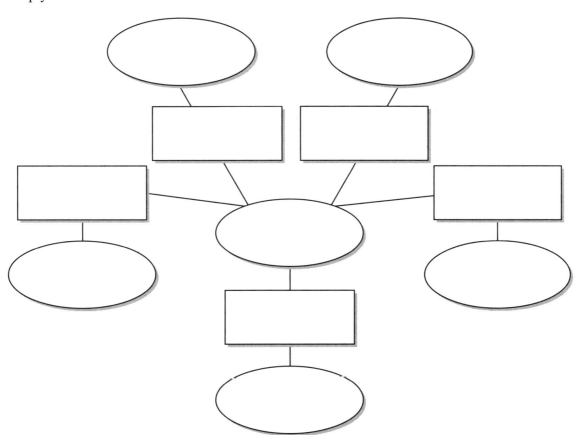

# 4B: Reading Comprehension

**Study Skill** Attitude is everything.

**Read the paragraph below and answer the questions that follow.**

The amount of solid waste produced by the United States has doubled in the last 30 years. Solid waste is the trash you create every day. One tenth of this trash is food and yard waste, $\frac{7}{25}$ is containers and packaging, $\frac{8}{25}$ is durable goods, and $\frac{3}{10}$ is nondurable goods. Durable goods are things like washing machines that are made to last a long time. Nondurable goods are not made to last long, like newspapers and napkins. In recent years, Americans have produced more than 232 million tons of trash a year. Most of our waste is disposed of in landfills, about $\frac{3}{20}$ is burned, and another $\frac{3}{10}$ is recycled.

1. How is most of the waste produced in the U.S. disposed of?

   _____

2. What fraction of solid waste is disposed of in this way?

   _____

3. How much waste does the U.S. produce each year?

   _____

4. What fraction of waste is burned?

   _____

5. How many tons of waste are burned each year?

   _____

6. How many tons of durable good waste are produced each year?

   _____

7. Estimate how many tons of durable good waste were produced 30 years ago.

   _____

8. **High-Use Academic Words** In Exercise 7, what does it mean to *estimate*?

   **a.** to identify something          **b.** to approximate

Name _____ Class _____ Date _____

# 4C: Reading/Writing Math Symbols    For use after Lesson 4-5

**Study Skill** Write assignments down; do not try to rely only on your memory.

**Match each expression with its product.**

| Column A | Column B |
|---|---|
| 1. $\frac{3}{5}$ of $\frac{3}{4}$ | A. $20\frac{1}{4}$ |
| 2. $\frac{1}{2} \cdot \frac{1}{3}$ | B. $\frac{2}{5}$ |
| 3. $3\frac{3}{8} \times 6$ | C. $\frac{9}{20}$ |
| 4. $9\frac{3}{5} \cdot \frac{1}{3}$ | D. $3\frac{1}{5}$ |
| 5. $1\frac{3}{5} \times \frac{1}{4}$ | E. $\frac{1}{6}$ |

**Match each expression with its quotient.**

| Column A | Column B |
|---|---|
| 6. $3\frac{1}{5} \div 2$ | A. $4\frac{1}{2}$ |
| 7. $\frac{5}{8} \div \frac{5}{16}$ | B. $2\frac{18}{35}$ |
| 8. $\frac{1}{4} \div \frac{1}{2}$ | C. $\frac{1}{2}$ |
| 9. $\frac{3}{4} \div \frac{1}{6}$ | D. $1\frac{3}{5}$ |
| 10. $4\frac{2}{5} \div 1\frac{3}{4}$ | E. $2$ |

**Match the equation with the value of its variable.**

| Column A | Column B |
|---|---|
| 11. $x - 3\frac{1}{5} = \frac{2}{5}$ | A. $60$ |
| 12. $c + 4\frac{4}{5} = 8$ | B. $56$ |
| 13. $\frac{g}{15} = 4$ | C. $28$ |
| 14. $\frac{3}{4}y = 21$ | D. $3\frac{3}{5}$ |
| 15. $\frac{a}{8} = 7$ | E. $3\frac{1}{5}$ |

# 4D: Visual Vocabulary Practice

For use after Lesson 4-4

**Study Skill** When a math exercise is difficult, try to determine what makes it difficult. Is it a word that you don't understand? Are the numbers difficult to use?

## Concept List

| | | |
|---|---|---|
| mixed number | improper fraction | denominator |
| numerator | divisor | dividend |
| quotient | equivalent fractions | model |

**Write the concept that best describes each exercise. Choose from the concept list above.**

| 1. 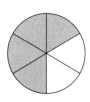 _____ | 2. The letter $x$ represents this in the equation $3 \div \frac{1}{4} = x$ _____ | 3. $120\frac{5}{6}$ _____ |
|---|---|---|
| 4. The number 6 represents this in the fraction $\frac{5}{6}$ _____ | 5. The fraction $\frac{1}{6}$ represents this in the expression $1\frac{1}{3} \div \frac{1}{6}$ _____ | 6. $\frac{4}{10}$ and $\frac{24}{60}$ _____ |
| 7. The number $3\frac{1}{2}$ represents this in the expression $3\frac{1}{2} \div \frac{1}{4}$ _____ | 8. $\frac{34}{15}$ _____ | 9. The number 7 represents this in the fraction $\frac{7}{8}$ _____ |

Name _____ Class _____ Date _____

# 4E: Vocabulary Check

For use after Lesson 4-5

• • • • • • • • • • • • • • • • • • • • • • • • • • • • •

**Study Skill** Strengthen your vocabulary. Use these pages and add cues and summaries by applying the Cornell Notetaking style.

**Write the definition for each word or term at the right. To check your work, fold the paper back along the dotted line to see the correct answers.**

_____

_____

_____     equivalent fractions

_____

_____

_____     mixed number

_____

_____

_____     reciprocals

_____

_____

_____     improper fraction

_____

_____

_____     proper fraction

_____

_____

Vocabulary and Study Skills

© Pearson Education, Inc., publishing as Pearson Prentice Hall. All rights reserved.

Vocabulary and Study Skills          *Course 1* Chapter 4          **191**

# 4E: Vocabulary Check (continued)

**Write the vocabulary word or term for each definition. To check your work, fold the paper forward along the dotted line to see the correct answers.**

fractions that name the same amount

_____

the sum of a whole number and a fraction

_____

two numbers whose product is 1

_____

a fraction whose numerator is greater than or equal to its denominator

_____

a fraction that has a numerator that is less than the denominator

_____

# 4F: Vocabulary Review Puzzle

For use with the Chapter Review

**Study Skill** Take notes while you study. They will provide you with a helpful outline when you study for a quiz or test.

**Complete the crossword puzzle. For help, use the glossary in your textbook.**

## Across

**1.** the number that is to be divided

**3.** a number that makes an equation true

**6.** a number that results from dividing

**7.** a mathematical phrase containing numbers and operation symbols

**8.** a number that can be used to indicate part of a whole

**9.** one of two numbers whose product is 1

**11.** fractions or decimals that name the same amount

## Down

**1.** the bottom number in a fraction

**2.** operations that undo one another

**4.** the top number in a fraction

**5.** a mathematical sentence with an equal sign

**10.** a fraction whose numerator is greater than or equal to its denominator

Name _____ Class _____ Date _____

# Practice 5-1 ............................................. Ratios

**Write each ratio in three ways.**

**1.** saws to pliers

_____

**2.** hammers to nails

_____

**3.** saws to nails

_____

**4.** nails to saws

_____

**5.** hammers to pliers

_____

**6.** pliers to saws

_____

**7.** pliers to nails

_____

**8.** saws to hammers

_____

**9.** nails to hammers

_____

**Describe the ratio shown in each tape diagram.**

**10.** Pears
Apples

_____
_____
_____

**11.** Blue Buttons
Yellow Buttons

_____
_____
_____

**Describe the ratio shown in each double number line diagram.**

**12.** Cups of Red Paint

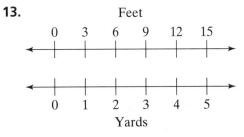

_____
_____
_____

**13.** Feet

Yards

_____
_____
_____

# 5-1 • Guided Problem Solving

**GPS** Student Page 163, Exercise 12:

A typical adult cat has 12 fewer teeth than a typical adult dog. An adult dog has 42 teeth. Write the ratio of an adult cat's teeth to an adult dog's teeth.

## *Understand*

1. What are you being asked to do?

   _____

   _____

2. What does *ratio* mean?

   _____

   _____

## *Plan and Carry Out*

3. Which number goes in the numerator, cat's teeth or dog's teeth?

   _____

4. How many teeth does a typical adult cat have? _____

5. How did you find the number of cat's teeth?

   _____

6. Write the ratio of cat's teeth to dog's teeth as a fraction. _____

7. What are two other ways to write the ratio? _____

8. Describe the ratio.

   _____

## *Check*

9. Which have fewer teeth, cats or dogs? Does this agree with your ratio? Explain.

   _____

## Solve Another Problem

10. The faculty softball league has 56 female players and 84 male players. Write the ratio of female players to male players in three ways. Then describe the ratio.

    _____

# Practice 5-2

**Unit Rates**

**Find the unit rate for each situation.**

**1.** 44 breaths in 2 minutes

_____

**2.** 72 players on 9 teams

_____

**3.** 60 miles in 2 hours

_____

**4.** 15 pages in 30 minutes

_____

**5.** 48 questions in 4 quizzes

_____

**6.** $3 for 4 packages

_____

**Use the unit rate and multiplication to solve each problem.**

**7.** There are 12 inches in a foot. Find the number of inches in 6 feet.

_____

**8.** The cost is $8.50 for 1 shirt. Find the cost of 4 shirts.

_____

**9.** There are 365 days in a year. Find the number of days in 3 years.

_____

**10.** There are 6 cans per box. Find the number of cans in 11 boxes.

_____

**11.** There are 5 students in a group. Find the number of students in 5 groups.

_____

**12.** There are 70 pages in a notebook. Find the number of pages in 8 notebooks.

_____

**Find each unit cost.**

**13.** $5 for 10 pounds _____

**14.** 40 ounces for $12 _____

**15.** $6 for 10 pens _____

**16.** $60 for 5 books _____

**17.** $27 for 3 shirts _____

**18.** $35 for 25 tapes _____

# 5-2 • Guided Problem Solving

**GPS Student Page 169, Exercise 22:**

**Jump Rope** Crystal jumps 255 times in 3 minutes. The United States record for 11-year-olds is 882 jumps in 3 minutes.

    **a.** Find Crystal's unit rate for jumps per minute.

    **b.** Find the record holder's unit rate for jumps per minute.

    **c.** How many more times per minute did the record holder jump than Crystal?

## Understand

  **1.** What are you being asked to do in part (a) and part (b)?

    _____

    _____

  **2.** What is a unit rate?

    _____

    _____

## Plan and Carry Out

  **3.** What is Crystal's rate? _____

  **4.** What is Crystal's unit rate? _____

  **5.** What is the record holder's rate? _____

  **6.** What is the record holder's unit rate? _____

  **7.** How many more times did the record holder jump per minute?

    _____

## Check

  **8.** How can you check your answer for parts (a) and (b)?

    _____

    _____

    _____

## Solve Another Problem

  **9.** Mike can make 60 egg sandwiches in 1.25 hours. What is his unit rate?

    _____

# Practice 5-3

**Equivalent Ratios and Rates**

**Use a multiplication table to write 4 ratios equivalent to each ratio.**

**1.** 2 to 4

_____

**2.** 3 : 8

_____

**3.** 7 to 3

_____

**4.** $\frac{5}{2}$

_____

**5.** 1 : 9

_____

**6.** $\frac{6}{5}$

_____

| × | 1 | 2 | 3 | 4 | 5 | 6 | 7 | 8 | 9 |
|---|---|---|---|---|---|---|---|---|---|
| 1 | 1 | 2 | 3 | 4 | 5 | 6 | 7 | 8 | 9 |
| 2 | 2 | 4 | 6 | 8 | 10 | 12 | 14 | 16 | 18 |
| 3 | 3 | 6 | 9 | 12 | 15 | 18 | 21 | 24 | 27 |
| 4 | 4 | 8 | 12 | 16 | 20 | 24 | 28 | 32 | 36 |
| 5 | 5 | 10 | 15 | 20 | 25 | 30 | 35 | 40 | 45 |
| 6 | 6 | 12 | 18 | 24 | 30 | 36 | 42 | 48 | 54 |
| 7 | 7 | 14 | 21 | 28 | 35 | 42 | 49 | 56 | 63 |
| 8 | 8 | 16 | 24 | 32 | 40 | 48 | 56 | 64 | 72 |
| 9 | 9 | 18 | 27 | 36 | 45 | 54 | 63 | 72 | 81 |

**For Exercises 7–9, use a multiplication table, a double number line, or a tape diagram to help you solve.**

**7.** Hudson reads 4 pages in 9 minutes. At that rate how many pages will he read in 27 minutes?

_____

**8.** The cost of 4 pounds of potatoes is $3.50. How many pounds of potatoes can you buy with $14?

_____

**9.** Cheryl mixed a 32-cup batch of orange juice and pineapple juice using a ratio of 3 cups of orange juice to 5 cups of pineapple juice. How many cups of pineapple juice did she use?

_____

# 5-3 • Guided Problem Solving

## GPS Student Page 173, Exercise 19:

**Number Sense** A recipe calls for 2 cups of flour to make 3 dozen cookies. Are 4 cups of flour enough to make 70 cookies? Explain.

### Understand

1. What are you being asked to do?

   _____

   _____

2. What will you need to know to solve this problem?

   _____

   _____

### Plan and Carry Out

3. How many cookies are in 3 dozen?

   _____

   _____

4. How will you find the number of cookies you can make with 4 cups of flour?

   _____

   _____

5. How do you know if 4 cups of flour is enough to make 70 cookies?

   _____

   _____

### Check

6. How can you check to make sure that 2 : 36 and 4 : 72 are equivalent ratios?

   _____

   _____

### Solve Another Problem

7. A recipe calls for 3 teaspoons of cinnamon to make 24 muffins. Is 6 teaspoons of cinnamon enough to make 50 muffins? Explain.

   _____

   _____

Guided Problem Solving

# Practice 5-4 ............................................ **Using Ratios to Convert Measurement Units**

**Convert each measurement.**

**1.** 500 centimeters to meters

_____

**2.** 5 feet to inches

_____

**3.** 24 cups to quarts

_____

**4.** 4 grams to milligrams

_____

**5.** 2 miles to feet

_____

**6.** 6 pounds to ounces

_____

**7.** 2.5 meters to millimeters

_____

**8.** 8 pints to quarts

_____

**9.** An ant walks 30 feet in 6 minutes. How long will it take the ant to walk 35 yards?

_____

**10.** You need 2 cups of orange juice to make 3 quarts of punch. How many cups of orange juice do you need to make 3 gallons of punch?

_____

**11.** Becky used 5 teaspoons of mustard to make 32 ounces of potato salad. How many teaspoons of mustard does she need to make 4 pounds of potato salad?

_____

# 5-4 • Guided Problem Solving

**GPS** **Student Page 177, Exercise 19:**

**Number Sense** A faucet leaks 75 milliliters of water per minute. How many liters of water does the faucet leak in $3\frac{1}{2}$ hours?

## Understand

1. What are you being asked to find?

   _____

2. What do you need to know to solve this problem?

   _____

## Plan and Carry Out

3. How will you solve the problem?

   _____

4. Write ratios to convert 75 milliliters to liters and $3\frac{1}{2}$ hours to minutes. Then, write a ratio to find the number of liters in $3\frac{1}{2}$ hours. Remember: Write the new units in the numerator.

   Convert 75 milliliters to liters.   Convert $3\frac{1}{2}$ hours to minutes.   Write a ratio to solve.

   |  |  |  |
   |---|---|---|
   |  |  |  |

5. How many liters of water does the faucet leak in $3\frac{1}{2}$ hours? _____

## Check

6. How can you check that your answer is correct?

   _____

   _____

   _____

   _____

## Solve Another Problem

7. Suzy drinks 3 quarts of water every 4 days. How many days will it take her to drink 6 gallons of water? _____

Name _____ Class _____ Date _____

# Practice 5-5 ·················································· **Understanding Percents**

**Shade each grid to represent each of the following percents.**

**1.** 53%

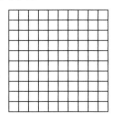

**2.** 23%

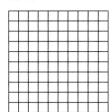

**3.** 71%

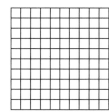

**Write each ratio as a percent.**

**4.** $\frac{4}{5}$ _____

**5.** $\frac{3}{5}$ _____

**6.** $\frac{9}{10}$ _____

**7.** $\frac{3}{10}$ _____

**8.** $\frac{6}{25}$ _____

**9.** $\frac{7}{100}$ _____

**10.** $\frac{9}{50}$ _____

**11.** $\frac{9}{25}$ _____

**12.** $\frac{2}{5}$ _____

**13.** $\frac{7}{10}$ _____

**14.** $\frac{4}{25}$ _____

**15.** $\frac{16}{25}$ _____

**16.** $\frac{11}{20}$ _____

**17.** $\frac{19}{20}$ _____

**18.** $\frac{27}{50}$ _____

**19.** 41 : 50 _____

**Write a percent for each shaded figure.**

**20.**

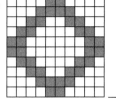

_____

**21.**

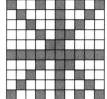

_____

**22.**

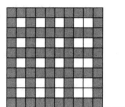

_____

**Complete the following.**

Ancient Egyptians did not write the fraction $\frac{4}{5}$ as "$\frac{4}{5}$". Instead, they
used *unit fractions*. The numerator of a unit fraction is always 1. No
denominator used to represent a given fraction can be repeated. For
this reason, Egyptians would have written $\frac{4}{5}$ as $\frac{1}{2} + \frac{1}{5} + \frac{1}{10}$ and not as
$\frac{1}{2} + \frac{1}{10} + \frac{1}{10} + \frac{1}{10}$. Write each of the following as a sum of unit fractions.

**23.** $\frac{3}{4}$ _____

**24.** $\frac{5}{8}$ _____

**25.** $\frac{9}{10}$ _____

**26.** $\frac{7}{12}$ _____

···················································

*Course 1 Lesson 5-5*

# 5-5 • Guided Problem Solving

**GPS** **Student Page 182, Exercise 30:**

**History** Before the Battle of Tippecanoe, nineteen twentieths of General William Harrison's troops had never before been in a battle. What percent of the troops had previously been in a battle?

## Understand

1. What is the relevant information?

   _____

   _____

2. What are you being asked to do?

   _____

   _____

## Plan and Carry Out

3. What fraction of the troops had never before been in a battle? _____

4. What fraction of the troops had previously been in a battle? _____

5. To write a number as a percent, first write an equivalent ratio with a denominator of what number? _____

6. Write an equivalent ratio of $\frac{1}{20}$. _____

7. Convert the fraction to a percent. _____

## Check

8. What percent is nineteen twentieths? Does the sum of the percent you found in Step 7 and the equivalent percent of nineteen twentieths equal 100%?

   _____

   _____

## Solve Another Problem

9. A marathon runner has run two fifths of the race. What percent of the race is left to run?

   _____

Name _____ Class _____ Date _____

# Practice 5-6 ................................................ Percents, Fractions, and Decimals

**Write each percent as a decimal and as a fraction in simplest form.**

**1.** 46% _____   **2.** 17% _____   **3.** 90% _____   **4.** 5% _____

**Write each decimal as a percent and as a fraction in simplest form.**

**5.** 0.02 _____   **6.** 0.45 _____   **7.** 0.4 _____   **8.** 0.92 _____

**Write each fraction as a decimal and as a percent.**

**9.** $\frac{3}{5}$ _____   **10.** $\frac{7}{10}$ _____   **11.** $\frac{13}{25}$ _____   **12.** $\frac{17}{20}$ _____

The table shows the fraction of students who participated in
extracurricular activities in a school from 1975 to 2010. Complete the table by
writing each fraction as a percent.

### Students' Extracurricular Choices

| Year | 1975 | 1980 | 1985 | 1990 | 1995 | 2000 | 2005 | 2010 |
|------|------|------|------|------|------|------|------|------|
| Student participation (fraction) | $\frac{3}{4}$ | $\frac{8}{10}$ | $\frac{17}{20}$ | $\frac{39}{50}$ | $\frac{21}{25}$ | $\frac{19}{25}$ | $\frac{87}{100}$ | $\frac{9}{10}$ |
| Student participation (percent) | | | | | | | | |

Write each fraction or decimal as a percent. Write the percent
(without the percent sign) in the puzzle.

**ACROSS**

**1.** $\frac{3}{5}$

**2.** $\frac{1}{5}$

**3.** 0.55

**5.** 0.23

**6.** $\frac{7}{20}$

**7.** 0.17

**9.** 0.4

**10.** $\frac{9}{25}$

**DOWN**

**1.** $\frac{13}{20}$

**2.** 0.25

**3.** $\frac{1}{2}$

**4.** $\frac{3}{20}$

**5.** 0.24

**6.** $\frac{3}{10}$

**7.** 0.1

**8.** $\frac{4}{25}$

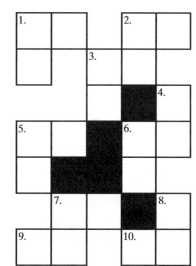

# 5-6 • Guided Problem Solving

GPS **Student Page 187, Exercise 46:**

**Biology** At least ninety-nine percent of all the kinds of plants and animals that have ever lived are now extinct. Write ninety-nine percent as a fraction and as a decimal.

## Understand

1. What percent of plants and animals are extinct?

   _____

2. A percent is a ratio of a number to what other number?

   _____

## Plan and Carry Out

3. Ninety-nine percent means 99 out of what number?

   _____

4. Write this number as a fraction.

   _____

5. Which decimal place is the hundredths place?

   _____

6. Write ninety-nine percent as a decimal.

   _____

## Check

7. Explain how you can check your answer.

   _____

   _____

   _____

## Solve Another Problem

8. Sixty-one percent of a school's students participate in extra-curricular activities. Write this number as a fraction and as a decimal.

   _____

# Practice 5-7 · · · · · · · · · · · · · · · · · · · · · · · · · · · · · · · · · · · · · · · · · · · · · · · · · Finding a Percent of a Number

**Find each answer.**

**1.** 15% of 20

**2.** 40% of 80

**3.** 20% of 45

_____

_____

_____

**4.** 90% of 120

**5.** 65% of 700

**6.** 25% of 84

_____

_____

_____

**7.** 60% of 50

**8.** 45% of 90

**9.** 12% of 94

_____

_____

_____

**10.** 37% of 80

**11.** 25% of 16

**12.** 63% of 800

_____

_____

_____

**13.** 55% of 250

**14.** 18% of 420

**15.** 33% of 140

_____

_____

_____

**Solve each problem.**

**16.** Teri used 60% of 20 gallons of paint. How much did she use? _____

**17.** The Badgers won 75% of their 32 games this year. How many games did they win? _____

**18.** Vivian earned $540 last month. She saved 30% of this money. How much did she save? _____

**19.** A survey of the students at Lakeside School yielded the results shown below. There are 1,400 students enrolled at Lakeside School. Complete the table for the number of students in each activity.

### How Lakeside Students Spend Their Time on Saturday

| Activity | Percent of Students | Number of Students |
|---|---|---|
| Baby-sitting | 22% | |
| Sports | 26% | |
| Job | 15% | |
| At home | 10% | |
| Tutoring | 10% | |
| Other | 17% | |

## 5-7 • Guided Problem Solving
..............................................................

**GPS** Student Page 191, Exercise 34a:

**Vision** In the United States, about 46% of the population wear glasses or contact lenses. A sample of 85 people is taken.

a. About how many people would you expect to wear contact lenses?

### *Understand*
..................

1. Circle the information you will need to solve.

2. What are you being asked to do?

   _____

   _____

3. What method can you use to solve this problem?

   _____

   _____

### *Plan and Carry Out*
.........................

4. Write 46% as a decimal. _____

5. Multiply the decimal by × 85. _____

6. About how many people would you expect to wear glasses or contact lenses? _____

### *Check*
..........

7. How can you check your answer? Does your answer check?

   _____

   _____

   _____

### **Solve Another Problem**

8. About 77% of all band members received either an A or a B on the last test. If this trend continues throughout the entire school of 1,260 students, about how many students do you expect to receive A's or B's?

   _____

# Practice 5-8

**Finding the Whole**

**Solve each problem.**

1. 43 is 10% of what number?

2. 32 is 16% of what number?

3. 6 is 60% of what number?

4. 24 is 80% of what number?

5. 75 is 20% of what number?

6. 16 is 40% of what number?

7. 85 is 50% of what number?

8. 9 is 12% of what number?

9. Twelve boys were playing soccer. If 60% of the children playing soccer were boys, how many children were playing soccer?

10. Marci has read 195 pages in a book. This is 65% of the pages in the book. How many pages are in the book?

11. Quinn has solved 20 problems on the math quiz. If this is 80% of the problems on the quiz, how many more problems does he have left to solve?

12. Sarah has made 21 bracelets to sell at the craft fair. If this is 70% of the bracelets she wants to make, how many more bracelets does she need to make?

# 5-8 • Guided Problem Solving

**GPS** **Student Page 195, Exercise 17:**

**Shopping** The discounted price of a book is 85% of the original price. This is a savings of $3. A sales tax of 8% will be added to the discounted price. How much sales tax will be added?

## *Understand*

**1.** What are you being asked to find?

_____

_____

**2.** How are the discounted price, the original price, and the savings related?

_____

_____

## *Plan and Carry Out*

**3.** How will you solve the problem?

_____

_____

**4.** What percent of the original price is the savings? Explain.

_____

_____

**5.** Solve the problem.
   Find the original price.       Find the discounted price.       Find the tax.

## *Check*

**6.** How can you check that your answer is reasonable?

_____

_____

## Solve Another Problem

**7.** The discounted price on a pair of shoes is 75% of the original price. This is a savings of $10. A sales tax of 7% will be added to the discounted price. How much sales tax will be added? _____

# 5A: Graphic Organizer

**Study Skill** Preview the chapter material. Make a list of new formulas, properties, and vocabulary. Add to this list as your teacher covers each new concept.

**Write your answers.**

1. What is the chapter title? _____

2. How many lessons are there in this chapter? _____

3. What is the topic of the Test-Taking Strategies page? _____

4. Complete the graphic organizer below as you work through the chapter.

    • In the center, write the title of the chapter.

    • When you begin a lesson, write the lesson name in a rectangle.

    • When you complete a lesson, write a skill or key concept in a circle linked to that lesson block. When you complete the chapter, use this graphic organizer to help you review.

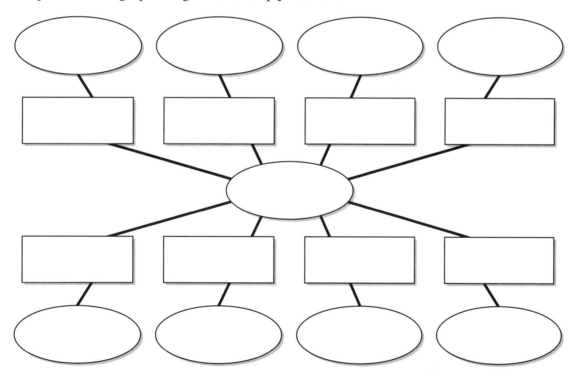

# 5B: Reading Comprehension

**Study Skill** Use tables and charts when you need to organize complex information.

Food coloring comes in red, blue, green, and yellow colors. By mixing these standard colors, you can make many different colors.

**Use the chart below to answer the questions.**

## Number of Drops Required

| Blended Shades | RED | YELLOW | BLUE | GREEN |
|---|---|---|---|---|
| Turquoise | 0 | 0 | 4 | 1 |
| Brown | 7 | 4 | 0 | 2 |
| Grape | 5 | 0 | 1 | 0 |
| Lime | 0 | 3 | 0 | 1 |
| Pistachio | 0 | 1 | 0 | 4 |
| Orange | 2 | 3 | 0 | 0 |
| Peach | 1 | 2 | 0 | 0 |
| Salmon | 3 | 2 | 0 | 0 |

1. What information is contained in the chart?

   _____

2. What colors are needed to make salmon? _____

3. If you use 6 drops of yellow to make lime,
   how many drops of green will you need? _____

4. To make brown, how many colors
   will you need to mix together? _____

5. Of the eight blended shades listed, which one
   requires the greatest number of drops (total)? _____

6. Which shades do not require any red? _____

7. What is the ratio of blue drops to
   red drops required to make grape? _____

8. How many total drops are needed to
   make brown if 8 yellow drops are used? _____

9. **High-Use Academic Words** What does it mean to *organize*
   information, as mentioned in the study skill?

   **a.** to arrange information so that      **b.** to store information on
       it is more easily understood          a computer

## 5C: Reading/Writing Math Symbols

**For use after Lesson 5-4**

**Study Skill** Use word clues such as rhyming words and pictures of familiar places and things to prompt your memory.

**Write the meaning of each mathematical expression in word form. Use a dictionary or go online to help you find the word for any abbreviation you don't know.**

**1.** 4 qt : 1 gal _____

**2.** 1 yd : 3 ft _____

**3.** 16 oz : 1 lb _____

**4.** $\dfrac{1{,}760 \text{ yd}}{1 \text{ mile}}$ _____

**5.** $\dfrac{1\text{T}}{2{,}000 \text{ lb}}$ _____

**6.** $\dfrac{2 \text{ c}}{1 \text{ pt}}$ _____

**7.** 1 m : 100 cm _____

**Write each of the following as a ratio or rate.**

**8.** 1 mile to 5,280 feet

_____

**9.** 72 hours to 3 days

_____

**10.** 2,000 milligrams to 2 grams

_____

**11.** 9 square feet to 1 square yard

_____

**12.** 4 quarts to 8 pints

_____

**13.** 62 miles per hour

_____

**14.** 203 calories per serving

_____

**15.** $1.25 per pound

_____

Vocabulary and Study Skills

# 5D: Visual Vocabulary Practice

**For use after Lesson 5-6**

**Study Skill** Mathematics is like learning a foreign language. You have to know the vocabulary before you can speak the language correctly.

## Concept List

| | | |
|---|---|---|
| convert | double number line diagram | equivalent ratios |
| percent | rate | ratio |
| tape diagram | unit cost | unit rate |

**Write the concept that best describes each exercise. Choose from the concept list above.**

| 1. A pie was sliced into 5 equal pieces and 3 slices remain. This is represented by the variable $x$ in the equation $\frac{3}{5} = \frac{x}{100}$. <br><br> _____ | 2. Jared can run 6 miles in 50 minutes. This can also be represented as $\frac{6 \text{ miles}}{50 \text{ minutes}}$. <br><br> _____ | 3. $\$6 : \$4$ and $\frac{\$15}{\$10}$ <br><br> _____ |
|---|---|---|
| 4. 9 to 11 <br><br><br> _____ | 5. Tables ▭ <br> Chairs ▭▭▭▭ <br><br> _____ | 6. Jesse purchased 2.5 lb of bananas for $2.00. The amount $0.80/lb represents this. <br><br> _____ |
| 7. Xavier biked 36 miles in 3 hours. $\frac{12 \text{ miles}}{1 \text{ hour}}$ or 12 mi/h represents this. <br><br> _____ | 8. Niles will do this to find the number of centimeters in 3.5 meters. <br><br> _____ | 9. 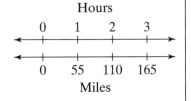 <br><br> _____ |

# 5E: Vocabulary Check

**Study Skill** Strengthen your vocabulary. Use these pages and add cues and summaries by applying the Cornell Notetaking style.

**Write the definition for each word or term at the right. To check your work, fold the paper back along the dotted line to see the correct answers.**

_____  unit rate
_____
_____


_____  ratio
_____
_____


_____  unit cost
_____
_____


_____  percent
_____
_____


_____  rate
_____
_____

# 5E: Vocabulary Check (continued)

**Write the vocabulary word or term for each definition. To check your work, fold the paper forward along the dotted line to see the correct answers.**

the rate for one unit of
a given quantity

_____

a comparison of two
quantities by division

_____

a unit rate that gives the
cost per unit

_____

a ratio that compares a
number to 100

_____

a ratio that compares two
quantities that are measured
in different units

_____

# 5F: Vocabulary Review Puzzle

**For use with the Chapter Review**

**Study Skill** Turn off the television, music, and cell phone while studying or doing homework.

**Read the definition, determine the word, and then find the hidden words in the puzzle. Once you have found a word, draw a circle around it and cross out the word definition. Words can be displayed forwards, backwards, up, down, or diagonally.**

```
K F L R A T I O K G N A Q H E J Z V O G
P O L K O C X E M A H Z U R S D N F J E
D N L C R R F Q I R S H U U E E E F S Z
P O S E E F A D G V E T H V S N P I O L
I I N D C J M S N N C K I B M O R V L V
E T D G I J R U S E R T T S A M O F U A
I A J Q P K A E J O U X D I L I A Q T D
K U O V R N F N W B C I T N E N O N I N
E Q H J O I O B I Y T I V X G A R C O R
E E H U C C H R I M N L A I B T T J N E
V K O O A I T V G N E N W T M O P N P B
I E S G L S K V S O C U H W I R O O U M
T S K K I X V P H B R M R I I V N I N U
A R C D S O L O O B E E S S D G E T Q N
T E C O A Q S E Y L P R O E Z S Z C X D
U V N K Z T I E B P Y A G X E H C A W E
M N L D W W S V X P A T V L H N N R U X
M I N H I J G F F B E O Q B S P W F W I
O Y K A U X Z J M U R R X D A E J U C M
C U V X X E T A R K A X K O W N F P R V
```

- comparison of two numbers by division
- $4(8 + 6) = 4(8) + 4(6)$ is an example of this property.
- ratio that compares a number to 100
- The variable $b$ in the fraction $\frac{a}{b}$ is known as this.
- ratio that compares two quantities measured in different units
- one of two numbers whose product is 1
- a number that describes a part of a set or a part of a whole that is divided into equal parts
- $12 + (3 + 6) = (12 + 3) + 6$ is an example of this property.
- The number 4 in the fraction $\frac{4}{7}$ is referred to as this.
- $7 + 8 = 8 + 7$ is an example of this property.
- a number that makes an equation true
- mathematical statement that contains an equal sign
- operations that undo one another
- shows the sum of a whole number and a fraction

Name _____ Class _____ Date _____

# Practice 6-1 •••••••••••••••••••••••••••••••••••••••••••••••••••••••••••••• Exploring Integers

**Use an integer to represent each situation.**

**1.** spent $23 _____   **2.** lost 12 yards _____   **3.** deposit of $58 _____

**Write the opposite of each integer.**

**4.** 16 _____                    **5.** −12 _____

**6.** the opposite of the opposite of −7 _____

**Find each absolute value.**

**7.** $|-5|$ _____   **8.** $|13|$ _____   **9.** $|25|$ _____   **10.** $|-7|$ _____

**11.** The temperature in Fargo, North Dakota, was 6°F at noon. By
4 P.M. the temperature dropped to −10°F. What integer
represents the change in temperature?

_____

**12.** A snail climbs 3 inches up a wall. Then it slides 6 inches down the
wall. What integer represents the distance the snail traveled from
its original position?

_____

**13.** Graph these integers on the number line: −4, 9, 1, −2, 3.

$$\xleftarrow{\hspace{1cm}} \begin{array}{ccccccccccc} -10 & -8 & -6 & -4 & -2 & 0 & 2 & 4 & 6 & 8 & 10 \end{array} \xrightarrow{\hspace{1cm}}$$

**Write an integer for each point on the number line.**

$$\begin{array}{ccccccc} M & & J & N & PL & K \\ \bullet & & \bullet & \bullet & \bullet\bullet & \bullet \\ \hline -6 & -4 & -2 & 0 & 2 & 4 \end{array}$$

**14.** $J$ _____                     **15.** $K$ _____

**16.** $L$ _____                     **17.** $M$ _____

**Write two numbers that have the given absolute value.**

**18.** 4 _____                   **19.** 38 _____

**20.** 260 _____                 **21.** 4,092 _____

**Think of the days of a week as integers. Let today be 0, and let days
in the past be negative and days in the future be positive.**

**22.** If today is Tuesday, what integer stands for last Sunday? _____

**23.** If today is Wednesday, what integer stands for next Saturday? _____

**24.** If today is Friday, what integer stands for last Saturday? _____

**25.** If today is Monday, what integer stands for next Monday? _____

•••••••••••••••••••••••••••••••••••••••••••••••••••••••••••••••••••••
Practice                                    *Course 1 Lesson 6-1*   **219**

# 6-1 • Guided Problem Solving

**GPS** **Student Page 208, Exercise 26:**

Starting at the fourth floor, an elevator goes down 3 floors and then up 8 floors. At which floor does the elevator stop?

## Understand

1. Circle the information you will need to solve the problem.

2. What are you being asked to do?

   _____

3. What is a good way to set up the problem visually?

   _____

## Plan and Carry Out

4. At which floor does the elevator start?

   _____

5. When the elevator goes down 3 floors, at which floor does it stop?

   _____

6. When the elevator goes up 8 floors, at which floor does it stop?

   _____

7. At which floor does the elevator stop?

   _____

## Check

8. Write a numerical expression you can use to check your answer.

   _____

## Solve Another Problem

9. A football team is on their opponents' 15-yard line. The quarterback throws a pass, but his team gets a penalty of 10 yards. During the next play, the quarterback passes the ball and the player runs the ball 8 yards. Which yard line is the team on for the next play?

   _____

# Practice 6-2

**Comparing and Ordering Integers**

**Compare, using < or >.**

**1.** $2 \boxed{\phantom{x}} -9$    **2.** $-5 \boxed{\phantom{x}} -4$    **3.** $10 \boxed{\phantom{x}} -10$    **4.** $-2 \boxed{\phantom{x}} 5$

**5.** $-33 \boxed{\phantom{x}} 2$    **6.** $-50 \boxed{\phantom{x}} -60$    **7.** $-9 \boxed{\phantom{x}} 0$    **8.** $-9 \boxed{\phantom{x}} -4$

**Order each set of integers from least to greatest.**

**9.** $-7, -5, -12, -4$ _____    **10.** $0, -6, 6, 4, -4$ _____

**11.** $15, -36, 4, -50$ _____    **12.** $-3, -12, 9, -27$ _____

**13.** Order the temperatures from least to greatest. _____
   - The temperature was 25°F below zero.
   - The pool temperature was 78°F.
   - Water freezes at 32°F.
   - The low temperature in December was –3°F.
   - The temperature in the refrigerator was 34°F.

**Write an integer that is located on a number line between the given integers.**

**14.** $-2,$ ____, $9$    **15.** $3,$ ____, $-12$    **16.** $-7,$ ____, $-11$

**17.** $0,$ ____, $-5$    **18.** $2,$ ____, $-1$    **19.** $-25,$ ____, $-16$

**Complete with an integer that makes the statement true.**

**20.** $-9 >$ ____    **21.** $0 >$ ____    **22.** $-1 >$ ____

**23.** $3 <$ ____    **24.** $-5 <$ ____    **25.** $-50 <$ ____

**26.** During scuba lessons, Sue dove 30 feet, Harriet dove 120 feet, and Kathy dove 90 feet. What integers represent these depths? Order the integers from least to greatest.

_____

# 6-2 • Guided Problem Solving

## GPS Student Page 212, Exercise 24:

**Weather** Order the temperatures below from least to greatest.

- Normal body temperature is about 37°C.
- An average winter day on the polar ice cap is −25°C.
- The warmest day on record in Canada was 45°C.
- The coldest day on record in Texas was −31°C.

### Understand

1. What are you being asked to do?

   _____

2. Are the integers all positive, all negative, or are they a mix of positive and negative?

   _____

### Plan and Carry Out

3. What are the positive integers?

   _____

4. What are the negative integers?

   _____

5. Order each group of integers separately.

   _____

6. Combine the lists, ordering from least to greatest.

   _____

### Check

7. Plot the integers on a number line to check the order.

   _____

### Solve Another Problem

8. A porpoise dives 300 meters below the ocean's surface.
   A Weddell seal dives 600 meters below the ocean's surface.
   Which dives farther below the ocean's surface?

   _____

Name _____ Class _____ Date _____

# Practice 6-3
## Rational Numbers

Show that each number is a rational number by writing it as the quotient of two integers.

**1.** 37 _____

**2.** $-3\frac{1}{5}$ _____

**3.** $-\frac{4}{6}$ _____

**4.** 3.87 _____

**5.** $-0.23$ _____

**6.** 9.2 _____

**7.** $8\frac{1}{9}$ _____

**8.** $\frac{2}{15}$ _____

Plot each fraction on a number line.

**9.** $-\frac{5}{6}$

**10.** $-4\frac{2}{3}$

**11.** $\frac{3}{5}$

**12.** $-2\frac{1}{2}$

**13.** $-\frac{7}{8}$

**14.** $3\frac{1}{4}$

Plot each decimal on a number line.

**15.** $-3.25$

**16.** 5.4

**17.** 1.6

**18.** 0.7

**19.** $-0.2$

**20.** $-1.3$

Plot each rational number on a vertical number line.

**21.** $-0.62$

**22.** $-3.2$

**23.** $7\frac{1}{6}$

# 6-3 • Guided Problem Solving

**GPS** Student Page 216, Exercise 30:

**Number Sense** Between what two integers on a number line does −3.425 lie? Between what two rational numbers, in tenths, does it lie? Between what two rational numbers, in hundredths, does it lie? Explain.

## Understand

1. What do you need to do? _____

_____

2. What types of numbers do you need to find?

_____

## Plan and Carry Out

3. Draw a number line. Divide it into tenths and plot −3.425. ⟵━━━━━⟶

4. Between what two integers on a number line does −3.425 lie?

_____

5. Which rational number, in tenths, is to the left of −3.425? _____

6. Between what two rational numbers, in tenths, does −3.425 lie?

_____

7. Which rational number, in hundredths, is to the left of −3.425?

_____

8. Between what two rational numbers, in hundredths, does
   −3.425 lie? _____

## Check

9. How can you check your answers? _____

_____

_____

_____

## Solve Another Problem

10. Between what two integers on a number line does −2.643 lie? Between what two rational numbers, in tenths, does it lie? Between what two rational numbers, in hundredths, does it lie? Explain.

_____

_____

_____

# Practice 6-4
**Comparing and Ordering Rational Numbers**

**Compare the decimals using <, =, or >.**

**1.** $-7.14 \,\square\, -6.19$

**2.** $-0.65 \,\square\, -0.6$

**3.** $-3.8 \,\square\, -4.6$

**4.** $-12.08 \,\square\, -12.8$

**5.** $-0.72 \,\square\, -0.27$

**6.** $-2.01 \,\square\, -2.18$

**Compare the fractions using <, =, or >.**

**7.** $-\frac{2}{3} \,\square\, -\frac{3}{5}$

**8.** $-\frac{2}{5} \,\square\, -\frac{7}{8}$

**9.** $-4\frac{3}{8} \,\square\, -4\frac{6}{7}$

**10.** $-1\frac{1}{5} \,\square\, -1\frac{5}{8}$

**11.** $-1\frac{1}{8} \,\square\, -1\frac{3}{4}$

**12.** $-\frac{1}{3} \,\square\, -\frac{1}{6}$

**Compare the fractions and decimals using <, =, or >.**

**13.** $-\frac{4}{5} \,\square\, -0.6$

**14.** $-3.9 \,\square\, -3\frac{4}{5}$

**15.** $-\frac{1}{2} \,\square\, -0.5$

**16.** $-1.2 \,\square\, -1\frac{1}{10}$

**17.** $-0.75 \,\square\, -\frac{8}{10}$

**18.** $-3.6 \,\square\, -3\frac{3}{5}$

**19.** The city measures the water level in a lake and considers the average depth of the lake to be 0 feet. After Week 1, the water level was $-3.1$ feet. In Week 2, the water level was $-3\frac{2}{3}$ feet. Compare the numbers. In which week was the water lower?

_____

**Order each set of rational numbers from least to greatest.**

**20.** $-4.5, -4\frac{6}{10}, -4.06$ _____

**21.** $\frac{25}{5}, -5.2, -5\frac{5}{20}$ _____

**22.** Nicholas researched the elevations of various places around Long Beach, California. He found these elevations.

$-5.28$ ft, $-5\frac{3}{8}$ ft, $-5.6$ ft, $-7$ft, $6.4$ ft, $-5\frac{3}{4}$ ft

Order the elevations from least to greatest.

_____

Name _____ Class _____ Date _____

# 6-4 • Guided Problem Solving

**GPS** Student Page 222, Exercise 21:

**Number Sense** The students in Mrs. Metz's science class are growing plants under different light, soil, and water conditions. The average plant growth during a week was 3.5 inches. The table shows the difference from the average for some of the students' plants. Order the students' plants from least to greatest. (Recall that 1 in. = 2.54 cm.)

| Student | Difference |
|---------|------------|
| Ji Sun | $2\frac{1}{4}$ in. |
| Gayle | $-2\frac{7}{10}$ in. |
| Stefan | 1.5 cm |
| Ricardo | −2.4 cm |

## Understand

1. What are you being asked to find?

   _____

2. What is the average growth for a plant during a week?

   _____

## Plan and Carry Out

3. How do you convert the centimeter measurements to inches?

   _____

4. To compare plant heights, convert all centimeter measurements to inches. _____

5. How do you find the actual height of each plant?

   _____

6. What are the actual plant heights in inches?

   _____

7. Order the students' plants from least to greatest.

   _____

## Check

8. How can you check that your answer is reasonable?

   _____

## Solve Another Problem

9. The students in Mr. Theo's science class are measuring the amount of rain received each week compared to the average. The table shows the difference from the average for different weeks. Order the weeks' rainfall from least to greatest. (Recall that 1 in. = 2.54 cm.)

| Week | Difference |
|------|------------|
| 1 | $1\frac{1}{4}$ in. |
| 2 | $-1\frac{3}{10}$ in. |
| 3 | 2.5 cm |
| 4 | −3.4 cm |

Name _____ Class _____ Date _____

# Practice 6-5 ............................................................ Inequalities

**Graph each inequality on a number line.**

**1.** $x \le 3$

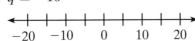

**2.** $t < -1$

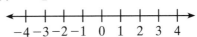

**3.** $q \ge -10$

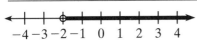

**4.** $m < 50$

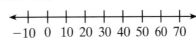

**For each inequality, tell whether the number in bold is a solution.**

**5.** $x < 7; \textbf{7}$ _____

**6.** $p > -3; \textbf{3}$ _____

**7.** $r < 4; \textbf{-3}$ _____

**8.** $z \le 12; \textbf{4}$ _____

**9.** $n > 3; \textbf{6}$ _____

**10.** $g \ge 3; \textbf{-1}$ _____

**Write an inequality for each graph.**

**11.** _____

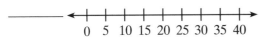

**12.** _____

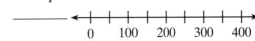

**Write a real-world statement for each inequality.**

**13.** $d \ge 60$ _____

**14.** $w \le -10$ _____

**Write and graph an inequality for each statement.**

**15.** You can walk there in 20 minutes or less.

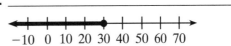

**16.** Each prize is worth over $150.

**17.** A species of catfish, *Malapterurus electricus*, can generate up to 350 volts of electricity.

  **a.** Write an inequality to represent the amount of electricity generated by the catfish.

  _____

  **b.** Draw a graph of the inequality you wrote in part (a).

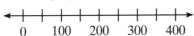

# 6-5 • Guided Problem Solving

**GPS** **Student Page 226, Exercise 16:**

**Football** You must weigh 120 pounds or less to play in a junior football league. Use the table at the right. Who qualifies to play?

| Name | Weight |
|------|--------|
| Aaron | 118 lb |
| Steve | 109 lb |
| Mark | 131 lb |
| James | 120 lb |

## Understand

1. What are you being asked to determine?

   _____

2. What is the weight requirement for playing in the junior football league?

   _____

## Plan and Carry Out

3. Write the weight requirement as an inequality. Use $p$ to represent a player's weight.

   _____

4. Substitute each player's weight for the inequality's variable to determine if the weight makes the inequality true or false.

   _____

   _____

5. Which players' weights make the inequality true?

   _____

6. Who qualifies to play?

   _____

## Check

7. Compare each player's weight to the weight requirement by plotting each weight on a number line.

   _____

## Solve Another Problem

8. Dave ran less than 5 miles. How many miles could Dave have run? Define a variable and write an inequality.

   _____

Guided Problem Solving

# Practice 6-6 ·············································· Solving One-Step Inequalities

**Solve each inequality.**

**1.** $x - 5 < 15$

**2.** $m + 7 \geq 12$

**3.** $k + 5 < -10$

_____

_____

_____

**4.** $g - (-4) \geq 0$

**5.** $-6 > b - 24$

**6.** $f - 6 < 12$

_____

_____

_____

**7.** $q + 9 < 60$

**8.** $h + (-1) > -1$

**9.** $42 + p \geq 7$

_____

_____

_____

**Write an inequality for each sentence. Then solve the inequality.**

**10.** Five is greater than a number minus 2. _____

**11.** Twenty is less than or equal to a number plus 4. _____

**12.** A number minus 5 is greater than 25. _____

**13.** A number plus 18 is less than or equal to 20. _____

**Write an inequality for each problem. Then solve the inequality.**

**14.** You and the chess teacher have been playing chess for 18 minutes.
To make the chess club, you must win the game in less than
45 minutes. How much time do you have to win the chess game?

_____

**15.** Your phone card allows you to talk long distance for up to 120
minutes. You have been on a long-distance call for 72 minutes.
How much longer do you have to talk before your phone card
expires?

_____

**Solve each inequality mentally.**

**16.** $x - 28 < 108$

**17.** $s - 18 \geq 12$

**18.** $t + 5 < -15$

_____

_____

_____

**19.** $g + 12 > 20$

**20.** $k - 4 \geq 25$

**21.** $24 > b + 16$

_____

_____

_____

# 6-6 • Guided Problem Solving

**GPS** **Student Page 230, Exercise 22:**

**Budgeting** You want to spend less than $30 on two T-shirts and a pair of shorts. The pair of shorts costs $13. Each of the T-shirts costs the same amount. Write and solve an inequality to find how much money you can spend on each T-shirt.

## Understand

1. What are you being asked to find?

   _____

   _____

2. Which symbol do you need to use in the inequality, < or >? ___

## Plan and Carry Out

3. Given that shorts cost $13, write an expression for the phrase "2 T-shirts and a pair of shorts." Let $t$ represent the cost of one T-shirt. _____

4. Use the expression in Step 3 to write an inequality for less than 30. _____

5. What do you do first to each side of the inequality? _____

6. Simplify each side of the inequality. _____

7. What do you do to each side of the inequality to solve for $t$? _____

8. What is the solution? _____

9. How much money can you spend on each T-shirt? _____

## Check

10. Can you spend exactly the amount you found in Step 9? Explain.

    _____

    _____

## Solve Another Problem

11. Suppose you are able to spend $10 more. How much money can you spend on each T-shirt now?

    _____

# 6A: Graphic Organizer

**For use before Lesson 6-1**

**Study Skill** Take notes when your teacher presents new material in class. Organize those notes as a way to study, reviewing them as you go.

**Write your answers.**

1. What is the chapter title? _____

2. How many lessons are there in this chapter? _____

3. What is the topic of the Test-Taking Strategies page? _____

4. Complete the graphic organizer below as you work through the chapter.

   • In the center, write the title of the chapter.

   • When you begin a lesson, write the lesson name in a rectangle.

   • When you complete a lesson, write a skill or key concept in a circle linked to that lesson block.

   • When you complete the chapter, use this graphic organizer to help you review.

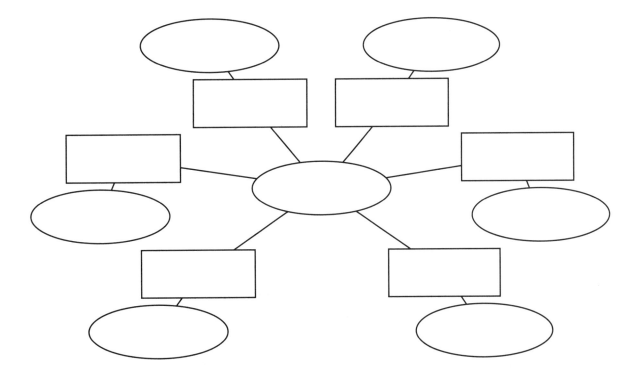

Vocabulary and Study Skills

# 6B: Reading Comprehension

**Study Skill** Finish one assignment before beginning another. Sometimes it helps to start with the most difficult assignment first.

**Read the paragraph below and answer the questions.**

> The surface temperatures of the solar system's planets vary greatly. The coldest planet is Neptune, where the average temperature is approximately $-373°F$. The warmest planet is Mercury, where the temperature can reach $950°F$. By comparison, the average temperature on Earth is $59°F$. Even more amazing is Earth's moon, where the temperature can change more than $700°F$ from day to night. During the day, the average temperature on the moon is $417°F$, while at night the temperature drops to $-299°F$. Interestingly, the temperature at each of the moon's poles is a constant $-141°F$.

1. What is the paragraph about?

   _____

   _____

2. What is the average temperature on Earth?

   _____

3. Which of the planets is the warmest?

   _____

4. What is the difference between the highest temperature and the lowest temperature on the moon?

   _____

5. Which temperature is warmer: the average nightly temperature of the moon or the temperature of one of the moon's poles?

   _____

   _____

6. How much colder is Neptune than Earth? _____

7. **High-Use Academic Words** What does it mean to *explain*?

   **a.** to look for similarities          **b.** to make understandable

# 6C: Reading/Writing Math Symbols

**For use after Lesson 6-5**

**Study Skill** Use abbreviations, formulas, and symbols to write mathematical statements quickly and with less complicated wording.

**Write the meaning of each mathematical statement.**

1. $y < 5$ _____

2. $-10$ _____

3. $6 - x$ _____

4. $y \geq 4$ _____

5. $4 : 5$ _____

6. $|-4| = 4$ _____

7. $\dfrac{3}{4} = 75\%$ _____

8. $y \leq 5$ _____

9. $3^2 = 9$ _____

10. $x - 6$ _____

11. $x + 3 = 9$ _____

12. $|4| = 4$

_____

13. $2 : 3 = 6 : 9$ _____

14. $y > 4$ _____

15. $\dfrac{2}{3} \approx 66.6\%$

_____

16. $y \leq -5$

_____

17. $\dfrac{7}{8}n = 42$

_____

18. $28\% = 0.28$

_____

Name _____  Class _____ Date _____

# 6D: Visual Vocabulary Practice

For use after Lesson 6-6

**Study Skill** When interpreting an illustration, look for the most specific concept represented.

**Concept List**

| | | |
|---|---|---|
| absolute value | integers | solution of an inequality |
| graph of an inequality | opposites | |
| inequality | rational number | |

**Write the concept that best describes each exercise. Choose from the concept list above. Some terms may be used more than once.**

| 1. $-5\frac{2}{3}$ | 2. $\frac{3}{19}$ and $-\frac{3}{19}$ | 3. The numbers $-2, 0, 3,$ and $5$ are examples. |
|---|---|---|
| 4. $|-10| = 10$ | 5. A statement that uses one of these symbols: $<, >, \leq, \geq$ | 6. 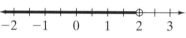 |
| 7. $x - 7 > 12$ | 8. $-6$ and $6$ | 9. $x + 5 < 9$<br>$x + 5 - 5 < 9 - 5$<br>$x < 4$<br>The number 3. |

# 6E: Vocabulary Check

**For use after Lesson 6-5**

**Study Skill** Strengthen your vocabulary. Use these pages and add cues and summaries by applying the Cornell Notetaking style.

**Write the definition for each word or term at the right. To check your work, fold the paper back along the dotted line to see the correct answers.**

absolute value

integers

inequality

opposites

rational number

# 6E: Vocabulary Check (continued)

**For use after Lesson 6-5**

**Write the vocabulary word or term for each definition. To check your work, fold the paper forward along the dotted line to see the correct answers.**

the distance of a number from 0 on the number line

_____

the set of positive whole numbers, their opposites, and zero

_____

a mathematical sentence that contains $<, >, \leq, \geq,$ or $\neq$

_____

two numbers that are the same distance from 0 on the number line, but in opposite directions

_____

any number that can be written as the quotient of two integers where the denominator is not 0

_____

# 6F: Vocabulary Review

**For use with the Chapter Review**

**Study Skill** Vocabulary is an important part of every subject you learn. You may find it helpful to review new words and their definitions using flashcards.

**Match the word in Column A with its definition in Column B.**

| Column A | Column B |
| --- | --- |
| **1.** absolute value | **A.** a number that can be written as a quotient of two integers in which the denominator is not zero |
| **2.** integers | **B.** two numbers that are the same distance from 0 on the number line, but in different directions |
| **3.** opposites | **C.** the set of positive whole numbers, their opposites, and zero |
| **4.** rational number | **D.** a mathematical sentence that contains $<, >, \le, \ge,$ or $\ne$ |
| **5.** inequality | **E.** the distance a number is from zero on a number line |

**Match the word in Column A with an example in Column B.**

Column A

**6.** graph of an inequality

**7.** absolute value

**8.** opposites

**9.** rational number

**10.** inequality

Column B

**F.** $-8$ and $8$

**G.** $-5\frac{1}{2}$

**H.** $y \le 6$

**J.**

**K.** $|-8|$

Name _____ Class _____ Date _____

# Practice 7-1 ............................................ Points in the Coordinate Plane

**Name the point with the given coordinates in the coordinate plane at the right.**

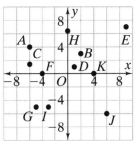

**1.** $(2, 3)$ _____   **2.** $(4, 0)$ _____

**3.** $(-3, -5)$ _____   **4.** $\left(0, 6\frac{1}{2}\right)$ _____

**Find the coordinates of each point at the right.**

**5.** $J$ _____   **6.** $E$ _____

**7.** $D$ _____   **8.** $A$ _____

**9.** $G$ _____   **10.** $C$ _____

**Graph each point on the coordinate plane at the right.**

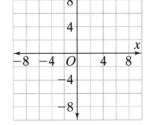

**11.** $A\ (8.5, -4)$   **12.** $B\ (-4, 8)$

**13.** $C\ (4, 8)$   **14.** $D\ (-8, -4)$

**15.** $E\left(8, 4\frac{1}{4}\right)$   **16.** $F\ (-4, -8)$

**17.** A taxi begins at $(4, -3)$. It travels 3 blocks west and 5 blocks north to pick up a customer. What are the customer's coordinates?

_____

**18.** A moving truck fills up a shipment at an old address, at $(-2, 1)$. It travels 7 blocks south and 6 blocks east to the new address. What is the location of the new address?

_____

**Use the coordinate plane at the right.**

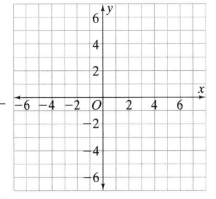

**19.** Graph four points on the coordinate plane so that when the points are connected in order, the shape is a rectangle. List the coordinates of the points.

_____

**20.** Graph four points on the coordinate plane so that when the points are connected in order, the shape is a parallelogram that is not a rectangle. List the coordinates of the points.

_____

# 7-1 • Guided Problem Solving

**Student Page 244, Exercise 31:**

**Geometry** A symmetrical four-pointed star has eight corner points. Seven of the points are $(-1, 1), (0, 3), (1, 1), (3, 0), (1, -1), (0, -3),$ and $(-1, -1)$. What are the coordinates of the missing point?

## Understand

**1.** What are you being asked to do?

_____

**2.** What is a good way to set up the problem visually?

_____

## Plan and Carry Out

**3.** What point is a reflection of $(-1, 1)$ over the $y$-axis?

_____

**4.** What point is a reflection of $(-1, -1)$ over the $y$-axis?

_____

**5.** What point is a reflection of $(3, 0)$ over the $y$-axis?

_____

**6.** What is the missing point?

_____

## Check

**7.** Does the point $(-3, 0)$ form a four-pointed star with the other seven points?

_____

## Solve Another Problem

**8.** A five-pointed star that is divided evenly in half by the $y$-axis has ten corner points. Eight of the points are $(-1, 1), (0, 3), (1, 1), (3, 1), (1, -1), (0, -1), (-2, -3),$ and $(-3, 1)$. What are the coordinates of the missing points?

_____

# Practice 7-2

**Polygons in the Coordinate Plane**

**Find the length of the line segment joining the two points.**

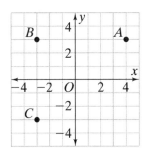

**1.** Find the length of a line segment joining points
   *A* and *B*. _____

**2.** Find the length of a line segment joining points
   *C* and *B*. _____

**3.** $(2,2), (4,2)$ _____

**4.** $(5,-1), (5,2)$ _____

**5.** $(0,3), (0,5)$ _____

**6.** $(-1,-4), (-3,-4)$ _____

**7.** $(1.5,6), (-2,6)$ _____

**8.** $(-7,-6), (-7,6)$ _____

**9.** $(2,3\frac{1}{2}), (-3,3\frac{1}{2})$ _____

**10.** $(1,4), (1,5)$ _____

**11.** $(-4,5.2)(2,5.2)$ _____

**12.** $(-8,1), (-8,-6)$ _____

**For Exercises 13–16, the two given points are connected to form the
diagonal of a rectangle. Find the perimeter of the rectangle.**

**13.** $(6,8), (-1,12)$ _____

**14.** $(-5,-3), (-10,-5)$ _____

**15.** $(-2,-5), (1,6)$ _____

**16.** $(7,-1), (6,4.5)$ _____

**17.** To show the location of the garden in her yard, Sandra graphs
a rectangle on a coordinate plane. The rectangle is formed by
the points $(15,4), (15,-8), (-4,-8),$ and $(-4,4)$. What is the
perimeter of the garden? Each unit is a foot.

_____

**For each pair, tell whether the point was reflected over the *x*-axis or the *y*-axis.**

**18.** $(4,13), (-4,13)$ _____

**19.** $(3,\frac{1}{2}), (-3,\frac{1}{2})$ _____

**20.** $(2,1), (2,-1)$ _____

**21.** $(12,6), (12,-6)$ _____

**22.** $(5,0), (-5,0)$ _____

**23.** $(-9,8), (9,8)$ _____

# 7-2 • Guided Problem Solving

**GPS** Student Page 249, Exercise 26:

**Reasoning** The point $(a, b)$ reflected over the $x$-axis, then the $y$-axis, then the $x$-axis again, and then the $y$-axis again. What are the coordinates of the new point? _____

## Understand

1. What does *reflected* mean? _____

   _____

2. What do you know about points when they are reflected over the $x$-axis?

   _____

3. What do you know about points when they are reflected over the $y$-axis?

   _____

## Plan and Carry Out

4. What are the coordinates of the new point when $(a, b)$ is reflected over the $x$-axis? _____

5. What are the coordinates of that point when it is reflected over the $y$-axis? _____

6. What are the coordinates of that point when it is reflected over the $x$-axis? _____

7. What are the coordinates of that point when it is reflected over the $y$-axis? _____

8. What are the coordinates of the new point? _____

## Check

9. Reflect the point $(3, 4)$ over the $x$-axis, then the $y$-axis, then the $x$-axis again, and then the $y$-axis again. What are the coordinates of the new point? _____

10. Does that confirm your answer? _____

## Solve Another Problem

11. The point $(a, b)$ is reflected over the $x$-axis 4 times. What are the coordinates of the new point? _____

Name _____ Class _____ Date _____

# Practice 7-3 **Functions**

**Complete the function table using the rule.**

**1.** Output = Input − 5

| Input | Output |
|-------|--------|
| 16 | |
| 9 | |
| 50 | |
| 71 | |

**2.** Output = Input · 11

| Input | Output |
|-------|--------|
| 10 | |
| 1 | |
| 4 | |
| 12 | |

**Identify the independent and dependent variables.**

**3.** the perimeter of a square and its side length

_____

_____

**4.** the dollars you are paid and the number of hours you work

_____

_____

**5.** the number of miles you drive and the number of gallons of gas
you need _____

_____

**Write an equation for each function table.**

**6.** Don is converting measurements in yards to measurements in inches. _____

| yards | inches |
|-------|--------|
| 2 | 72 |
| 5 | 180 |
| 9 | 324 |
| 10 | 360 |

**7.** Pablo is calculating how much is in his savings account each month. _____

| months | Total ($) |
|--------|-----------|
| 4 | 100 |
| 7 | 175 |
| 11 | 275 |
| 18 | 450 |

**8.** The number of sides on a polygon is greater than the number of diagonals drawn from one vertex. _____

| Sides | Diagonals |
|-------|-----------|
| 4 | 1 |
| 6 | 3 |
| 9 | 6 |
| 13 | 10 |

**9.** Abby is older than Caitlyn. _____

| Caitlyn's Age | Abby's Age |
|---------------|------------|
| 9 | 11 |
| 12 | 14 |
| 28 | 30 |
| 44 | 46 |

# 7-3 • Guided Problem Solving

**GPS** **Student Page 254, Exercise 16:**

**Reasoning** Aaron records how much he makes for different numbers of lawns he has mowed.

How many lawns were mowed if he earned $368? _____

| Lawns Mowed | $ Earned |
|:---:|:---:|
| 2 | 46 |
| 5 | 115 |
| 9 | 207 |
| ? | 368 |

## Understand

1. What are you being asked to do? _____

   _____

2. What do you need to know to find the number of lawns?

   _____

3. What do you need to show the relationship between the number of lawns mowed and the amount he earns? _____

## Plan and Carry Out

4. What is the relationship between the number of lawns and the amount he is paid? _____

   _____

5. What is the equation that represents that relationship? _____

6. For which variable will you substitute 368? _____

7. How will you solve that equation? _____

8. How many lawns were mowed? _____

## Check

9. How can you check your equation? _____

   _____

10. What equation will you solve to see if your answer is correct?

    _____

## Solve Another Problem

11. Jake records how much he makes for different numbers of cars he parks.

    How many cars were parked if he earned $124? _____

| Cars Parked | $ Earned |
|:---:|:---:|
| 4 | 16 |
| 6 | 24 |
| 10 | 40 |
| ? | 124 |

Name _____ Class _____ Date _____

# Practice 7-4

**Graph the data in the table. Determine whether the relationship is a linear function.**

**1.**

| Input | 1 | 2 | 3 | 4 | 5 |
|---|---|---|---|---|---|
| Output | 5 | 10 | 15 | 20 | 25 |

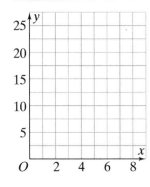

Is it linear? _____

**2.**

| Input | 10 | 20 | 30 | 40 | 50 |
|---|---|---|---|---|---|
| Output | 20 | 40 | 60 | 70 | 100 |

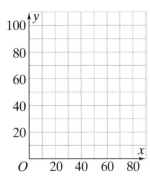

Is it linear? _____

**3.**

| Input | 3 | 4 | 5 | 6 | 7 |
|---|---|---|---|---|---|
| Output | 6 | 7 | 8 | 9 | 10 |

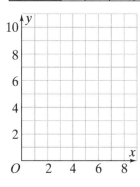

Is it linear? _____

**Make a table and graph each function. Use *x*-values of 0, 1, 2, 3 and 4.**

**4.** $y = x + 1$

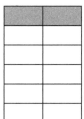
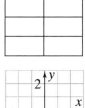

**5.** $y = 2x$

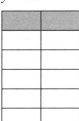

**6.** $y = \frac{x}{2} + 1$

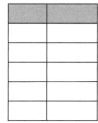

**7.** A parking garage charges $3.50 per hour to park. The function rule: $c = 3.5h$ shows how the number of hours $h$ relates to the parking charge $c$. Graph the function.

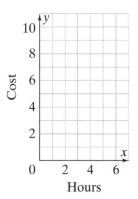

# 7-4 • Guided Problem Solving

**GPS** Student Page 259, Exercise 19:

**Business** You start a cookie business. You know that the oven and materials will cost $600. You decide to charge $.75 for each cookie. The function $p = 0.75c - 600$ relates profit $p$ to the number of cookies $c$ that you sell.

a. What will be your profit or loss if you sell 400 cookies? If you sell 500 cookies?

b. How many cookies must you sell to break even?

## Understand

1. What is *profit*?

   _____

   _____

2. How will you use the equation to answer part (a) and part (b)?

   _____

   _____

## Plan and Carry Out

3. Substitute 400 for $c$ and solve for $p$. What is the profit? _____

4. Substitute 500 for $c$ and solve for $p$. What is the profit? _____

5. What value represents breaking even? _____

6. Do you substitute this for $p$ or $c$? _____

7. How many cookies must you sell to break even? _____

## Check

8. What is $(0.75 \cdot 800) - 600$? _____

## Solve Another Problem

9. Distance is a function of time. Suppose you walk at a rate of 2 miles per hour. Write an equation for the distance $d$ you walk in $t$ hours, and use it to determine the distance you will have walked after 10 hours.

   _____

# Practice 7-5

**Functions in the Real World**

**Use the table for Exercises 1 and 2.**

Paige pet sits every weekend to earn extra spending money. She earns $11.50 per day.

| Days | $ Earned |
|------|----------|
| 2    | 23       |
| 4    | 46       |
| 7    | 80.50    |
| 13   | 149.5    |

1.  How much does she earn after working for 7 days? _____

2.  If she earns $46, how long did she work? _____

**Use the graph for Exercises 3 and 4.**

Pete graphs how much he spends on football game tickets.

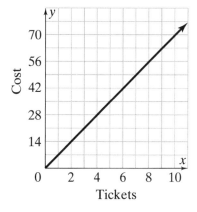

3.  How much does he spend on 4 games? _____

4.  If he has spent $42, how many tickets has he bought? _____

5.  When making punch, the number of cans of apple juice is 2 times the number of cans of pineapple juice. Write an equation to represent this situation. If George used 8 cans of apple juice, how many cans of pineapple juice did he use?

_____

6.  In a bag of marbles, there are four times as many small marbles as large marbles. Write an equation to represent this situation. If there are 16 large marbles, how many small marbles are there?

_____

# 7-5 • Guided Problem Solving

**GPS** Student Page 264, Exercise 16:

**Choose a Method** Juanita earns $5 for each subscription she sells. If she sells 25 subscriptions, will she make enough money to buy a new bicycle that costs $115? Explain. Use a table, graph, or equation to support your answer.

### Understand

1. What are you being asked to do?

   _____

   _____

2. What are the three ways you could find the amount?

   _____

### Plan and Carry Out

3. What variable will you use? _____

4. What does the variable stand for? _____

   _____

5. What equation can you use to represent how much she makes?

   _____

6. How can you use the equation to find how much she made?

   _____

7. How much does she make? _____

8. Does she have enough to buy the bicycle? _____

### Check

9. Is $125 enough to buy the bicycle? _____

### Solve Another Problem

10. Shawn earns $3 for each advertisement she sells for a theater's program. If he sells 41 advertisements, will he make enough money to buy a new gaming system that costs $125? Explain. Use a table, graph, or equation to support your answer.

    _____

    _____

Name _____ Class _____ Date _____

# 7A:  Graphic Organizer

**Study Skill**  Develop consistent study habits. Work in a quiet area where you can concentrate. Block off enough time for doing homework, so you do not have to rush through your assignments.

**Write your answers.**

1. What is the chapter title? _____

2. How many lessons are there in this chapter? _____

3. What is the topic of the Test-Taking Strategies page? _____

4. Complete the graphic organizer below as you work through the chapter.

   • In the center, write the title of the chapter.

   • When you begin a lesson, write the lesson name in a rectangle.

   • When you complete a lesson, write a skill or key concept in a circle linked to that lesson block.

   • When you complete the chapter, use this graphic organizer to help you review.

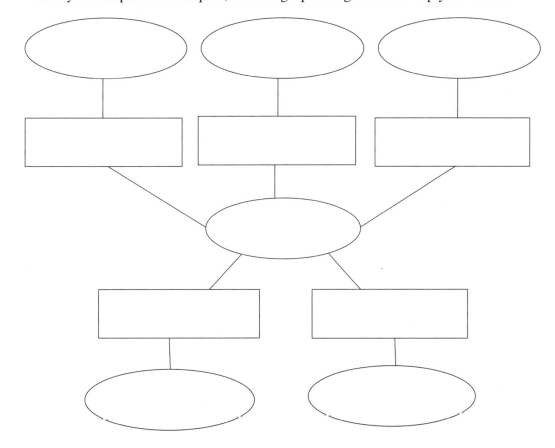

# 7B: Reading Comprehension

**Study Skill** Finish one assignment before beginning another.
Sometimes it helps to start with the most difficult assignment first.

**Read the paragraph below and answer the questions.**

> When Bobby first started working at the shop, he earned an hourly
> wage of $4.50. His main job at that time was to clean; he swept and
> mopped floors, wiped windows, and dusted shelves. After showing
> that he was reliable, he got a raise. At that time, he earned $6.25
> per hour and had the new responsibility of stocking shelves. Again,
> Bobby proved to be dependable, and after a short period of time,
> he was promoted to cashier. As a cashier, he earned $8.90 per hour.
> He worked as a cashier until he graduated from high school, when
> he became an assistant manager. At that time, he earned a salary of
> $2,750 per month. His perseverance had paid off.

1. What is the paragraph about?

   _____

   _____

2. How much did Bobby earn when he stocked shelves?

   _____

3. At what point was Bobby paid a salary, rather than an hourly wage?

   _____

4. What was the difference from a cleaner to a cashier in his pay
   for 20 hours of work? _____

5. How many hours would Bobby have to work as a cashier each
   month to make $2,750, his salary as an assistant manager?
   Justify your answer.

   _____

6. What function could represent how much Bobby is paid when he
   first starts his job? _____

7. **High-Use Academic Words** In Exercise 5, what does it mean to
   *justify*?

   **a.** to show your calculations

   **b.** to align your work to one side
      of the paper

Name_____ Class_____ Date_____

# 7C: Reading/Writing Math Symbols

For use after Lesson 7-5

**Study Skill** Prepare a set of flash cards to help you memorize symbols and their meanings.

**Match the function representation in Column A with the representation of the same function in Column B.**

| Column A | Column B |
|---|---|

**1.** Carrie makes 110 muffins per hour.

**A.**

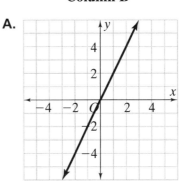

**2.** $y = 2x$

**B.**

| x | y |
|---|---|
| 3 | 330 |
| 6 | 660 |
| 10 | 1100 |

**3.**

| x | y |
|---|---|
| −4 | 5 |
| 2 | 11 |
| 11 | 20 |

**C.** the club members rappelled downward at a rate of 1 meter per second.

**4.**

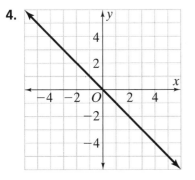

**D.** $y = x + 9$

# 7D: Visual Vocabulary Practice

**For use after Lesson 7-4**

**Study Skill** Math symbols give us a way to express complex ideas in a small space.

**Concept List**

| | | |
|---|---|---|
| absolute value | equation | origin |
| coordinate plane | polygon | quadrants |
| function | ordered pair | reflected points |

**Write the concept that best describes each exercise. Choose from the concept list above.**

| 1. $y = 1.5x$ _____ | 2. A hot dog vendor makes $1.50 for each hot dog she sells. Let $n$ represent the number of hot dogs sold in a day. If $P$ represents the profit for the day, this can be represented by $P = 1.5n$. _____ | 3. 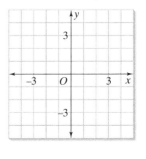 _____ |
|---|---|---|
| 4. $\lvert -10 \rvert = 10$ _____ | 5. $\left(4, \dfrac{3}{19}\right)$ and $\left(4, \dfrac{-3}{19}\right)$ are this with respect to the $x$-axis. _____ | 6. $(-5, 2)$ _____ |
| 7. 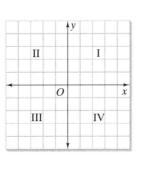 _____ | 8. $(0, 0)$ represents this point. _____ | 9. The line segments connecting the points $(1, 1), (1, 7), (7, 1)$ and $(7, 7)$ form this. _____ |

# 7E: Vocabulary Check

**Study Skill** Strengthen your vocabulary. Use these pages and add cues and summaries by applying the Cornell Notetaking style.

**Write the definition for each word or term at the right. To check your work, fold the paper back along the dotted line to see the correct answers.**

quadrants

ordered pair

origin

vertical line

function

# 7E: Vocabulary Check (continued)

For use after Lesson 7-5

Write the vocabulary word or term for each definition. To check your
work, fold the paper forward along the dotted line to see the correct
answers.

the four regions of the
coordinate plane

_____

describes the location of a
point in a coordinate plane

_____

the point of intersection of the
$x$- and $y$-axes on a coordinate plane

_____

a straight line that extends
up and down

_____

a relationship that assigns
exactly one output value for
each input value

_____

# 7F: Vocabulary Review

**For use with the Chapter Review**

**Study Skill** Vocabulary is an important part of every subject you learn. You may find it helpful to review new words and their definitions using flashcards.

**Match the word in Column A with its definition in Column B.**

| Column A | Column B |
|---|---|
| **1.** vertical line | **A.** has a graph that is a straight line |
| **2.** horizontal line | **B.** a pair of numbers that describes the location of a point in a coordinate plane |
| **3.** origin | **C.** the point where the *x*- and *y*-axes intersect |
| **4.** linear function | **D.** a straight line that extends left and right |
| **5.** quadrants | **E.** the surface formed by the intersection of two number lines |
| **6.** coordinate plane | **F.** the four regions of a coordinate plane |
| **7.** ordered pair | **G.** a rule that assigns exactly one output value to each input value |
| **8.** function | **H.** a straight line that extends up and down |

Vocabulary and Study Skills

Name _____ Class _____ Date _____

# Practice 8-1 · · · · · · · · · · · · · · · · · · · · · · · · · · · · · · · · · · · · · Areas of Parallelograms and Triangles
· · · · · · · · · · · · · · · · · · · · · · · · · · · · · · · · · · · · · · · · · · · · · · · · · · · · · · · · · · ·

**Find the area of each parallelogram.**

1.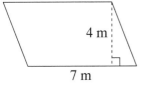

2.

3.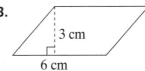

_____   _____   _____

**Find the area of each triangle.**

4.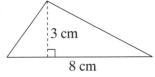

5.

6.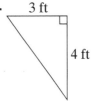

_____   _____   _____

**Find the area of each complex figure.**

7.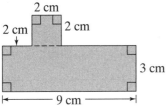

8.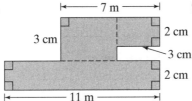

9.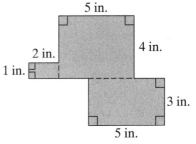

_____   _____   _____

10. Draw and label a triangle and a parallelogram that each have an area of 20 square units.

**Tell whether each statement is *true* or *false*.**

11. A parallelogram and triangle can have the same base and area. _____

12. Two triangles that have the same base always have the same area. _____

13. Any obtuse triangle has a greater area than any acute triangle. _____

· · · · · · · · · · · · · · · · · · · · · · · · · · · · · · · · · · · · · · · · · · · · · · · · · · · · · · · · · · ·

Name _____ Class _____ Date _____

# 8-1 • Guided Problem Solving

**GPS** Student Page 278, Exercise 19:

**Algebra** A parallelogram has an area of 66 in.$^2$ and a base length of 5 inches. What is the height of the parallelogram?

## Understand

1. What are you being asked to find?

_____

2. What information are you given?

_____

_____

## Plan and Carry Out

3. Write the formula you will use to find the area of a parallelogram.

_____

4. Substitute the values you know into the formula.

_____

5. What operation do you use to find the height?

_____

6. What is the height of the parallelogram?

_____

## Check

7. Check your answer. Explain your method.

_____

_____

## Solve Another Problem

8. A parallelogram has an area of 96 cm$^2$ and a height of 4 cm. What is the base length of the parallelogram?

_____

# Practice 8-2 ·············································· Areas of Polygons

**Find the area of the shaded polygon.**

1.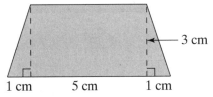

2.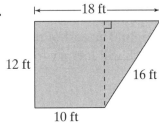

_____     _____

**Find the total area of the shaded polygons.**

3.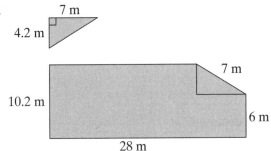

4.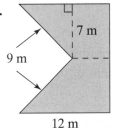

_____     _____

**Find the area of the shaded polygon.**

5.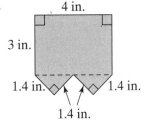

6.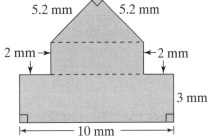

_____     _____

7. Martha is covering this trapezoid-shaped board with fabric. How many square feet of fabric does Martha need?

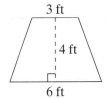

_____

8. A garden in the shape of a regular hexagon has sides that are each 5 meters long. If the height of each of the congruent triangles within the hexagon is about 4.33 meters, what is the area of the garden?

_____

## 8-2 • Guided Problem Solving

**GPS  Student Page 283, Exercise 16:**

Joe is having a concrete patio installed in the shape of the regular pentagon shown at the right. The cost of the finished patio is $2.75 per square foot. How much will Joe pay for the patio?

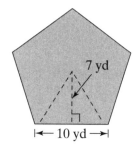

7 yd

|← 10 yd →|

### Understand

1. What are you being asked to do?

_____

2. What will you need to know to solve this problem?

_____

### Plan and Carry Out

3. The cost is given per square foot, so first convert yards to feet. What are the base and height of the triangle in feet?

_____

4. What is the area of the triangle-shaped section of the pentagon?

_____

5. How can you use the area of one triangle to find the total area?

_____

6. What is the total area of the patio?

_____

7. How can you find the total cost? What is the total cost?

_____

### Check

8. How can you check to make sure that your answer is correct?

_____

_____

### Solve Another Problem

9. Suppose the patio is in the shape of a regular pentagon with sides that are 12 yards long. The height of each triangle-shaped section is 8 yards. If the cost per square foot is $2.70, what is the total cost for the finished patio?

_____

Guided Problem Solving

# Practice 8-3

**Three-Dimensional Figures and Spatial Reasoning**

**Name each three-dimensional figure.**

**1.**

_____

**2.**

_____

**3.**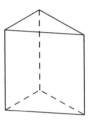

_____

**4.**

_____

**5.**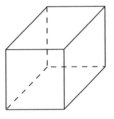

_____

**6.**

_____

**7.**

_____

**8.**

_____

**9.** In a square pyramid, what shape are the faces?

_____

**10.** How many faces does a rectangular prism have? How many
edges? How many vertices?

_____

# 8-3 • Guided Problem Solving

**GPS** **Student Page 289, Exercise 17:**

Name the figure. Then find the number of faces, vertices, and edges in the figure.

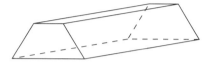

## Understand

1. What is a face?

   _____

2. What is a vertex?

   _____

   _____

3. What is an edge?

   _____

   _____

## Plan and Carry Out

4. How many bases does the figure have? _____

5. Does this make the figure a pyramid or a prism? _____

6. What is the shape of the bases? _____

7. Name the figure. _____

8. How many faces are there total? _____

9. How many vertices are there? _____

10. How many edges are there? _____

## Check

11. How do you know the figure is not a pyramid?

    _____

## Solve Another Problem

12. Name the figure. Then find the number of faces, vertices, and edges in the figure.

    _____

    _____

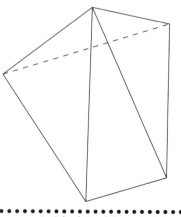

Guided Problem Solving

Name _____ Class _____ Date _____

# Practice 8-4

**Draw a net for each three-dimensional figure.**

**1.**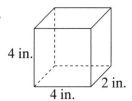
4 cm
8 cm
3 cm

**2.**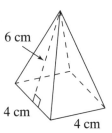
8 ft
6 ft
5 ft
10 ft

**3.**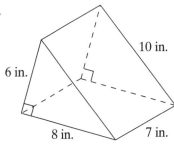
2 yd
2 yd
2 yd

**Find the surface area of each prism or pyramid.**

**4.**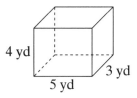
4 in.
4 in.
2 in.

**5.**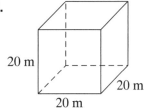
6 cm
4 cm
4 cm

**6.**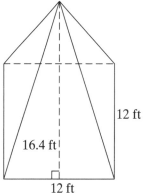
10 in.
6 in.
8 in.
7 in.

_____ _____ _____

**7.**
4 yd
5 yd
3 yd

**8.**
20 m
20 m
20 m

**9.**
12 ft
16.4 ft
12 ft

_____ _____ _____

**10.** Jan is making a pencil holder out of plastic canvas. The pencil holder will be 4 inches high. It will not have a top. Each edge of the square base is 3 inches long. How much plastic canvas does Jan need?

_____

# 8-4 • Guided Problem Solving

## GPS Student Page 295, Exercise 14:

**Writing in Math**  Suppose each dimension of a square pyramid is
doubled. How is the surface area affected?

### Understand

  **1.** Write the expression used to find the surface area of a square
  pyramid.

  _____

  **2.** To double a number means to multiply that number by what value?

  _____

### Plan and Carry Out

  **3.** Multiply each dimension by 2 and substitute it into the surface
  area expression from Step 1.

  _____

  **4.** Simplify the formula.

  _____

  **5.** By what number is the area of the square base and the area of
  each triangular face multiplied?

  _____

  **6.** How is the surface area affected when each dimension is
  doubled?

  _____

### Check

  **7.** Explain another way to solve this problem.

  _____

  _____

### Solve Another Problem

  **8.** Suppose each dimension of a square pyramid is tripled. How is
  the surface area affected?

  _____

Name _____ Class _____ Date _____

# Practice 8-5 ..................................... Volumes of Rectangular Prisms

**Choose an appropriate sized cube. Then count the cubes to find the volume of each rectangular prism.**

**1.**

$1\frac{1}{2}$

$1\frac{1}{2}$ 2

_____

**2.**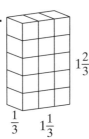

$1\frac{2}{3}$

$\frac{1}{3}$ $1\frac{1}{3}$

_____

**3.**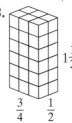

$1\frac{1}{2}$

$\frac{3}{4}$ $\frac{1}{2}$

_____

**Find the volume of each rectangular prism.**

**4.**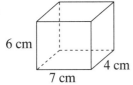

6 cm

7 cm 4 cm

_____

**5.**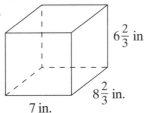

$6\frac{2}{3}$ in.

7 in. $8\frac{2}{3}$ in.

_____

**6.**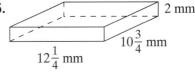

2 mm

$10\frac{3}{4}$ mm

$12\frac{1}{4}$ mm

_____

**7.** $l = 6$ cm, $w = 5\frac{4}{5}$ cm, $h = 12$ cm

_____

**8.** $l = 13$ in., $w = 7$ in., $h = 9\frac{3}{4}$ in.

_____

**9.** $l = 14\frac{1}{2}$ m, $w = 13$ m, $h = 19\frac{3}{8}$ m

_____

**10.** $l = 44\frac{2}{3}$ cm, $w = 27\frac{1}{6}$ cm, $h = 89$ cm

_____

**11.** $l = 2\frac{1}{2}$ ft, $w = 1.9$ ft, $h = 11.6$ ft

_____

**12.** $l = 48.1$ m, $w = 51.62$ m, $h = 3.42$ m

_____

**13.** A packing box is $1\frac{1}{5}$ m long, 0.8 m wide, and $1\frac{2}{5}$ m high. What is the volume of the box?

_____

**14.** A fish aquarium measures 3 feet long, 2 feet wide, and 24 inches high. What is the volume of the aquarium?

_____

**15.** A swimming pool is 25 feet wide, 20 yards long, and $7\frac{1}{2}$ feet deep. What is the volume of the pool?

_____

# 8-5 • Guided Problem Solving

**GPS** **Student Page 302, Exercise 22:**

A truck trailer has a length of 20 feet, a width of $8\frac{1}{2}$ feet, and a height of $7\frac{1}{2}$ feet. A second trailer has a base area of 108 square feet and a height of $8\frac{1}{2}$ feet. Which trailer has a greater volume? How much greater is it?

## Understand

1. Circle the information you will need to solve the problem.

2. Write the formula used to find the volume of a rectangular solid.

   _____

## Plan and Carry Out

3. Substitute the values for the length, width, and height of the first trailer into the formula for the volume of a rectangular solid. What is the volume?

   _____

4. Repeat Step 3 for the second trailer.

   _____

5. What are the units for the volume of this solid?

   _____

6. Which trailer has the greater volume?

   _____

7. How much greater is the volume?

   _____

## Check

8. How can you check your answer?

   _____

   _____

## Solve Another Problem

9. A building is $32\frac{1}{2}$ feet tall and has a base area of 420 square feet. What is the volume of the building?

   _____

## 8A: Graphic Organizer

For use before Lesson 8-1

**Study Skill** Develop consistent study habits. Block off approximately the same amount of time each evening for schoolwork. Plan ahead by setting aside extra time when you know you have a test or big project coming up.

**Write your answers.**

1. What is the chapter title? _____

2. How many lessons are there in this chapter? _____

3. What is the topic of the Test-Taking Strategies page? _____

4. Complete the graphic organizer below as you work through the chapter.

   • In the center, write the title of the chapter.

   • When you begin a lesson, write the lesson name in a rectangle.

   • When you complete a lesson, write a skill or key concept in a circle linked to that lesson block.

   • When you complete the chapter, use this graphic organizer to help you review.

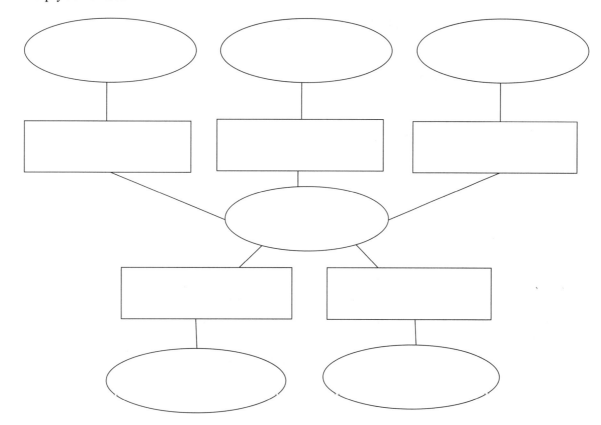

# 8B: Reading Comprehension

For use after Lesson 8-1

**Study Skill** Take a few minutes to relax before and after studying. Your mind will absorb and retain more information if you alternate studying with brief rest intervals.

**Read the paragraph below and answer the questions.**

The first paper money in the United States was printed during a coin shortage in 1862. The denominations of the first bills printed were 1, 5, 25 and 50 cents. In the late 1920s, the size of the paper bills was reduced from 3.1 by 7.4 inches to 2.6 by 6.1 inches. Currently, 50% of the bills printed are one-dollar bills, and they last only about a year and a half. For this reason, approximately 93% of the money printed each year replaces worn-out bills.

**1.** How many years ago was the first paper money printed in the United States?

_____

**2.** What was the area of a paper bill before the 1920s?

_____

**3.** What was the area of a paper bill after the 1920s?

_____

**4.** Write an inequality that relates the old area to the new area.

_____

**5.** Approximately how many months does a one-dollar bill last?

_____

**6.** What percent of bills printed each year is not for replacing old bills?

_____

**7.** What fraction of bills printed each year is not one-dollar bills?

_____

**8.** **High-Use Academic Words** In the paragraph, what does it mean to *reduce*?

    **a.** to make smaller                **b.** to make more durable

Name _____ Class _____ Date _____

# 8C: Reading/Writing Math Symbols

For use after Lesson 8-5

**Study Skill** Use flashcards to learn equations, facts, and formulas.

**Specific letters are used to represent parts of formulas for area, perimeter, volume, etc. Identify the type of measurement that each of the following letters typically represents in a geometric formula.**

**1.** $l$ _____

**2.** $A$ _____

**3.** $w$ _____

**4.** $b$ _____

**5.** $s$ _____

**6.** S.A. _____

**7.** $h$ _____

**8.** $V$ _____

**Match the expression in Column A with its meaning in Column B.**

| Column A | Column B |
|---|---|
| **9.** $s^2$ | **A.** surface area of a square pyramid |
| **10.** $bh$ | **B.** area of a square |
| **11.** $lw + \frac{1}{2}(bh) + \frac{1}{2}(bh) + \frac{1}{2}(bh) + \frac{1}{2}(bh)$ | **C.** surface area of a rectangular prism |
| **12.** $\frac{1}{2}bh$ | **D.** area of a triangle |
| **13.** $lwh$ | **E.** area of a parallelogram |
| **14.** $2lw + 2lh + 2wh$ | **F.** volume of a rectangular prism |

# 8D: Visual Vocabulary Practice

## *High-Use Academic Words*

**Study Skill** When you feel you're getting frustrated, take a break.

**Concept List**

| | | |
|---|---|---|
| explain | acronym | illustrate |
| represent | abbreviate | classify |
| property | approximate | dimensions |

**Write the concept that best describes each exercise. Choose from the concept list above.**

| 1. $0.8, 80\%, \frac{4}{5}$ _____ | 2. 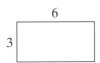 The area is $3 \times 6 = 18$ units. _____ | 3. Write in. for inches. _____ |
|---|---|---|
| 4. Pentagons, squares, octagons, and triangles are all polygons; circles are not. _____ | 5. $9.6\%$ of $25.36 \approx 10\%$ of $25$ _____ | 6. $l \times w \times h$ _____ |
| 7. $(a + b) + c = a + (b + c)$ _____ | 8. Write LCM for least common multiple. _____ | 9. 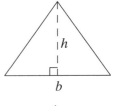 $A = \frac{1}{2}b \times h$ _____ |

# 8E: Vocabulary Check

**For use after Lesson 8-5**

**Study Skill** Strengthen your vocabulary. Use these pages and add cues and summaries by applying the Cornell Notetaking style.

**Write the definition for each word or term at the right. To check your work, fold the paper back along the dotted line to see the correct answers.**

_____    pyramid

_____

_____

_____    prism

_____

_____

_____    height of a
                                            parallelogram
_____

_____

_____    surface area

_____

_____    volume of a
                                            three-dimensional
_____    figure

_____

_____

# 8E: Vocabulary Check (continued)

**Write the vocabulary word or term for each definition. To check your work, fold the paper forward along the dotted line to see the correct answers.**

a three-dimensional figure with one polygon for a base and all other faces are triangles that meet at one vertex

_____

a three-dimensional figure with two parallel and congruent faces that are polygons

_____

the perpendicular distance between opposite bases

_____

the sum of the areas of all the surfaces of a three-dimensional figure

_____

the number of cubic units needed to fill the space inside the figure

_____

Name _____ Class _____ Date _____

## 8F: Vocabulary Review Puzzle

**For use with the Chapter Review**

**Study Skill** Get plenty of rest before a major quiz or test. If you're well rested, you may be able to concentrate better and retain more of what you hear or see in class.

**Below is a list of words grouped by number of letters. Fit each word into the puzzle grid. Use each word only once.**

| 3 letters | 4 letters | 5 letters | 6 letters | 7 letters |
|---|---|---|---|---|
| net | area | prism | height | pyramid |
| | cone | | sphere | |
| | edge | | square | |
| | face | | vertex | |
| | | | volume | |

| 8 letters | 9 letters | 13 letters |
|---|---|---|
| cylinder | decompose | parallelogram |
| | | perpendicular |

Name _____ Class _____ Date _____

## Practice 9-1

**Finding the Mean**

**Find the mean of each data set.**

**1.** 4, 5, 7, 5, 6, 3 _____

**2.** 72, 76, 73, 74, 75 _____

**3.** 85, 91, 76, 85, 93 _____

**4.** 2.1, 3.2, 1.6, 2.4 _____

**For each set of data, identify any outliers. Then determine the effect that the outlier has on the mean.**

**5.** 64, 65, 62, 69, 59, 23, 61, 67 _____

**6.** 8.1, 8.3, 7.8, 7.9, 8.4, 6.8, 8.0 _____

**7.** 1230, 1225, 1228, 1232, 1233, 1321, 1229, 1231 _____

**8.** 18.66, 18.75, 18.69, 18.67, 18.99, 18.64, 18.73 _____

**Use the table for Exercises 9–11.**

| Name | Hourly Wage |
|---|---|
| Julia | $8.75 |
| Ron | 7.50 |
| Miguel | 25.00 |
| Natasha | 11.00 |
| Robert | 10.50 |

**9.** Whose wage is an outlier in the data set?

_____

**10.** Find the mean hourly wage with and without the outlier.

_____

**11.** What effect does the outlier have on the mean?

_____

**Fill in the blanks to find the mean of each data set.**

**12.** 4, 6, 2, 8, 5: $\dfrac{25}{\boxed{\phantom{0}}} = \boxed{\phantom{0}}$

**13.** 10, 4, 2, 12, 6, 8: $\dfrac{\boxed{\phantom{000}}}{6} = \boxed{\phantom{0}}$

# 9-1 • Guided Problem Solving ••••••••••••••••••••••••••••••••••••••••

**GPS** **Student Page 314, Exercise 23:**

Shelby made a list of her test scores: 88, 100, 92, 80, 85, 94, and 90. What is the lowest score she can get on her next test to have a mean score of 90?

## Understand

1. What are you being asked to do?

_____

_____

2. If you already know the mean and all her test scores but one, how can you find the missing test score?

_____

_____

## Plan and Carry Out

3. What is her mean score right now?

_____

4. Does her next test score need to be higher or lower than 90?

_____

5. How many tests will there be, including the next test? Multiply that number by 90.

_____

6. Subtract the first seven scores from your answer to Step 5.

_____

## Check

7. Take all her test scores, including the one that you found, and find the mean. Is it 90?

_____

## Solve Another Problem

8. The mean of five numbers is 55. If four of the numbers are 86, 77, 14, and 12, what is the other number?

_____

# Practice 9-2                                    **Median and Mode**

**Find the median and the mode of each data set.**

**1.** 6, 10, 12, 5, 7, 12, 9

**2.** 19.32, 19.44, 19.54, 19.44, 19.33, 19.27, 19.31

**3.** 24, 24, 28, 32, 40, 42

**4.** 2, 4, 5, 4, 3, 4, 2, 3, 3

**5.** 86.4, 87.2, 95.7, 96.4, 88.1, 94.9, 98.5, 94.8

**6.** 12.2, 12.8, 12.1, 12.2, 12.3 12.5, 12.4

**Use the table for Exercises 7–10.**

| Last Year's Monthly Rainfall | |
|---|---|
| **Month** | **Rainfall (inches)** |
| January | 5 |
| February | 4.5 |
| March | 6 |
| April | 15 |
| May | 5 |
| June | 3 |
| July | 2 |
| August | 2 |
| September | 1 |
| October | 2 |
| November | 3 |
| December | 4.5 |

**7.** What was the mean monthly rainfall last year? _____

**8.** What is the median rainfall of all the months listed? _____

**9.** What is the mode of all the months listed? _____

**10.** Does the mean, median, or mode best describe last year's rainfall? _____

**Each student in a class has taken five tests. The teacher allows the students to pick the mean, median, or mode of each set of scores to be their final score. Which measure should each of these students pick in order to have the highest final score?**

**11.** 100, 87, 81, 23, 19

**12.** 79, 78, 77, 76, 85

**12.** 80, 80, 70, 67, 68

**14.** 75, 78, 77, 70, 70

# 9-2 • Guided Problem Solving

**GPS** **Student Page 318, Exercise 21:**

**Number Sense** The median of four numbers is 48. Three of the numbers are 42, 51, and 52. What is the other number?

## Understand

1. What are you being asked to do?

   _____

2. What is the median?

   _____

3. How do you find the median when there is an even number of data items?

   _____

## Plan and Carry Out

4. Order the three numbers. _____

5. Between which two numbers does the missing number belong?

   _____

6. 48 is the number between the missing number and which other number? _____

7. What is the difference between the answer to Step 6 and 48?

   _____

8. What is the difference between the missing number and 48? Why?

   _____

9. What is the missing number? _____

## Check

10. Explain how to check your answer.

    _____

    _____

## Solve Another Problem

11. The median of six numbers is 37. If five of the numbers are 29, 38, 34, 38, and 40, what is the other number?

    _____

# Practice 9-3

Frequency Tables and Dot Plots

**1. a.** Choose a page from a book you are reading. Choose 50 words on that page. Using these 50 words, complete the frequency table.

| Letter | Tally | Frequency |
|--------|-------|-----------|
| t      |       |           |
| s      |       |           |
| r      |       |           |
| n      |       |           |
| d      |       |           |

**b.** Make a dot plot for your frequency table.

**c.** Which letter occurred most frequently in your sample? least frequently?

**Use the dot plot at the right for Exercises 2–5.**

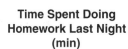

Time Spent Doing
Homework Last Night
(min)

**2.** What information is displayed in the line plot?

_____

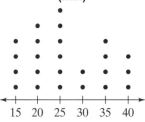

15  20  25  30  35  40

**3.** How many students spent time doing homework last night?

_____

**4.** How many students spent at least half an hour on homework?

_____

**5.** What is the range of time spent on homework last night?

_____

**6.** A kennel is boarding dogs that weigh the following amounts (in pounds).

| 5 | 62 | 43 | 48 | 12 | 17 | 29 | 74 |
|---|----|----|----|----|----|----|----|
| 8 | 15 | 4  | 11 | 15 | 26 | 63 |    |

**a.** What is the range of the dogs' weights?

_____

**b.** How many of the dogs weigh under 50 pounds?

_____

# 9-3 • Guided Problem Solving

## GPS Student Page 321, Exercise 13:

**Speed Limits** On a highway, the minimum speed allowed is 40 miles per hour. The maximum speed is 65 miles per hour. What is the range of speeds allowed on the highway?

### Understand

1. Underline the words that indicate which numbers you are to use to answer this question.

2. What is the mathematical meaning of range?

   _____

   _____

### Plan and Carry Out

3. What is the least possible highway speed allowed?

   _____

4. What is the greatest possible highway speed allowed?

   _____

5. Write a subtraction expression to answer the question.

   _____

6. What is the range?

   _____

### Check

7. How can you check your answer? Does your answer check?

   _____

   _____

### Solve Another Problem

8. You have to be at least 36 inches tall to ride the rides at Kiddie Land, but you cannot be any taller than 48 inches. What is the range of heights for these rides?

   _____

# Practice 9-4

**Box-and-Whisker Plots**

**Tell how many observations are in the data set. Then construct a box-and-whicker plot to represent the data.**

1. The number of cars coming into a parking garage each hour:

    35, 40, 34, 25, 50, 35, 39. _____

2. The length in miles of the trails in one county park:

    5, 3, 4.5, 8, 10, 1.5, 8, 2, 6.5, 7, 6. _____

3. The number of tickets to the dance recital sold by some students:

    4, 2, 7, 10, 10, 5, 2, 20. _____

4. The box and whisker plot represents the cost of a lunch special at 10 different places.

    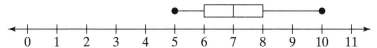

    **a.** One half of the lunch specials cost between $____ and $____.

    **b.** What fraction of the lunch specials cost more than $8? _____

    **c.** What fraction of the lunch specials cost less than $5? Explain.

    _____

Name _____ Class _____ Date _____

## 9-4 • Guided Problem Solving

**Student Page 326, Exercise 11:**

The number of words per minute that students can type at the end of
the first semester are shown in the dot plot.

**a.** How many observations are
in the data set?

**b.** Construct a box-and-whisker
plot to represent the data.

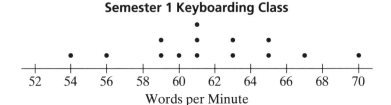

### Understand

1. What are you being asked to do? _____

2. How do you use the dots to tell you the number of observations? _____

### Plan and Carry Out

3. Write the data values in order.

   _____

4. How many observations are there? _____

5. What are the least value and the greatest value? _____

6. Construct the box-and-whisker plot
for the data. What are the lower
quartile, the median, and the
upper quartile?

   _____

### Check

7. How can you check your answer?

   _____

   _____

### Solve Another Problem

8. Construct a box-and-whisker plot from the data in the dot plot.

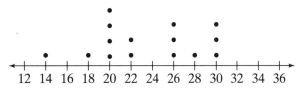

Guided Problem Solving

Name _____ Class _____ Date _____

# Practice 9-5

Histograms

The histograms below summarize the number of commuter trains that depart one station on weekday mornings and weekend mornings.

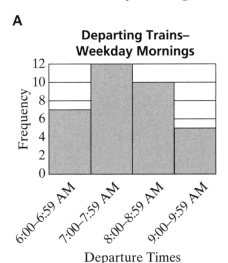

**A**

Departing Trains–
Weekday Mornings

**B**

Departing Trains–
Weekend Mornings

**Use histogram A for Exercises 1–3.**

1.  What are the intervals in these data sets?

    _____

2.  How many observations were made in this data set? _____

3.  What do the observations represent?

    _____

**Use histogram B for Exercises 4–6.**

4.  Can the histogram tell you how many trains departed at 6:30 AM? Explain.

    _____

    _____

5.  Compare Histograms A and B. Which graph showed more frequent trains between 6 and 10 AM? _____

6.  What conclusions can you make? _____

    _____

    _____

7.  The frequency table shows the frequency of customers at a snack bar at the train station. Construct a histogram to display the data.

| Time (AM) | 8:00–8:14 | 8:15–8:29 | 8:30–8:44 | 8:45–8:59 |
|-----------|-----------|-----------|-----------|-----------|
| Frequency | 20 | 15 | 10 | 15 |

# 9-5 • Guided Problem Solving

**GPS** **Student Page 331, Exercise 12:**

The table shows the number of songs Owen purchased online during each of 20 weeks. Construct a histogram for the data.

| Songs Purchased Each Week | | | | | | | | | |
|---|---|---|---|---|---|---|---|---|---|
| 0 | 4 | 1 | 7 | 2 | 0 | 0 | 5 | 9 | 1 |
| 3 | 2 | 1 | 0 | 8 | 5 | 5 | 0 | 1 | 6 |

    **a.** Explain how you chose your intervals.

    **b.** Describe any patterns you see in the data.

## Understand

  **1.** What are you being asked to do? _____

  **2.** What does each observation represent? _____

  **3.** How can making a tally chart and frequency table help you organize the observations?

    _____

    _____

## Plan and Carry Out

  **4.** What are convenient intervals that you can use to group the data?

    _____

  **5.** Make a frequency table and draw a graph.

  **6.** What patterns do you see?

    _____

    _____

## Check

  **7.** How can you check your answer?

    _____

## Solve Another Problem

  **8.** Construct a box-and-whisker plot from this data that represents the number of times a month people eat dinner at a restaurant: 0, 0, 4, 2, 1, 2, 2, 1, 1, 1, 4, 4, 8, 5, 3, 1. Describe any patterns you see in the data.

    _____

# Practice 9-6

**Variability of Data**

**Find the mean absolute deviation for the data. Round your answer to the nearest tenth if necessary.**

**1.** 2, 8, 5, 8, 7, 3, 8, 7

    **a.** Find the mean.

        **b.** Find the MAD.

_____

_____

**2.** 41, 47, 30, 46, 48, 46

    **a.** Find the mean.

        **b.** Find the MAD.

_____

_____

**3.** 11, 16, 4, 17, 18, 10, 13, 18, 10

    **a.** Find the mean.

        **b.** Find the MAD.

_____

_____

**Find the interquartile range for each data set.**

**4.** 12, 19, 15, 22, 9, 8, 20 _____

**5.** 2, 0, 1, 0, 5, 12, 2, 3, 4, 9, 2 _____

**6.** 300, 50, 80, 100, 100, 250, 230, 80 _____

**Find the mean absolute deviation and the interquartile range for each data set. Round your answer to the nearest tenth if necessary.**

**7.** 11, 1, 2, 6, 8, 4, 1, 7

    MAD =

    IQR =

**8.** 8, 10, 8, 13, 12, 8, 11

    MAD =

    IQR =

**9.** Compare the variability of the sets in Exercises 7 and 8.

_____

_____

# 9-6 • Guided Problem Solving

**GPS** Student Page 338, Exercise 19:

**Use the table and information below.**

| Daily Exercise | | | | | | | | |
|---|---|---|---|---|---|---|---|---|
| **Day** | 1 | 2 | 3 | 4 | 5 | 6 | 7 | 8 |
| **Talia's Exercise (min)** | 40 | 60 | 45 | 4̶0̶ | 20 | 32 | 30 | 45 |

The MAD is 8.75 and the IQR is 13.

**Reasoning** Using Talia's 8-Day exercise schedule, what effect would it have on the measures of variability if the value for Day 4 changed from 40 to 0? Explain.

## *Understand*

1. What are you being asked to do? _____

2. Cross out and change the number in the table.

3. What statistical name can you call 0 in the new data set? _____

## *Plan and Carry Out*

4. Without calculating, predict the effect of the new data on the mean. Explain.

   _____

5. What effect will this have on the MAD? Why?

   _____

6. What effect will the new data have on the IQR? Why?

   _____

7. Overall, how does the new data affect the variability of the data set? _____

## *Check*

8. How can you check your answer?

   _____

9. Is your answer reasonable?

   _____

## Solve Another Problem

10. Using Talia's original exercise schedule for 8 days, what effect would reducing each value by 10 minutes have on the measures of variability? Explain.

    _____

    _____

Guided Problem Solving

Name _____ Class _____ Date _____

# Practice 9-7

**Shape of Distributions**

**Match the shape of each distribution with the description that best fits it.**

**A**

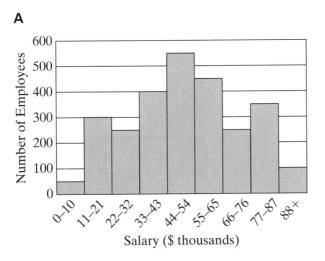

**B**

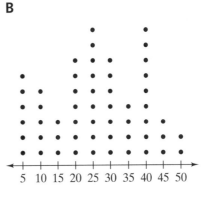

**C**

Patient satisfaction score

**D**

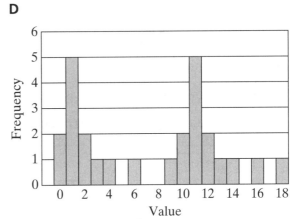

**1.** Data has 2 modes, gaps, and peaks. _____

**2.** Data is not symmetrical, has 2 modes, has no peaks, and clusters around the modes. _____

**3.** Data has no gaps, has 2 modes, is not symmetrical, and is spread over a large range. _____

**4.** Data has one mode, has a large range, and is not symmetric. _____

**5.** How can you make dot plot C above symmetric?
Describe and sketch it.

_____

_____

Name _____ Class _____ Date _____

# 9-7 • Guided Problem Solving

12. Two age groups were surveyed about the hours per week they spend on the Internet. The results are shown in the histograms below.
   a. Describe the shape of each distribution.
   b. In which range of hours would you expect to find the median for each distribution?

## Understand

1. What are you being asked to do?

   _____

2. What are some words that are used to describe distributions in graphs?

   _____

## Plan and Carry Out

3. What do the intervals describe? _____

4. What do the observations represent? _____

5. Describe the shape of each distribution.

   _____

   _____

6. In which range of hours would you expect to find the median for each distribution?

   _____

## Check

7. Explain how you can check you answer to Question 6?

   _____

## Solve Another Problem

8. Makayla and Oscar work at a kitchen store. The plots show each person's sales of small kitchen appliances in 6 months. Use the shape of the data to compare their sales.

   _____

   _____

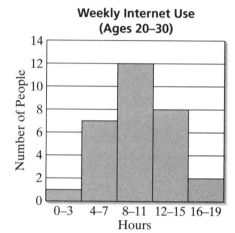

**Weekly Internet Use (Ages 20–30)**

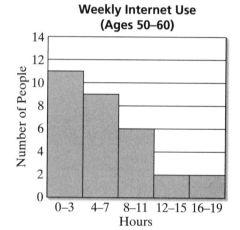

**Weekly Internet Use (Ages 50–60)**

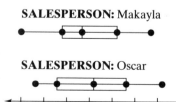

SALESPERSON: Makayla

SALESPERSON: Oscar

# Practice 9-8

**Tell whether the question is a statistical question. If it is, identify likely answers. If not, explain why not.**

1. What is my middle name?

   _____

2. Which is the most frequent girl's name in your school?

   _____

3. Which flavor of potato chips do you like?

   _____

4. Where would you like to go on your next vacation?

   _____

5. How many colds have you had this year?

   _____

6. Do I know how to figure skate?

   _____

**Is the survey question biased? If so, explain why. Then rewrite the question so it is unbiased.**

7. Which pet do you prefer: a hamster or a playful kitten?

   _____

   _____

8. Do you like plain mustard or messy sauerkraut and relish on a hot dog?

   _____

   _____

9. Do you use an umbrella, a raincoat, both, or neither when you go out in the rain?

   _____

10. Do you prefer to swim in a pool, a lake, or the ocean? _____

11. Would you paint your room sky blue, sunny yellow, or boring beige?

   _____

   _____

# 9-8 • Guided Problem Solving

**GPS** **Student Page 347, Exercise 17:**

Pauline collects the results at the right from a survey.
   **a.** Is it likely that Pauline asked a statistical question? Explain.
   **b.** What question might Pauline have asked?

| Survey Results | |
|---|---|
| 12 miles | 28 miles |
| 15 miles | 48 miles |
| 10 miles | 6 miles |
| 2 miles | 36 miles |

## Understand

**1.** What are you being asked to do?

_____

_____

**2.** How can you analyze the data in order to answer the question?

_____

## Plan and Carry Out

**3.** What would it mean if all the answers or almost all the answers were the same?

_____

_____

**4.** Describe the data that resulted from Pauline's question.

_____

**5.** Is it likely that it was a statistical question? Why?

_____

**6.** What question might result in the data?

_____

## Check

**7.** How can you check your answer?

_____

_____

## Solve Another Problem

**8.** The results of a survey are in the box at the right.
   **a.** Is it likely that the survey asked a statistical question? Explain. _____
   **b.** What question might have been asked?

_____

| Survey Results | | |
|---|---|---|
| fried | omelet | fried |
| hard | fried | omelet |
| boiled | | |
| fried | scrambled | scrambled |

# 9A: Graphic Organizer

**For use before Lesson 9-1**

**Study Skill** Take notes when your teacher presents new material in class. Organize those notes as a way to study, reviewing them as you go.

**Vocabulary and Study Skills**

**Write your answers.**

1. What is the chapter title? _____

2. How many lessons are there in this chapter? _____

3. What is the topic of the Test-Taking Strategies page? _____

4. Complete the graphic organizer below as you work through the chapter.

   • In the center, write the title of the chapter.

   • When you begin a lesson, write the lesson name in a rectangle.

   • When you complete a lesson, write a skill or key concept in a circle linked to that lesson block.

   • When you complete the chapter, use this graphic organizer to help you review.

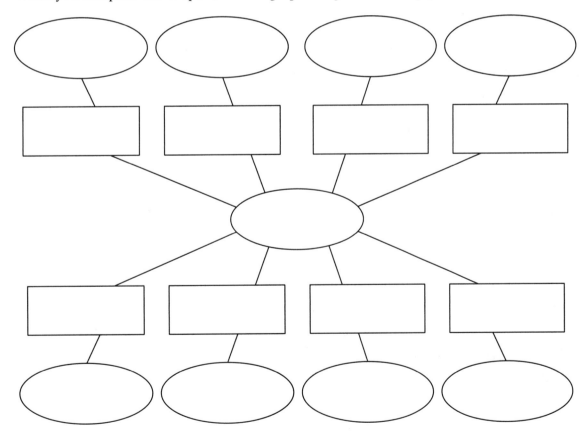

# 9B: Reading Comprehension

**Study Skill** Read direction lines carefully before beginning an exercise set.

**Read the paragraph and answer the questions.**

According to the National Gardening Association, Americans spent $37.7 billion in 2001 decorating and maintaining their lawns and gardens. The most popular flowering plants used in landscaping are impatiens, petunias, and pansies. Eighteen percent of all flowering plants sold in the United States are impatiens, 13% are petunias, and 8% are pansies. Twenty-three percent of all garden vegetables sold are tomatoes.

The average amount of money spent per household on lawn and garden projects in 2001 is shown.

| | | | |
|---|---|---|---|
| Flower bulbs | $40 | Flower gardening | $58 |
| Indoor houseplants | $40 | Insect control | $60 |
| Landscaping | $174 | Lawn care | $220 |
| Tree care | $97 | Vegetable gardening | $58 |

1. What is the paragraph about? _____

2. What was the total amount of money that Americans spent on their lawns and gardens in 2001?

   _____

3. What is listed as the most popular flowering plant in the United States?

   _____

4. How many projects are listed in the article? _____

5. Which project had the greatest average amount of money spent?

   _____

6. On average, how much more was spent per household on lawn care projects than landscaping projects in 2001?

   _____

7. How much did the average American household spend on *all* lawn and garden projects in 2001?

   _____

8. **High-Use Academic Words** In Exercise 7, what does it mean to *determine*?

   **a.** to give examples          **b.** to find a result

# 9C: Reading/Writing Math Symbols

**For use after Lesson 9-2**

**Study Skill** Learning is when you figure out how to get past an obstacle.

**Match each number with its word form.**

**1.** 6.8
**2.** 2.16
**3.** 860
**4.** 0.218
**5.** 0.8

**A.** two and sixteen hundredths
**B.** eight tenths
**C.** eight hundred sixty
**D.** six and eight tenths
**E.** two hundred eighteen thousandths

**Write a mathematical expression for each word description.**

**6.** seven plus three hundredths

_____

**7.** Two tenths is greater than six hundredths.

_____

**8.** Ten divided by four equals two and five tenths.

_____

**9.** three and one tenth multiplied by ten and one half

_____

**10.** seven minus eleven and four thousandths

_____

**Write out the following numbers in a word form.**

**11.** 3.9 _____

**12.** 4.01 _____

**13.** 0.039 _____

**14.** 0.5 _____

**15.** 60.908 _____

# 9D: Visual Vocabulary Practice

**Study Skill** Mathematics builds on itself, so build a strong foundation.

**Concept List**

| | | |
|---|---|---|
| mean | median | mode |
| range | outlier | line graph |
| dot plot | frequency table | histogram |

**Write the concept that best describes each exercise. Choose from the concept list above.**

| 1. | 2. | 3. |
|---|---|---|
| **Number of Pets** <br><br> | **Test Scores in English Class** <br> 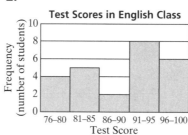 | The prices of the same item at five stores are $1.15, $2.05, $1.35, $2.25, and $1.65. <br><br> What does the amount $2.25 − $1.15 = $1.10 represent for this set of prices? |

**Number of Pets**

| Pets | Tally | Frequency |
|---|---|---|
| 0 | ℍℍ | 5 |
| 1 | ℍℍ Ⅰ | 6 |
| 2 | ‖ | 2 |

| 4. | 5. | 6. |
|---|---|---|
| **Books Purchased** <br> 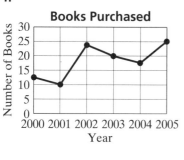 | The high temperatures in a city over five days included 64°F, 61°F, 67°F, 82°F, and 64°F. <br><br> What does the temperature of 82°F represent for this set of temperatures? | The ages of five employees at a company are 32, 25, 28, 37, and 28. <br><br> What does the number $\frac{32 + 25 + 28 + 37 + 28}{5} = 30$ represent for this set of ages? |

| 7. | 8. | 9. |
|---|---|---|
| Sandra's grades in math class are 80, 82, 100, 96, 90, and 82. <br><br> What does the number $\frac{82 + 90}{2} = 86$ represent for this set of grades? | The number 3 represents this in the data set {1, 3, 4, 1, 3, 8, 2, 3}. | **Runs Batted In** <br>  |

# 9E: Vocabulary Check

For use after Lesson 9-3

**Study Skill** Strengthen your vocabulary. Use these pages and add cues and summaries by applying the Cornell Notetaking style.

**Write the definition for each word or term at the right. To check your work, fold the paper back along the dotted line to see the correct answers.**

_____     mean

_____

_____

_____     median

_____

_____

_____     mode

_____

_____

_____     outlier

_____

_____

_____     range

_____

_____

_____

Vocabulary and Study Skills

# 9E:  Vocabulary Check (continued)

For use after Lesson 9-3

**Write the vocabulary word or term for each definition. To check your work, fold the paper forward along the dotted line to see the correct answers.**

the sum of the data divided by the number of data items

_____

the middle value of a data set that is arranged in numerical order

_____

the item in a data set that occurs with the greatest frequency

_____

a data item that is much higher or lower than the other item in the set

_____

the difference between the greatest and least values in a data set

_____

Name _____ Class _____ Date _____

# 9F: Vocabulary Review

**For use with the Chapter Review**

**Study Skill** Pay attention in class. Some concepts are very difficult to grasp unless you devote your full attention to learning them.

**Circle the word that best completes the sentence.**

1. The (*median, mean*) is the sum of the data values divided by the number of items.

2. A (*line, bar*) graph is used to show a change in data over time.

3. You can use the (*commutative, associative*) property to change the order in an addition or multiplication expression.

4. (*Standard form, Expanded form*) is a way to write a number to show the place and value of each digit.

5. The (*Associative, Commutative*) Property of Addition states that changing the grouping of the addends does not change the sum.

6. To find the (*mode, range*) of a data set, you must subtract the least value from the greatest value.

7. If a data set has an outlier that is very far apart from the rest of the data, the (*mean, mode*) may not be the best way to describe that data.

8. The (*median, mode*) is the middle number in a set of ordered data.

9. A (*spreadsheet, cell*) is a table made up of rows and columns used to organize data.

10. The (*mean, mode*) of a data set is the data item that appears most often.

11. A (*frequency table, dot plot*) is a graph that shows the shape of the data set by stacking dots above each data value on a number line.

**Vocabulary and Study Skills**